Lizzie Borden and the Massachusetts Axe Murders

Ronald Bartle

❈ WATERSIDE PRESS

Lizzie Borden and the Massachusetts Axe Murders
Ronald Bartle

ISBN 978-1-909976-43-6 (Paperback)
ISBN 978-1-910979-33-4 (Epub E-book)
ISBN 978-1-910979-34-1 (Adobe E-book)

Copyright © 2017 This work is the copyright of Ronald Bartle. All intellectual property and associated rights are hereby asserted and reserved by the author in full compliance with UK, European and international law. No part of this book may be copied, reproduced, stored in any retrieval system or transmitted in any form or by any means, including in hard copy or via the internet, without the prior written permission of the publishers to whom all such rights have been assigned worldwide.

Cover design © 2017 Waterside Press by www.gibgob.com Front cover image from an original in the possession of Waterside Press.

Printed by Lightning Source.

Main UK distributor Gardners Books, 1 Whittle Drive, Eastbourne, East Sussex, BN23 6QH. Tel: +44 (0)1323 521777; sales@gardners.com; www.gardners.com

North American distribution Ingram Book Company, One Ingram Blvd, La Vergne, TN 37086, USA. Tel: (+1) 615 793 5000; inquiry@ingramcontent.com

Cataloguing-In-Publication Data A catalogue record for this book can be obtained from the British Library.

e-book *Lizzie Borden and the Massachusetts Axe Murders* is available as an ebook and also to subscribers of Ebrary, Ebsco, Myilibrary and Dawsonera.

Published 2017 by
Waterside Press Ltd
Sherfield Gables
Sherfield on Loddon, Hook
Hampshire RG27 0JG.

Telephone +44(0)1256 882250
Online catalogue WatersidePress.co.uk
Email enquiries@watersidepress.co.uk

Table of Contents

Copyright and publication details *ii*
About the author *v*
Acknowledgements *vi*
Dedication *vii*
Lizzie Borden in Popular Culture *ix*
Floorplans *x*

1	The Case Against Lizzie Borden	13
2	The Background	19
3	Before the Holocaust	35
4	Lizzie's Visit to Alice	43
5	The Inquest	49
6	The Scene is Set	81
7	The Murder of Abby Borden	89
8	The Murder of Andrew Borden	111
9	The Evidence of Hannah Reagan	119
10	The Blood Mystery	127
11	The Murder Weapon	135
12	The Burning of a Dress	147
13	The Alibi	171
14	The Exclusion of the Inquest Evidence	193
15	The Exclusion of the Prussic Acid Evidence	201
16	Lizzie's Failure to Give Evidence	211
17	Closing Speeches and Charge to the Jury	217
18	The Conclusion	231

Select Bibliography *245*

Index *246*

Lizzie Borden and the Massachusetts Axe Murders

About the author

The author in the Garrick Club Library

Ronald Bartle was Deputy Chief Stipendiary Magistrate (now District Judge) for Inner London and earlier practised as a barrister. His books include *The Telephone Murder: The Mysterious Death of Julia Wallace* (2012); *The Police Witness: A Guide to Presenting Evidence in Court* (1984 onwards); *Three Cases that Shook the Law* (2016); and *Bow Street Beak* (re-issued 2016).

Acknowledgements

I wish to express my sincere thanks to Mr John Bernard for kindly creating and supplying the author's photograph for this work.

Sources which have helped me in my research are noted in the *Select Bibliography* at the end of the book.

To my wife Molly,
With grateful thanks for all her
enthusiastic support and encouragement

Lizzie Borden in Popular Culture

Lizzie Borden took an axe
And gave her mother forty whacks.
When she saw what she had done,
She gave her father forty-one.

Skipping/Nursery Rhyme—Traditional.

…you can't chop your Papa up in Massachusetts
Not even if it's planned as a surprise…
No, you can't chop your Papa up in Massachusetts
You know how neighbors love to criticise.

…you can't chop your Mama up in Massachusetts
Not even if you're tired of Her cuisine…
No you can't chop your Mama up in Massachusetts
You know it's almost sure to cause a scene.

Extracts from *Lizzie Borden*—Chad Mitchell Trio (1962).

Lizzie Borden and the Massachusetts Axe Murders

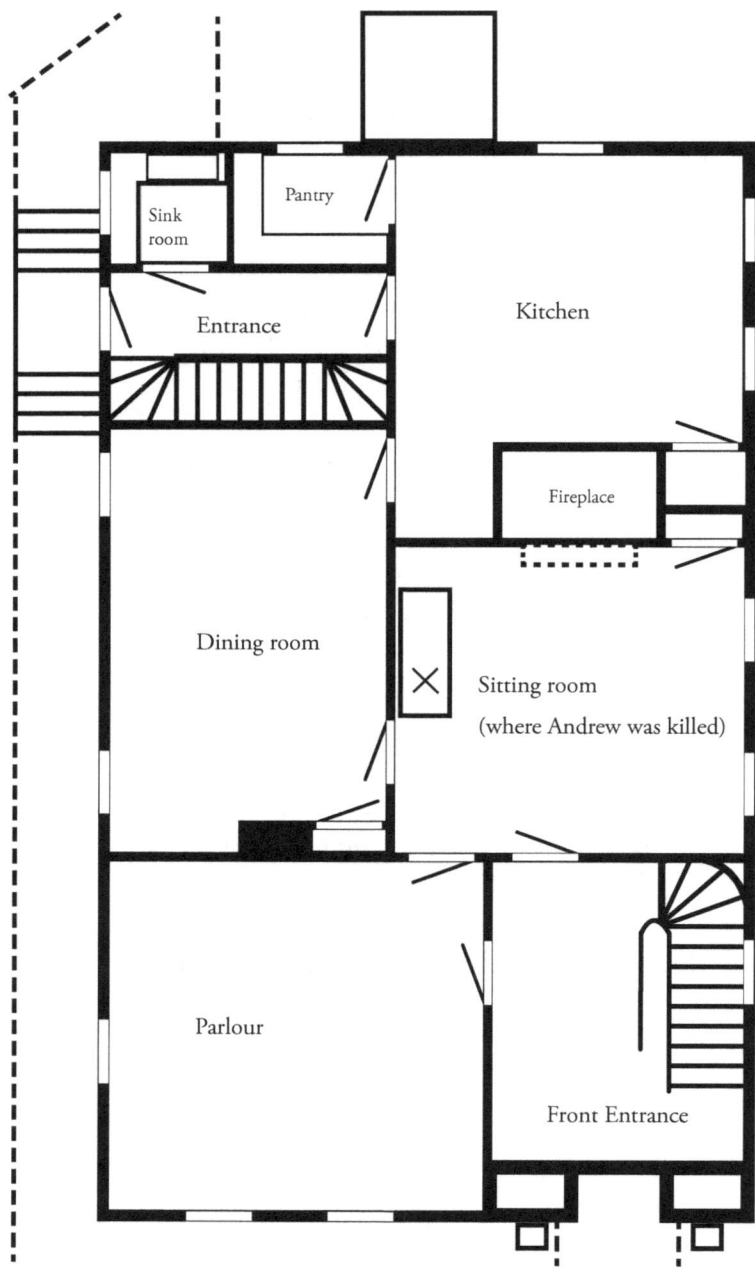

Ground floor, Borden House

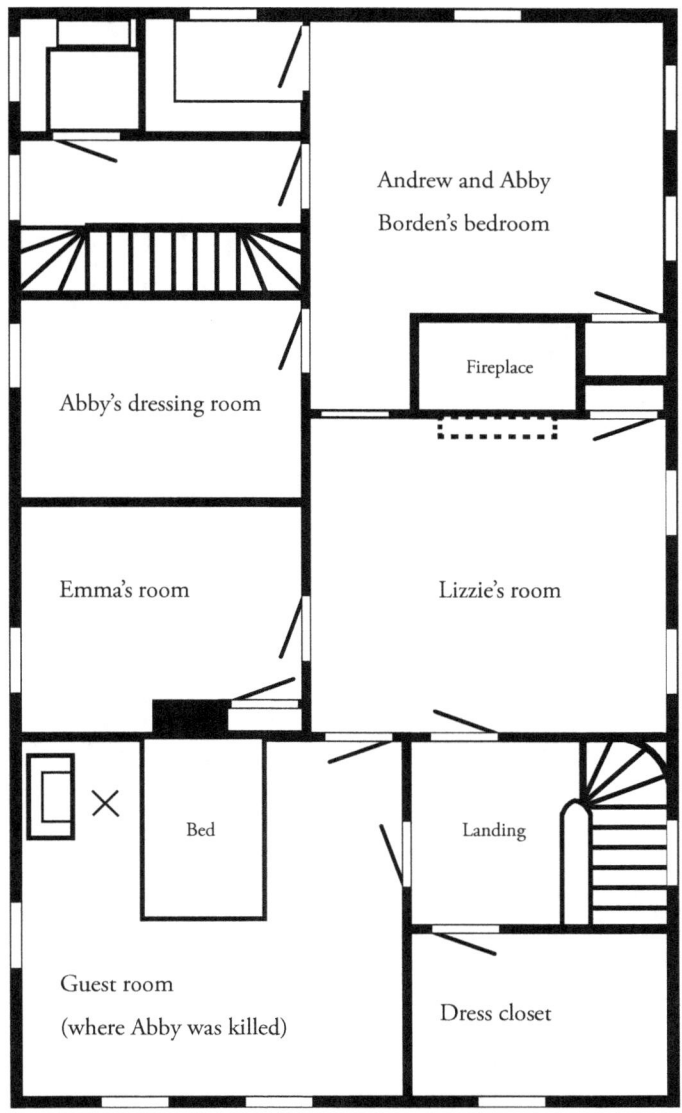

Second floor, Borden House

CHAPTER ONE

The Case Against Lizzie Borden

"Here is a candle to light you to bed and here comes a chopper to chop off your head."

Old English rhyme.

It has been said that for sheer altitude in the illustrative peaks of crime, the bloodstained palm goes to Miss Lizzie Borden of Fall River Massachusetts, and her inseparable symbol, the hatchet. The case is no ordinary murder mystery. Amid the welter of violent crime which fills the newspapers today, a few terrible murder trials have survived year upon year to retain their hold on the imagination of successive generations of readers and students of legendary homicide.

The study of the dreadful crime of murder is always a gruesome exercise, but some instances contain elements which place them in a category of their own. This may be because of the uniquely, almost unnaturally, shocking nature of the facts, the element of mystery contained in the circumstances or the degree of dispute concerning the conclusion of the jury at the trial. An example of the former is the UK's Moors Murders in April 1966, perpetrated by Ian and Myra Hindley upon several children. An instance of the latter is the *Wallace Case* heard before the Liverpool Assizes in April 1931 (*see Chapter Twelve*).

The Lizzie Borden trial which came before the Superior Court of Massachusetts in 1893 combines both of these elements. Patricide and Matricide are acts of infinite wickedness. But to commit both within an hour and a half of each other is of such incredible evil that it defies words adequately to describe such an unsurpassable deed. Yet this was the charge levelled against Miss Lizzie Andrew Borden of Fall River on the 2nd day of December 1892. The grand jury of the county of Bristol returned an indictment against her charging her with the murder of her step-mother Abby Durfee Borden, and her father Andrew Jackson Borden.

Few cases of murder have been subject to the same degree of analysis as this one. This is particularly true with reference to the United States of America and the State of Massachusetts, since Fall River in Massachusetts is the where the terrible events occurred. Dating from the time of the trial itself manifold books and legal articles have been written on the subject, lectures delivered, debates and seminars held and endless opinions, some by learned men of the law, expressed. Every aspect of this landmark case has been dissected and the house which was once occupied by the Borden family has been visited over the years by countless tourists.

Yet the arguments continue over the question of Lizzie's guilt or innocence. Numerous authors and legal experts still differ on this crucial question. If she was innocent, a woman of a spotless character was rescued from the gallows. If, however, she was guilty, the verdict constitutes a disgraceful denial of justice where justice was desperately required.

A Controversial Case

Much of the controversy has centred upon the reported events of the 4th August 1892. The lay-out of the Borden's house, the members of the family who were present at the time and their various movements together with the element of time and moments of opportunity to carry out the murders have been endlessly discussed. The only person who has been arrested as being the murderer and indeed charged as such is Lizzie herself. Neither of the other possible candidates for the deed, namely John Vinnicum Morse, Lizzie's uncle or Bridget Sullivan the family maid has been seriously posed as the guilty party. Indeed there has rarely been a celebrated case of murder where suspicion fell within such a narrow compass; both were effectively eliminated as suspects. If Lizzie herself was not the killer it had to be an intruder from outside, yet there is no evidence at all that this happened. Indeed the intense security the Borden family exercised made such a suggestion unlikely in the extreme.

Lizzie herself seemed anxious to present a credible theory that her father had enemies. She impressed this view upon her friend Alice Russell a few days before the killings and expressed to others that this was her opinion. But the whole pattern of the homicide spoke volumes against this theory. Why should someone bent on dispatching Andrew Borden kill Abby Borden first? There was a time lapse of at least an hour between the killings. The medical evidence is of vital importance for two reasons. Firstly, because of the fact that Abby Borden was murdered an hour to an hour and a half before her husband; secondly because the first blow received by Mrs Borden was delivered when she was facing her assailant. In the light of these two facts the theory of the defence that the murderer chased Abby up the stairs to her room in order to eliminate a witness to the killing of Andrew is patently unsound.

Since Andrew Borden was killed within a short period of arriving at home it may be presumed, from the medical evidence, that Abby was murdered well before he was on the premises. An interloper who had a grudge against Andrew would have no reason to make his task doubly difficult by killing Abby—against whom in any event he had no cause for ill-feeling. He would have been unfamiliar with the layout of the house and would have created greater peril for himself by the necessity of spending an hour hiding on the premises before carrying out the second homicide. His whole plan would have been the assassination of his victim and a rapid escape. Why should he complicate the exercise in this way?

Besides, it is universally the case that it is a witness to the killing which has to be eliminated. To slay a potential witness an hour before the bloody deed has occurred is surely unheard of. Since there was an appreciable period of time between the murders the further consideration arises as to why the alleged intruder should unleash such a furious assault upon a harmless woman who by common consent was most probably killed by the first blow which felled her. Yet the views of the medical experts, which the defence did not seek to contradict, was that Abby's assailant stood astride her body and rained blow after blow upon her head in what can only be described as a frenzied attack.

The term "assassination" has been employed for the Borden murders, but there is nothing of the cold ruthless efficiency of the planned assassination about them. These are killings in which emotion and personal hatred dominate the picture. The butchering of Abby Borden, like that of Andrew, bears all the hallmarks of a prior personal relationship, and one in which the highest emotions are involved. Would business differences and resentment be adequate to explain this? Further, would the attacker, who wanted to eliminate a witness to a future deed, have cause to rain a series of blows on the head of the victim which provides a rich source of clues to his or her identity?

The Theory of an Intruder

There are other factors which call into question the theory of the intruder. This was a house on a busy thoroughfare where there were likely to be witnesses to anyone entering or leaving the house. Moreover it was a residence in which the outer doors were kept locked as a matter of course as were some of the inner doors. An intruder who was prepared to risk running the gauntlet of possible witnesses would have no knowledge of which of the doors were locked on the outside of the building and which of the rooms were secured inside.

Unless he or she was a regular visitor to the house they would not be familiar with the layout of the premises nor whether anyone was likely to be present in some part of them when he or she gained entry. Surely, faced with these almost unsurpassable risks the killer, assuming that his or her hatred of Mr Borden was such as to drive him or her to murder both he and his wife, would have chosen a more suitable venue for the assault.

The identity of the supposed intruder has never been seriously mooted, let alone discovered. Lizzie herself expressed the view from the start that her father had enemies and that the deed must be accounted to one of these. She told Alice Russell, before the fatal day, that she had a premonition it would be one of these persons who would attack her father. The words she first used after the murder of her father were to the maid: "Come down quick father's dead. *Somebody came in and killed him*". She continued to maintain this viewpoint after the police investigation had begun.

These are all matters which this author proposes to deal with more fully later in this work. They are important issues in the Lizzie Borden case. In the years succeeding the trial a welter of speculation has taken place. The Borden house has been minutely examined, so also have the movements of the principal participants in the drama. But these degrees of analysis can all too easily befog the subject to the extent that many significant points are obscured in a sea of controversy. This applies particularly in the Borden case in which mass sentiment and opinion was formed on the basis of prejudices and emotion which contributed to a result which many students of criminology and practitioners of the law regard as dubious at best and a denial of justice at worst.

Miscarriages of Justice and Criminal Trials

In deciding whether or not there has been a miscarriage of justice in any criminal case, the place to concentrate is the trial itself. It is on this that the present author intends to place the emphasis. All too often miscarriages of justice occur, not from newspapers misreporting, excessive sentiment on behalf of a defendant with a good character or poor police investigation but from a defect in the trial, perhaps in the role played by the judge such as the wrongful admission or rejection of evidence or the failure of either or both sides to bring forward certain important evidence.

It is the considered view of this author that the criminal trial which is common to the English-speaking world is the best of all legal procedures and in particular is superior to the continental inquisitorial system. It is slanted in favour of the defendant — the term now favoured rather than "the accused" or "the prisoner". However since the issue of guilt or innocence is left in the hands of 12 men and women of no legal expertise, but only with common sense, this method of trial places a huge responsibility upon ordinary citizens who are without any special qualifications for the task of assessing the validity of the arguments of counsel, the credibility of witnesses or the directions of the judge on matters of law. It is true that counsel may, for reasons with or without cause, object to the presence of certain jurors, but the fact remains that those brought in as substitutes may be no more competent for the task than others who have been removed.

The whole philosophy of a trial in Britain or America is based upon the belief that it is better that many guilty persons are acquitted than that a single innocent one should be convicted. The consequence is that in keeping with this philosophy of prudence, in fact a great many guilty persons are set free as against a very small number of innocent ones who have been convicted. When a miscarriage of justice is spoken of it is almost invariably an injustice to the defendant not the prosecution. But the latter sometimes occurs, and when it does it is not only justice itself that suffers, but society as a whole. The judicial system is made to look ineffective and confidence in the administration of justice is lowered. It is the contention of this author that such a case is the trial of Lizzie Borden.

This I know will always be contentious, but I am convinced that:
- the trial was unreasonably biased in favour of the defence;
- the judge acted wrongly in the exclusion of important and highly relevant evidence;
- defence counsel was less than accurate in his presentation of his case to the jury;
- the significance and validity of circumstantial evidence was improperly depreciated; and
- the jury were moved by emotion and sentiment.

In reaching this conclusion I draw on my 17 years of forensic and 27 years of judicial expertise, together with my years of writing books on the subject of the Criminal Law of England and Wales. Nevertheless it could not be argued that on the state of the evidence as a whole the jury in the Borden trial had no reasonable cause to reach the verdict that they did.

CHAPTER TWO

The Background

Much has been written and discussed regarding the history and character of the Borden family in the hope that there may be found a clue to the motive which may have led Lizzie Borden to commit the murders of her father and step-mother. The build-up of emotional turmoil, which can happen in a family situation, leading to an explosion resulting from years of bottled up feelings, has been identified as the root cause of the trouble. Likewise the too common financial motive has been singled out as a reason why Andrew and Abby Borden met their terrible deaths.

There is some basis for both or either of these being the catalyst of disaster. Yet as motive for murder in this particular case they hardly seem, on the known facts, to qualify. Bridget the maid was definite that she had never seen or heard Lizzie and her father or step-mother quarrelling, and although there was some dissatisfaction on the part of Lizzie and her sister Emma regarding their father's disposition of some property, Andrew Borden had acted subsequently to correct the cause of complaint.

The absence of a motive commensurate with the unprecedented violence of the crime is one of the mysterious features of the whole extraordinary drama. It will not be necessary to enter into these matters in depth at this stage, since we shall see how, in the forensic battle of the trial, the various points are developed by both sides in the form of witnesses, examination and cross examination, the addresses of counsel to the jury, and ultimately the summing up by the judge. We shall consider certain strange features of the Borden household—such as the fact that doors, both exterior and interior were kept routinely locked, that the daughters did not join their parents at meal times and that although, according to reports, the members of the family were civil to one another, there seems to have been a strange lack of warmth and affection. The atmosphere, while not openly hostile, appears to have been cold and loveless.

This is something which the prosecution sought to emphasise in order to set a backdrop to the events which followed and which, conversely, the defence tried to minimise as lacking the significance which the Commonwealth, represented by William H Moody and Hosea M Knowlton, placed upon it.

Fall River and the Borden's Home and Social Position

In 1892 the Borden family lived in Fall River, Massachusetts. This was a cotton mill town, with a busy industry and a population of around 75,000. The social class of the people was sharply divided. On the one hand there were old New England families with their privileged lifestyle, their large houses and their servants. At the other end of the scale were the foreign arrivals, mostly from Ireland or European countries. They often found employment as labourers and as workers in the local industries and houses of the wealthy citizens. The Borden family had a name which had long been known in Fall River. There were in fact a great many Bordens, but the surprising and somewhat elusive fact is that notwithstanding that Andrew J Borden, the father of the two girls Lizzie and Emma, was a wealthy man by any standards, the family lived in a house and vicinity which by the measure of the affluent in Fall River, who mostly occupied houses on "The Hill", was comparatively modest. Not only was their dwelling without the trappings of the rich, but they had a lifestyle to match.

Let us take a look first at the Borden house and then consider the members of the family who lived there. The layout of the building is important since the position of the rooms and their relationship to one another has a significant bearing upon the question of whether the defence suggestion that an interloper from outside murdered Mr and Mrs Borden is a reasonable possibility. It must be born in mind at the very start of one of the most celebrated murder trials in American history, that under the criminal law, which broadly speaking prevails in the

English speaking world, however strong the prosecution feels it's case to be, and however fervently those presenting it believe that it should lead to a conviction, if the defence can raise a reasonable doubt in the minds of the jury the defendant must be acquitted.

Under the rules of evidence in both American and English courts it is a legitimate strategy for the defence to raise the possibility of the crime having been committed by someone other than the defendant. This may be no more than an alternative explanation. It may have no real evidence to support it, but provided no attempt is made by counsel to mislead the court by pretending that there is such evidence, when in fact none exists, the tactic is not unethical.

The Borden house was, and is, since it remains basically unchanged to this day, of an unusual oblong design. One end of the oblong faces a road, which was the busy thoroughfare known as Second Street. That is also an important consideration, since at no time during the relevant period of the murder was an interloper seen entering or leaving the premises.

The front of the house abuts onto the street. Behind the rear was a barn, which contained items which were not suitable for inclusion in the house. There were two entrances, one at the front and one at the rear on the side adjacent to another house occupied by a Mrs Adelaide Churchill, a lady who figures in the events of the day of the homicides. At the back of the house there was a door leading into a cellar. Besides the barn there was a yard and a pear orchard. As to the interior of the house, one cannot do better than to quote the clear description given by Judge Robert Sullivan in his book *Goodbye Lizzie Borden*.

> "As one entered the front door from Second Street, there was a large hall. Immediately to the right of the door was a small coat closet, also to the right of the side of the hall was a curving flight of stairs leading up to the bedroom floor. From this hall one could go straight into the sitting room and then through to the kitchen. But from this front entry, one could take a rather zig zag route to the kitchen by turning left into the more formal parlour, going through doors set at right angles in the corner of the sitting room to reach the dining room, and from there go into the kitchen. In addition to the sink room and pantry, the back hall next to the kitchen held back

stairs which led up to the second floor and down into the cellar...From the front entry one reached the bedroom floor by going up the front stairs, at the top of which was a landing".

This part of the description of the premises is highly relevant to the murder of Abby Borden. Sullivan then described the rest of the house. To the left, above the parlour was a guest room. Doors from both the guest room and the landing led to Lizzie's room, which was directly above the sitting room. In Lizzie's room was the only entrance to Emma's smaller bedroom. Beyond Lizzie's room was a large bedroom used by Mr and Mrs Borden, whose dressing room was directly behind Emma's room. There was a connecting door between Lizzie's room and that of the older Borden's. But on the 4th August 1892 and for a long time previously—this door was locked and blocked with heavy furniture. As a result the only means of access to and from the bedroom and anteroom used by Mr and Mrs Borden was by means of the back stairway leading from the kitchen entry on the first floor.

In addition Andrew Borden locked his bedroom door at the top of these stairs whenever he and his wife were out of the room, though he left the key on the sitting room mantelpiece. Access to the older Borden's room was to be a significant piece of evidence at the trial, as was the fact that it had become family practice to keep locked all outside doors on the ground floor—even on the briefest errand to the yard around the house—as was also the case with the second floor bedrooms. Under the pitched roof was an attic where Bridget Sullivan, the maid, slept in a partitioned space or room at the rear of the house, and which could be reached only by the back stairway.

Having examined the Borden house, let us now take a look at the family. Accounts of the character of Mr and Mrs Borden, Emma and Lizzie have agreed to a surprising extent as also have descriptions of the relationship between them. It is also fair to say that photographs of the two most striking and dominant figures in the drama, namely Andrew Borden and Lizzie coincide remarkably with those descriptions provided by contemporaries who knew them well.

Andrew Borden

Let us begin with Andrew. Lizzie's father, in his portrait photograph, looks cold and humourless. The mouth is set tight; the eyes contain no hint of gentleness or generosity. The picture contains the face of a man who was ruthless and relentless in achieving his targets in life; who would not yield an inch to considerations of kindness nor would he compromise for a moment with any kind of sentimentality. One should not read too much into a photograph but the fact remains that a person's character may frequently be mirrored in their facial appearance. Andrew Borden, like Bordens before him, was a rich man by the standards of those days, but he had acquired his wealth by years of effort and single-minded struggle. The sum of a quarter of a million dollars, which is the amount he is alleged to have been worth, would rank as a minor acquisition today, but in 1892 it counted as a fortune.

Mr Borden had begun as a funeral director and his later reputation may be gauged by the somewhat gruesome rumour that he would amputate the feet of a tall cadaver rather than go to the expense of having a longer coffin built. A more reliable, and certainly factual, report is that at the height of his opulence he would carry a basket of eggs from a farm of his and personally sell them in the town. Further instances of his complete lack of generosity of heart are his failure, or more properly refusal, to equip his house with basic amenities, such as adequate heating and plumbing. For Andrew Borden money was an end in itself, not a means to a materially better life.

For some time Borden attended church, but unlike his daughter Lizzie there was no great commitment on his part. When the tax assessor who was an official of his church, raised the valuation on some of his properties he stopped attending in response. It was his boast that he had never been in debt and there can be little reason to doubt that this was true.

With the money derived from his undertaking business Andrew invested in real estate in the town and in farms in the countryside and also possessed substantial shareholdings in the most profitable of the growing cotton mills. The upshot of his single minded pursuit of financial success was that by the time of his murder he was President of the

Union Savings Bank, director of the First National Bank, director of the Safe Deposit and Trust Company, director of the Farm Mills Company, director of the Troy Cotton and Woolen Manufacturing Company, and director of the Merchants Manufacturing Company.

To the end of his life he was never known to give to charity and in his business dealings he drove a hard bargain (though as described later in this chapter he could be generous). Although Lizzie claimed that her father had enemies there is a dearth of evidence as to who, in particular, they were, and whether their antipathy towards Andrew was of the type that prompted a person to murder. The fact has to be that Mr Borden's position in the community merited respect for such a prominent figure and the bearer of an honoured name in Falls River. But that being said there is not a jot of evidence that he was popular. Indeed the reverse would seem to have been the case. Whatever the qualities that had brought him his prosperity, benevolence was clearly not one of them. There are reports that, like his younger daughter, he involved himself in charitable causes. He employed ruthless tactics in his business dealings, and only grudgingly parted with money, even when it was for the benefit of his own family. The picture is the not unfamiliar one of the self-made man who, whatever his subsequent wealth, cannot forget the penury of his early days and yet never achieves the sense of security which his success should have brought him.

There were no parks, libraries, schools or hospitals in Fall River to which he devoted his services or his money. For this reason on the occasion of his death there was no outpouring of grief—only shock and surprise and, perhaps on the part of some, a degree of malicious satisfaction. No doubt this was due to the fact that in human affairs success brings envy and envy in its turn promotes animosity.

Lizzie and Emma

Andrew Borden married twice. The first time this was to Sarah J Morse in 1845. Sarah was the mother of Lizzie and Emma. Emma Leonora was born in 1849 and Lizzie Andrew in 1860. Sarah had a tragically early death in 1862, by which time Emma was 13 and Lizzie two. The tragedy of the

Borden household was that for the daughters, young as they were at the time of their mother's death, the second wife who arrived on the scene was merely a replacement. There are times where a step-mother is much loved by the children of a former wife. This was not one of them. One clear fact from the story of this family is that Abby Durfee Gray Borden was never fully accepted by Lizzie and Emma. So far as Emma is concerned, her feelings are harder to discern than are Lizzie's. Perhaps this is due to the fact that her personality and character are over-shadowed by the stronger and more colourful Lizzie. It is significant that in the works researched by this author no photographs of Emma appear anywhere.

No doubt Emma's attitude towards her step-mother coincided in some measure with that of her sister, but probably not to the same extent. In the case of Lizzie her frame of mind can only be described as downright hostility. In the course of Lizzie's subsequent trial for the murder of her father and step-mother the prosecution, in the hope of raising a motive for murder, called witnesses to statements made by Lizzie concerning her relationship with Abby. Mrs Hannah M Gifford, a dressmaker who for seven or eight years had been making clothing for Lizzie, deposed to a conversation she had with Lizzie in the spring of 1882. "I was speaking to Lizzie of a garment I had made for Mrs Borden, and instead of saying "Mrs Borden" I said "Mother" and Lizzie says don't say that to me, she is a mean good-for-nothing" "I said 'Oh Lizzie, you don't mean that' and she said 'Yes, I don't have much to do with her, I stay in my room most of the time' I said, you come down to your meals, don't you and she said, 'Yes, but we don't eat with them if we can help it'".

Another witness is Miss Anna H Borden (no relative) who had accompanied Lizzie on a steam ship to Europe in 1890. According to Anna, Lizzie had expressed extreme resentment towards Abby and was reluctant to return to her "unhappy home". This evidence was excluded on the proper grounds of ambiguity and remoteness of time. Adverse remarks may well depict the situation in the Borden's household but they do not constitute even circumstantial evidence of intent to murder.

Bridget Sullivan, the family maid, stated in her evidence at the trial that she had never heard a quarrel or an argument involving Lizzie and Abby Borden in the years she had spent in the Borden household. Two things must be born in mind however: firstly this was a period when emotions were held in check, especially among people of good family, more firmly than is the case today. Secondly, family quarrels were not conducted in front of servants. The evidence of Mrs Gifford is to some extent supported in the trial by that of John Fleet, the Deputy City Marshall of Fall River, who said, that during the murder investigation he was having a conversation with Lizzie: "I then asked her if she had any idea who could have killed her father and mother". Then she said, "She is not my mother sir, she is my step-mother, my mother died when I was a child." But it seems little weight should be given to these remarks.

Potential Suspects

The allegation of a financial motive will be dealt with later in this work. The three potential suspects to the murder, John Vinnicum Morse, Bridget Sullivan and Emma Lenora Borden were all, after careful police investigation, eliminated from the murder enquiry. This left two possibilities only, an unknown intruder or Lizzie herself. The likelihood of an intruder having committed the murder was reduced for several reasons. First and foremost was the fact the Mrs Borden was also killed. Why should an enemy of Andrew Borden, and there is little doubt that he may well have had some, have slain his harmless and unoffending wife? Secondly, the theory that she was eliminated because she was a witness to the death of her husband is completely discredited on the grounds that she was the first of the two to die. The undisputed medical evidence was that there was a least one hour between the two deaths. Thirdly, the first blow was delivered when she was facing her assailant, which indicates that she was already in the guest bedroom when the assassin entered. There are other considerations. To carry out these murders, or indeed either of them, within the Borden house, was an enterprise full of risks.

Unlike the average home, 92 Second Street was something of a fortress. The front entry, the kitchen entry and the entry down to the cellar were all routinely locked and secured from the inside. They each were occasionally unlocked for a brief interval to enable members of the family household to leave or enter, and on the day of the murders the side entry was unlocked while Bridget was cleaning windows, but an intruder would have no knowledge of when this would be. Nor would the unknown interloper have any awareness of the geography of the interior of the premises. The rooms occupied by Lizzie, Emma and Mr and Mrs Borden were kept locked and although Mr Borden kept his keys on the mantelpiece in the sitting room their whereabouts would not be known to a trespasser. Once inside the house the infiltrator would have no possible way of knowing how he or she could avoid being observed by any member of the family in the house, or that they would have a suitable hiding place during the hour to an hour and a half between the two crimes. In fact at the time of any presumed entry, there would have been four people, Bridget, Lizzie and the two victims. Emma was away staying with friends.

The only apparent places where the killer might conceal himself were the large dress closet on the upstairs floor or the small one next to the front entry. The former was immediately next to the guest room where the body of Abby Borden was found. The discovery would have led to an immediate search of the adjoining rooms, including the first floor lobby. The latter was very small, and would have involved the killer descending the front stairs where he or she would have been exposed to recognition by anyone else in the house.

The Murder Weapon

Then there is the question of the murder weapon, which was clearly the same one used on both victims. This was a hatchet — though whether it was the one advanced by the prosecution at the trial is contentious. The only implements of this kind were locked in the cellar. How would the intruder have known of this, or whereabouts they were? Or did he or she enter the house armed with such a weapon, and carry it away covered with blood in a busy street?

Lizzie or an Intruder?

I have raised these issues at an early stage. They will be examined in more detail later in this work, but reduced to simple terms the bottom line in the Borden trial is that the culprit has to be an unknown intruder or Lizzie herself. At the time of the murders the only known occupants of 92 Second Street were Bridget the maid and Lizzie Borden. As one who has spent his entire career in criminal courts, first as a barrister and later as a judge this writer is familiar with the tactics of the prosecution when this is the scenario: if not the defendant, then who else could have committed the crime? In the system of trial employed in the English-speaking world the jury do not and must not convict a defendant if they have a reasonable doubt as to his or her guilt. What is "reasonable" is not defined in the Common Law tradition of both England and the United States of America. It is left as a question fact for the jury, after adequate and proper direction by the judge.

A great English Judge in a famous murder trial, the *Wallace Case* of 1931, told the jury that it was not their task to say that if the defendant did not commit the murder, who could have done? Their province was to ask the question, "Did this defendant commit the crime? The question is not who did this crime? The question is did the prisoner do it? Or rather, to put it more accurately, is it proved to your reasonable satisfaction and beyond all reasonable doubt that the prisoner did it? It is a fallacy to say 'If the prisoner did not do it, who did?'"

The same judge also said of his summing up, "So many strange things happen in life. I should not, and never did demand a motive for any crime. Very often the motive is merely impulse, and you must remember that Wallace was a highly strung man".

As I write I have before me four photographs of Lizzie Borden; one of these was taken when she was 17, one when she was 29, one at age 31 and one when she was probably in her late-30s. She is the only person involved in her trial for murder for whom so many photographs exist. What can one learn from a photo? Certainly not enough to decide whether or not the subject is capable of committing murder. Yet the human face is not without significance in some respects. Abraham Lincoln thought so:

questioned why he said he found a certain persons face objectionable he replied — "I hold every man over 40 responsible for his face". Lizzie at 17 presents as an alert, intelligent teenager. The monochrome films of the time fail to capture her red hair which was a striking feature, but the eyes and the mouth, always an important aspect of a person's countenance, have an aspect which is consistent in all the shots. The eyes are intelligent and imperious, yet at the same time cold and expressionless. The mouth is set and strong-willed. Only in one of the pictures is there the merest suspicion of a smile. The general impression has to be of someone who lacks the quality of warm humanity, though it is fair to add that in that era people did not smile for photos.

When she was questioned at the inquest about her relationship with her stepmother she prevaricated.

> **Hosea M Knowlton:** Were you always cordial with you stepmother?
> **Lizzie Borden:** That depends on your idea of cordiality.

Agnes de Mille, in her book *Lizzie Borden* provides us with the following picture:

> "And how did Miss Lizzie look? She was medium sized, five foot three inches, inclined to plumpness but not fat. Her hair was brown and worn on the crown".

Lewis F Grant, who was called upon to sketch her several times when she had become the centre of attention, said, "She was a very solid lady, short heavily built … You wouldn't have thought twice about her except for her jaw. Enormous, the largest jaw I ever saw in a woman." Mrs Gifford, the curator of the Fall River Historical Society in the 1960s, described her expression as not a pleasant one. "Not a face you would voluntarily address". "She was always neat and plainly but smartly dressed. She favoured blue. During the grand jury hearings she wore a top-tilted hat with cherry coloured ribbons, and when travelling a blue veil to conceal her face. During the trial she rubbed her button boots across one another in nervousness. The shoes were shined each morning. She had

had a great deal of dental work done and there was a gleam of gold when she opened her mouth wide when she laughed and her laugh was memorable — unexpected, mirthless and very loud. At school it had unnerved her classmates. Jokes were one of the things she did not choose to share".

Then follows this very significant account: "She was known in town for her peculiar look". Eva Kelly Betz said, "I saw Lizzie a few times when I was young. She had dreadful eyes, colourless and soul-less like those of a snake". Another neighbour unkindly remarked she was certain the lids came up from the bottom. She was given to staring, old women still remember how frightened they were as children, even though at first ignorant of her identity, whenever that face appeared with its peculiar unexplained look staring outside windows of stores or stations. It was her eyes, they said, the emptiness in her eyes. But for her eyes, her face would have been mild, even comely. She wore rimless *pince-nez*.

Another story is told involving a cat which annoyed Lizzie by rubbing against her skirt. She seized the animal by the tail and swung it around, letting it fly to a place about 50 feet away. There is little information regarding Lizzie's mental state, although hints that it gave rise to concern. It must be recounted that she took pity on another cat which had been injured by a scythe. Her wild swings of mood can be indicative of a psychopathic condition of mind.

More on Lizzie's Character and Relationships

During the inquest Lizzie was questioned about her relationship with her step-mother. The following continues from the previous exchange with counsel on the previous page:

> **Knowlton:** Was it cordial according to your idea of cordiality?
> **Lizzie Borden:** Yes, I did not regard her as my mother, though she came there when I was young. I decline to say whether my relationship between her and myself were those of a mother and daughter or not. I called her Mrs Borden and sometimes mother, I stopped calling her mother after the affair regards her half-sister.
> **Knowlton:** Why did you leave off calling her mother?

Lizzie Borden: Because I wanted to.
Knowlton: Have you any other answer to give me?
Lizzie Borden: No sir, I always went to my sister, she was older than I was.

These replies are self-confident, even arrogant. They present a portrait of a young woman very much in possession of herself which conflicts with Lizzie Borden the church going charity worker who taught at Sunday School and was active in the Women's Christian Union and the Christian Endeavour Society, and who became a close friend of the local clergymen the Reverend W Walker Jubb and the Reverend E A Buck. These two gentlemen played a considerable role in championing the wave of sentiment during the trial, which ultimately carried Lizzie to her triumphant acquittal. Yet after her release neither had anything further to do with her.

In his book *Goodbye Lizzie Borden* Robert Sullivan, a former Justice of the Massachusetts Superior Court, recounts an incident which Mrs Potter, the niece of Abby Borden, had told him was recounted by Abby.

> "Lizzie Borden had company and my aunt had a tabby cat and the cat was trained that it would touch the latch—you know it was latches in those days, she would touch the latch and the door would open. So the cat went in where Lizzie was entertaining and she took it out and shut the door again, and it came back so this is what she told aunt Abby and Abby told my mother…Lizzie Borden finally excused herself and went downstairs—took the cat downstairs, put it on the chopping block and chopped its head off. My aunt for days wondered where the cat was—all she talked about. Finally, Lizzie said you go downstairs and you'll find your cat. My aunt did".

Further talks regarding Lizzie's conduct in the past have been recounted which cast no further light on the crimes themselves, other than presenting a picture, if true, of a streak of cold callousness in the character of Lizzie. One story is to the effect that Lizzie and a companion were guests in the house of an acquaintance. The two girls slept overnight in their friend's house. In the morning Lizzie came down alone to breakfast.

About halfway through the meal she almost nonchalantly commented that the other girl had died during the night. A doctor was called but failed to identify the cause of death. On another occasion Lizzie was with a friend who expressed a wish to demolish a barn. Lizzie responded by saying "give me an axe and I will soon chop it down".

Yet another incident told to Robert Sullivan by Mrs Potter, a niece of Abby, was that after the trial was over Lizzie sent all the personal effects of Abby to Sarah Whitehead, a member of Abby's family, which included a photograph of Abby in her wedding gown.

Unusual Generosity from Andrew Borden

One other relevant matter should be referred to while surveying the background to the case. At some time between 1884 and 1887 Andrew showed some generosity, unusually for him, towards Abby's family, the Whiteheads. Lizzie was resentful about this. When Oliver Gray, the father of Sarah and Abby died, their Fourth Street house was divided four ways. One fourth went to Sarah, and one fourth to Abby, Abby gave her share to Sarah. Andrew Borden bought Mrs Gray's portion and gave this to Sarah. Lizzie and Emma took exception to what they regarded as generosity to Abby's family which should have been shown to them. However, Andrew compensated by making a present of property which exceeded the value of the gift about which they were complaining. He then repurchased this from them, only a short time before his death.

All in all, notwithstanding the evidence of ill-feeling that Lizzie bore towards her step-mother, there is little evidence that she felt even remotely the same way towards her father. This presented a problem for the prosecution in the trial. It was one which they never fully surmounted. The absence of any clear motive on Lizzie's part for murdering Andrew Borden was a stumbling block for advocates acting for the Commonwealth.

Two Other Key Participants

Now let us take a look at the other two people who figure in the drama of 4th August 1892. The maid Bridget Sullivan, who for obscure reasons was known to Lizzie and Emma as "Maggie", was an Irish girl. Like other immigrants from Ireland who had fled the conditions of famine in their home country she had entered the United States three years earlier. She was 26 at the time of the murders, single and by all accounts conscientious in carrying out her duties in the Borden household. She was also highly intelligent. During the trial she gave her evidence with coolness, frankness and obvious honesty. Although she was devoted to Lizzie it could not be said that she slanted her testimony to assist Lizzie's case.

Bridget had a small attic bedroom in the Borden house. Her duties were reasonable for a maid but not onerous and she was treated fairly by the family for whom she worked. Her duties were washing, ironing, cooking and some sweeping and scrubbing. She had to look after her own bedroom, the others being attended to by their occupiers. She was a devout Roman Catholic and had a blameless character. Bridget gave evidence at both the trial and the inquest. Her evidence was neither prejudicial to nor helpful for Lizzie, but it was crucial in eliminating Emma from suspicion because she confirmed that Emma and been away from the house some two weeks and had not returned in all that time. She had Sundays off and also a large part of Thursdays.

It was clear from the evidence that Bridget was in her attic bedroom at the time of the murders. At the inquest Lizzie herself exonerated Bridget from blame. We can ponder the reason why she did. Was it because Lizzie, who was a clever woman, knew that if she tried to throw suspicion on Bridget it would be to her own detriment?

Lizzie Borden and the Massachusetts Axe Murders

CHAPTER THREE

Before the Holocaust

August 3rd 1892 was another day in Fall River where the heat was relentless in a summer which, even in Massachusetts, was almost unprecedented. It was on that day, the one before the murders, that four significant events occurred in the Borden household. Firstly John Vinnicum Morse arrived for a short stay. He must have intended his visit to be a very brief one, because he had no overnight clothing or toiletries with him. He had been a visitor to the family on other occasions, but other than the fact that he was uncle to the girls, having been the brother of the deceased Sarah Morse and consequently brother-in-law to Andrew, there seems to have been little in common between John and the rest of the Bordens. There was however a certain degree of respect between Morse and his brother-in-law, notwithstanding that a horse trainer and a banker inhabited very different worlds. John had given Andrew some investment advice which had proved profitable to Andrew, something which in itself would secure for the former a degree of affection from the latter. There is little doubt that on this occasion Morse had no idea he was entering a hornet's nest.

The other three events concern Lizzie and Abby. The first was when Lizzie absented herself in the morning at around 11 am. She gave as the reason a need for some air, a not unreasonable motive on such a humid day. It was alleged by the prosecution however, that her real intention was to visit a chemist in order to purchase Prussic acid. We shall see in due course the evidence which the prosecution sought to call regarding this and the extraordinary way in which the court dealt with it.

The third incident was Mrs Borden's visit to Dr Bowen, who lived nearby, complaining of sickness and even expressing the belief that she had been poisoned—a suggestion which her doctor dismissed in favour of the greater likelihood that Abby had eaten food which had deteriorated in the heat.

Finally, there was Lizzie's departure in the evening to visit Alice Russell, a close friend of herself and her sister Emma. This was between seven and nine in the evening. It was an extraordinary visit. Lizzie spoke to her friend about strange and fearful forebodings she had that something was going to happen. She said her father had enemies and plainly implied that someone was planning to do something criminal. She could not shake off this grim premonition—or so she said. Lizzie told Alice that she believed the sickness from which the family had suffered was due to poisoning. She also spoke about things which had taken place in the house and the barn.

Alice was plainly disturbed and advised Lizzie to leave Fall River for a spell. This advice was not taken. When Lizzie arrived home she went straight to her room. She exchanged not a word with her uncle. Morse slept that night in the guest room which was later to be the scene of Abby's murder.

The Fatal Day

On the morning of the fatal day Bridget the maid was the first to come down. At seven o'clock Mr and Mrs Borden were eating breakfast together with Morse. By today's standards the food provided was somewhat extraordinary. This however, has little to do with the drama which followed. At about 8.45 am Morse left the house, he had several errands to make. He was told by Andrew Borden to be sure to come back for dinner (taken at lunchtime). Mrs Borden did some dusting.

Around 9 am Lizzie came down. She had a cup of coffee and nibbled a cookie. Lizzie had a few words with Abby while the latter was dusting in the dining room. Bridget, who also felt sick, returned from the garden where she had vomited. After Morse had left at about 8.45, Bridget was instructed by Abby to wash the windows. She got a bucket and brushes from the cellar and worked her way round the outside of the house. She had a clear view into each of the rooms. She saw no strangers. She had a brief chat with the servant of Dr Kelly next door. Lizzie left the side door unlocked while Bridget was cleaning the windows. At no time did Bridget see any strangers on the premises. After Morse had left the house, Andrew left at 9.15, and with Bridget outside washing the windows only Abby and Lizzie remained inside the building.

Mrs Borden tidied up the guest room and made the bed. She came downstairs and remarked to Lizzie that she was going up again to put fresh pillow slips on the bed. Bridget came in to close all the windows preparing to wash them inside. She entered the kitchen, dining room and sitting room, all were empty. About 9.30 Abby went upstairs with the pillow slips to the guest room — and was murdered.

At about 10.45 am Andrew returned home. He tried the side door unsuccessfully. He went to the front door. He had some difficulty. Bridget helped with the lock. Lizzie laughed — she was on the landing at the head of the front stairs. She gave widely varying accounts of where she was when her father returned. If in fact she was on the landing she would have been within 15 or 20 feet of Mrs Borden's dead body. Lizzie told her father "Mrs Borden has gone out — she had a note from somebody who is sick". No trace of the note has ever been found. No-one has answered an appeal for the author to come forward. No doctor in Fall River has admitted to having a patient who sent the note. The story of the note came from Lizzie alone.

When Andrew Borden came in he retrieved his key from the mantelpiece and went to his room. Shortly afterwards he returned to the sitting room. The two sitting room windows opened onto the Kellys' side of the house. The shades of both windows were drawn. According to the Kellys this was most unusual. Andrew was assisted by Lizzie to lie down on the couch.

Bridget finished washing the windows and Lizzie started to iron her handkerchiefs. Bridget went to her room for a rest. After anything from ten to 20 minutes she heard the city hall strike eleven. Suddenly she heard Lizzie's agitated voice, "Maggie! Come down".

"What's the matter?" said Bridget.

"Come down here! Father is dead. Someone came in and killed him."

Told by Lizzie to get a doctor Bridget ran across the street to Dr Bowen's house only to learn that he was out, She left the message of Andrew Borden's death and returned. She asked Lizzie where she was when this happened and received a reply which was inconsistent with a later account:

"I was out in the yard and heard a groan, and came in and the screen door was wide open". This, unlike the side door itself, was only secured by a hook.

Next on the scene was Mrs Churchill. She asked Lizzie where she was when her father was killed. Her reply: "I went to the barn to get a piece of iron...". This was the first time the barn had been mentioned—and there was no reference to a groan. If Lizzie had been in the barn there was no way that she could have heard a groan in the sitting room. Asked "Where is your mother?" Lizzie replied, "I don't know, she had a note to go to see somebody who is sick, but I don't know but that she is killed too, for I thought I heard her come in". This again is a strange reply. If Lizzie thought it was her father who was at risk why should she assume her mother had been murdered, even if she had heard her enter the premises. If on the other hand she had not heard Abby come in then she, Lizzie was not telling the truth.

The police were telephoned and City Marshall Hilliard received the message at 11.15 am. When Mrs Churchill returned to the house she was joined by Dr Bowen, who inspected the body of Andrew Borden. It is important to consider his report to the press at this early stage:

"Mr Borden lay partly on his right side, with his coat thrown over the arm of the sofa...his feet rested on the carpet. It was his custom to lie that way, I am satisfied that he was asleep when he received the first blow, which was necessarily fatal...his clothing was not disarranged, and his pockets had apparently not been touched...

The dead man's head and face were so hacked that the wounds and blood made him unrecognisable. The cuts extended from the eye and nose around the ear. In a small space there were at least eleven distinct cuts...Physician that I am and accustomed to all kinds of horrible sights, it sickened me to look upon the dead man's face. I am inclined to think that an axe was the instrument. The cuts were about four and a half inches in length, and one of them had severed the eye ball and socket. There was some blood on the floor and splatter on the wall, but nothing of a quantity to indicate the slaughter that had taken place. I calculated that all the blows were delivered from behind with great rapidity".

Alice Russell had arrived and joined Mrs Churchill. Lizzie suggested that someone look for Mrs Borden. Mrs Churchill and Bridget went upstairs. As soon as her eyes were level with the landing Mrs Churchill saw the body of Abby. She and Bridget returned downstairs and reported the discovery to Dr Bowen. Dr Bowen went and examined the corpse, which had similarly horrific injuries to those of her husband.

It became clear, after examination of the bodies, that Mrs Borden had been killed about 90 minutes before her husband. The difference in temperature between the bodies, and the more advanced coagulation of Mrs Borden's blood indicated this and it was confirmed by the autopsies.

If the murderer was an interloper from outside the house it was impossible that he had carried out one homicide, left the house and then returned to commit another. The only alternative was that somehow he had concealed himself, for that considerable period of time, about the interior of a house of which he had no knowledge, without being seen or heard by either Lizzie or Bridget. Furthermore he would have had to perform this feat in a building which was far from spacious, some of the doors to the main rooms being kept permanently locked. Finally, having gained entrance through outside doors which were also kept locked, save for the brief widow of opportunity when Bridget undid the catch on side door while she was working on the windows, he would have to escape into a street where he would quite possibly be seen by passers to be carrying a weapon and with blood on his clothing. Was this believable? Is it believable?

The jury at the subsequent trial of Lizzie Borden must presumably have thought so, since this fantastic story is the only alternative to Lizzie's guilt. Or were they prepared to accept any alternative possibility rather than send a "nice, religious and charitable girl to the gallows". Later in this work we shall have ample opportunity to consider the consequences for justice of such an approach by 12 jurymen who, for the duration of their task, were custodians of the law. In his seminal work on the case *Trial of Lizzie Borden* Edmund Pearson writes, "[I]t should be understood that all who came to the house after the discovery of the murders, whether they came as friends to fan 'the poor girl' and flutter around her, or whether they came as police officers to investigate and report, had but one idea. It was that some fiend, some unknown assassin, had entered and done these ghastly murders".

> "To everyone it seemed the deed of a maniac, of a Frankenstein monster, a senseless atrocity which could only be imagined by creatures from the infernal pit. Not long before, everyone had been reading of the Whitechapel Murders, within about a year newspaper reports had suggested—although erroneously—that Jack the Ripper had come to America. A visitation by someone like this, so everyone thought, was the explanation of the frightful event. Nobody had any other theory or belief puzzling as it was to think that there could be such enmity towards old people; or to explain why the foe of one of them should kill the other, or why, if the killer were a madman he should have spared Miss Lizzie and Miss Bridget; the belief that a 'criminal' from the outside was, for many hours, perhaps days, all but universal. Thus can ill-informed opinion based on misplaced sentiment if widely held, come to influence events".

Where Was Lizzie Borden?

Not surprisingly a number of people enquired of Lizzie where she was when the murders took place. One place where she certainly was without any doubt was within the precincts of the house, and excluding Bridget, who at relevant times was outside the house washing the windows or in her room during the attack, she was the only person who could have seen the murderer. We shall see, from the evidence of those persons who appeared as witnesses at the trial and the account given by Lizzie at the inquest, how inconsistent were the replies Lizzie gave to questions about her whereabouts. We shall also consider carefully the absence of blood on Lizzie's clothing and whether this should have been as decisive in her favour as it proved eventually to be.

In the course of their investigation the police were informed of the strange sickness suffered by Andrew and Abby Borden and Bridget on the Tuesday before the crimes. For this purpose, two police officers visited several chemists in the neighbourhood. Three employees of a shop near to the Borden's home deposed to the fact that a woman who they identified as Lizzie Borden had entered their shop and asked for ten cents worth of the deadly poison Prussic acid. The request was refused. When the Commonwealth sought to call these witnesses the court excluded the evidence on the astonishing grounds that because the murders were accomplished with an axe, evidence of the attempted purchase of poison was not sufficiently relevant.

CHAPTER FOUR

Lizzie's Visit to Alice

If the alleged visit of Lizzie to the chemist to purchase poison on the morning or early afternoon of 3rd of August is a matter of contention there is no such issue over her meeting with Alice Russell in the evening of the same day. Alice Russell is an important witness in the Borden trial. There are two reasons for this.

Firstly, Alice was one of the very few genuine friends that Lizzie had, the rest being acquaintances in social and church circles in Fall River.

Secondly, she was by common consent a wholly truthful and reliable witness. She was indeed one of the three soundest witnesses to be called by the prosecution; the others being Adelaide B Churchill and Bridget Sullivan. Alice was called for two reasons, one was to recount the events when Lizzie visited her and the other was to give her testimony regarding the burning of a dress by Lizzie which we shall come to in due course:

> "I have lived in Fall River a good many years, I am unmarried. Two years ago last October I lived in the house now occupied by Dr Kelly, I have lived there eleven years. All that time the Bordens occupied the house next door, I was acquainted with the whole family. On the fourth of last August I lived in the Bordens' street. I exchanged calls with Miss Lizzie Borden; she always received me upstairs in the guest room. About seven o'clock on the evening of Wednesday August third of last year she called upon me. She stayed until about nine".

The importance of this interview has been overlooked or minimised by previous authors. In the view of this writer it is of great significance.

Hence the value of a study of the conversation as recorded in the official court transcript:

William H Moody: Won't you state what was said by her and you and then go on and state the conversation which followed.

Alice Russell: I think when she came in she said "I have taken your advice and have written to Marion that I will come". I don't know what came in between. I don't know as this followed that, but I said I am glad you are going as I had urged her to go before and I don't know just what followed, but I said something about her having a good time and she said "well I don't know. I feel depressed. I feel as though something was hanging over me that I cannot throw off, it comes over me at times no matter where I am". And she says "when I was at the table the other day when I was at Marion's and the girls were laughing and talking and having a good time and this feeling came over me and one of them spoke and said "Lizzie why don't you talk?"

Moody: Well then go on then, and state how the conversation went taking your own method.

Alice Russell: I suppose it followed right on after that when she spoke she says "I don't know Father has so much trouble" Oh I am a little ahead of the story, she said "Mr and Mrs Borden were awfully sick last night and I said why what is the matter, something they have eaten" she said "we were all sick all but Maggie" and I said "something you have eaten?". She said "we don't know, we had some bakers bread and all ate of it but Maggie, and Maggie wasn't sick" and I said "well it couldn't have been the bread, if it had been bakers bread I should suppose other people would be sick and I haven't heard of anybody" and she says "that is so" and she says "sometimes I think our milk might be poisoned" and I said "well how do you get your milk, how could it be poisoned? And she said "we have the milk come in a can and set on the step, and we have an empty can, we put out the empty overnight, and the next morning when they bring the milk they take the empty can" and I said "well if they put anything in the can the farmer would see it". And then I said—I asked her what time the milk came in, if she knew. She said "I think about four o'clock" and I said "well, it is light at four, I shouldn't think anyone would dare to come then and tamper with the can for fear somebody would see them" and she said "I shouldn't think so" and then she said "they were awfully sick, and I wasn't sick, and didn't vomit, but I heard them vomiting and stepped to the door and asked if I could do anything, and they said no".

Moody: Now go on with the conversation.

Alice Russell: Well I think she told me that they were better in the morning and that Mrs Borden thought that they had been poisoned, and she went over to Dr Bowen's — she said she was going over to Dr Bowen's.

Moody: Well we won't follow that any further, is there any other thing that she began to talk about?. Proceed in your own way Miss Russell.

Alice Russell: I can't recall anything just now. Of course she talked about something else, because there were two hours, but I cannot think about it.

Moody: Anything about trouble with tenants, or anything of that sort?

Alice Russell: She says "I don't know" she says "I feel afraid sometimes, that father has got an enemy" for she said "he has so much trouble with his men that come to see him". She told me of a man who came to see him, and heard him say — she didn't see him, but heard her father say "I don't care to let my property for such business". And she said the man answered sneeringly "I shouldn't think you would care what you let your property for" and she said "father was mad and ordered him out of the house."

She told me of seeing a man running around the house one night when she went home. I have forgotten where she had been. She said "and you know the barn has been broken into twice" and I said "oh well you know that was somebody after pigeons, there is nothing in there for them to go after but pigeons" well she says "they have broken into the house in broad daylight, with Emma and Maggie and me there". And I said "I have never heard of that before" and she said "father forbade our telling it". So I asked her about it, and she said it was in Mrs Borden's room, what she called her dressing room. She said her things were ransacked, and they took a watch and chain and money and car tickets, and something else that I can't remember, and there was a nail left in the keyhole, and she didn't know why that was left; whether they got in with it or what. I asked her if her father did anything about it, and she said he gave it to the police, but they didn't find out anything, and she said father expected that they would catch the thief by the tickets. She remarked "just as if anybody would use those tickets".

Moody: Is there anything else that you recall? Anything about burning the house?

Alice Russell: She said "I feel as if I want to sleep with my eyes open half the time — for fear they will burn the house down over us".

Moody: Is there anything else that occurs to you in the conversation?

Alice Russell: Oh, she said "I am afraid somebody will do something; I don't know but somebody will do something". I think that was the beginning.

Moody: Please state that.

Alice Russell: "I think sometimes — I am afraid sometimes that someone will do something to him. He is so discourteous to people".

Lizzie's visit to Alice on the evening of Wednesday 3rd August has, in the view of this author, greater significance than it has sometimes been accorded by previous writers on the case. It is full of questions: Why did Lizzie who was a close friend of Alice and who has access to her at any time, choose that particular occasion to see her, so close to the time of the murders? Why had she not spoken to her father about her fears of some imminent disaster? For that matter, if her concerns were so grave, why had she not contacted the police? She informs Alice that she has decided to accept her advice and go to Marion, where she could be with her sister Emma — yet in fact she has changed her mind and will not be going on the somewhat strange pretext that wherever she may be she will get depressed and will experience "something hanging over me that I cannot throw off".

Why is it that whatever Alice says to set her mind at rest Lizzie refused to be reassured? She almost argues against each point made by Alice to suggest that there is no real cause for alarm. Lizzie very strongly asserts the likelihood of poison, notwithstanding the fact that Mrs Borden visited Dr Bowen in the earlier part of that day and expressed her fears of possible poisoning. Dr Bowen had dismissed these fears with assurances of his own. Moreover subsequent medical evidence at the trial revealed no traces of poison in the stomachs of either victim.

When Lizzie suggested that the bread might have been poisoned and Alice wisely pointed out that the symptom's would have been apparent in other people in the neighbourhood, Lizzie turned to the question of the milk. When she conceded that her parents were better in the morning, Lizzie expressed fears for her father. However she could only quote one argument between Andrew Borden and another man, whose name she did not know, nor had enquired, over the letting of some property belonging to Andrew. She referred to the barn having been broken into twice, but Alice pointed out that the object of this theft was some pigeons, and these were the most a burglar could hope for in the barn. Perhaps most significantly Lizzie spoke about a burglary in the house — of which Alice had never heard. She pointed out that this had taken place "in broad daylight" with "Emma and Maggie and me in there". Was she laying the foundation of a defence to murder that an interloper could have gained admittance to the house and carried out his or her crimes undetected. Notwithstanding the fact that Lizzie and Bridget were on the premises.

Most dramatic was her fear that, "They will burn the house down over us". Even more curious is Lizzie's statement that, "I am afraid somebody will do something; I don't know but someone will do something". What that something was and who that somebody could be Lizzie did not specify. She only gave reasons why her father might be under threat. Never as to why the unfortunate Abby might be in danger.

Lizzie Borden and the Massachusetts Axe Murders

CHAPTER FIVE

The Inquest

The inquest on the two victims was held on August 9th to 11th 1892. Lizzie underwent a thorough questioning by the District Attorney for the Southern District of Massachusetts, Hosea M Knowlton. Knowlton had graduated in law from Tufts College in 1867 and studied at Harvard. He was a representative on the lower house of the Massachusetts Legislature from 1867 to 1877 and a senator in 1878 and 1897. He was Attorney General of Massachusetts from 1894 to 1901, he died in 1902. His style of examination was firm and thorough, but not hectoring or bullying. Lizzie's evidence at the inquest was excluded at the trial, at which she never gave evidence. But let us see how it reflects on her truthfulness.

After some formal questions regarding Lizzie, the family and the house, Knowlton asked Lizzie about her father's wealth, in particular his real estate. She replied, "He owns two farms in Swansea, the place on Second Street, and the A G Borden Building and corner and the land on South Maine Street, where Mr McManus is; then a short time ago he bought some real estate further south that formerly he said belonged to a Mr Birch.

Knowlton then touched on a transaction which was alleged to have caused Lizzie and Emma to feel great resentment towards their father and thus provide a motive for subsequent violence.

> **Hosea M Knowlton:** Did you ever deed him any property?
> **Lizzie Borden:** He gave us, some years ago, grandfather Borden's house on Ferry Street and bought that back from us some weeks ago. I don't know just how many.
> **Knowlton:** As near as you can tell.

Lizzie Borden: Well, I should say in June, but I am not sure.
Knowlton: What do you mean by "bought it back"?
Lizzie Borden: He bought it off us and gave us the money for it.
Knowlton: How much was it?
Lizzie Borden: He gave us five thousand dollars for it.
Knowlton: Did you pay him anything when you took a deed from him?
Lizzie Borden: Pay him anything? No sir.
Knowlton: How long ago was it that you took a deed from him?
Lizzie Borden: When he gave it to us?
Knowlton: Yes.
Lizzie Borden: I can't tell you. I should think five years.
Knowlton: Did you have any other business transactions?
Lizzie Borden: No sir.
Knowlton: Never?
Lizzie Borden: Never.

Knowlton then turned to another matter which had been raised as a possible cause for ill-feeling between Andrew and his daughters, whether or not he had made or was about to make a will at the time of his death.

Knowlton: Did you ever know of your father making a will?
Lizzie Borden: No sir, except I heard somebody say once that there was one several years ago. That is all I ever heard.
Knowlton: Who did you hear say so?
Lizzie Borden: I think it was Mr Morse.
Knowlton: What Morse?
Lizzie Borden: Uncle John V Morse.
Knowlton: What did he say about it?
Lizzie Borden: Nothing except just that.
Knowlton: Did you ask your father?
Lizzie Borden: I did not.
Knowlton: Did he ever mention the subject of wills to you?
Lizzie Borden: He did not.
Knowlton: Did he have any marriage settlement with your step-mother that you know of?

Lizzie Borden: I never knew of any.
Knowlton: Have you heard anything of his proposing to make a will?
Lizzie Borden: No sir.

Knowlton's questions are so pertinent to the possibility of a future trial that one is forced to the conclusion that he already suspected Lizzie to be responsible for the murders. He now turns to the possibility of an intruder being the miscreant.

Knowlton: Do you know of anybody that your father was on bad terms with?
Lizzie Borden: There was a man that came there he had trouble with. I do not know who the man was.
Knowlton: When?
Lizzie Borden: I cannot locate the time exactly. It was within two weeks.
Knowlton: Tell all you heard and saw.
Lizzie Borden: I did not see anything. I heard the bell ring, and father went to the door and let him in. I did not hear anything for some time, except just the voices. Then I heard the man say "I would like to have that place. I would like to have the store". Father says "I am not willing to let your business go in there". And the man said "I thought with your reputation of liking money you would let your store for anything". Father said "you are mistaken". Then they talked a while and their voices were louder and I heard father order him out, and he went to the front door with him.
Knowlton: What did he say?
Lizzie Borden: He said he had stayed long enough and would thank him to go.
Knowlton: Did he say anything about coming again?
Lizzie Borden: No sir.
Knowlton: Have you any idea who that was?
Lizzie Borden: No sir, I think it was a man from out of town, because he said he was going home to see his partner.
Knowlton: Have you had any efforts made to find him?
Lizzie Borden: We have had a detective. That is all I know.

Knowlton: Besides that, do you know of anybody that had bad feelings towards your father?

Lizzie Borden: I know of one man that has not been friendly with him. They have not been friendly.

Knowlton: Who?

Lizzie Borden: Hiram C Harrington.

Knowlton: What relation is he to him?

Lizzie Borden: He is my father's brother-in-law.

Knowlton: Your mother's brother?

Lizzie Borden: My father's only sister married Mr Harrington.

Knowlton: Anybody else that was on bad terms with your father, or that your father was on bad terms with?

Lizzie Borden: Not that I know of.

As the questions continue there is little doubt that Knowlton foresaw that Lizzie was most probably guilty. He was laying the foundations of the case against her.

Lizzie denied that she harboured ill-feeling towards her step-mother, although Knowlton interrogated her closely on the matter. Lizzie said that five or six years ago she ceased to call Abby "mother" and began to call her "Mrs Borden". This was due to the affair with her step-sister. She said that in most matters she confided in her sister Emma. Knowlton was trying to build up a picture of motivation on Lizzie's part for the murder of her step-mother but it must be said that he made little progress. This was partly due to the fact that no clear motive could be found for such unbridled butchery and Lizzie proved a very skilful witness.

It is commonly said that the secret of investigating a murder is to find the motive. It has never been the law of Massachusetts or of England that motive has to be proved. George D Robinson counsel for Lizzie Borden in the trial, came close to saying in his closing argument for the defence at the conclusion of the trial, that the prosecution's case must fail because of their failure to prove motive:

"Now why is the Commonwealth in this case to show a motive for doing it? Merely for this, gentlemen: because they say, there are the crimes, there sits the defendant. Now in order to hold her responsible for the crimes, we have got to bind her up to the crimes. We have no direct evidence that puts her there, we have some circumstances that look as if she might get there, and so in order to bring her to it, we must show a reason why she should do it, what moved her to do it, and that is the motive". This is not the law. Circumstantial evidence, if sufficiently strong, is sufficient grounds for a conviction even though no motive has been proved.

The District Attorney then turned to a subject which proved to be a vital issue in the whole case. The question of which dress Lizzie was wearing on the day of the murders. Did she destroy that dress because it had blood stains?

> **Knowlton:** What dress did you wear the day they were killed?
> **Lizzie Borden:** I had on a navy blue, sort of india silk skirt, with a navy blue blouse. In the afternoon they thought I had better change it. I put on a pink wrapper.
> **Knowlton:** Did you change your clothing before the afternoon? [the victims were killed in the morning].
> **Lizzie Borden:** No sir.
> **Knowlton:** You dressed in the morning as you have described, and kept that clothing on until afternoon?
> **Lizzie Borden:** Yes sir.

These answers are crucial to the question of whether Lizzie burnt a dress on Saturday August 7th, because she wanted to destroy signs of blood. The burning, which was not disputed by the defence, took place three days after the murders. Witnesses who attended to Lizzie after the murders said at the trial that they saw no blood on her clothing. Mrs Churchill the neighbour of the Borden's, and a strong witness, affirmatively deposed to the fact that Lizzie was wearing a light blue cotton dress on the morning of the murders, not the dark blue silk dress which was produced at the trial as being her garb at that time.

Professor Edward Wood who examined the dress found no sign of blood on it, but this would have been after Lizzie's arrest on the 11th August. His examination of the dress would have been after that date, and would have been the dress produced at the trial, which the prosecution maintained was not the one which she wore at the time of the murders. The witnesses who saw no blood on the dress of Lizzie when they were trying to console and assist her were not looking for blood. In answer to the question as to why she should burn a dress with no blood stains must surely be the answer that even if there were none nevertheless if she believed there were this would indicate a guilty mind.

Dr Seabury Bowen who attended Lizzie shortly after the murders was unable to describe the dress she was wearing at that time. However he was clear that she changed into a pink wrapper. Lizzie, at the inquest denied that she changed dress before the afternoon. Either Mrs Churchill or Dr Bowen are wrong or Lizzie is lying. Lizzie said at the inquest: "They thought I had better change it" (the dark silk dress) — she does not say who thought so, who advised her to change her dress or what reason they gave.

At the trial Knowlton asked Bridget the maid, "Let me ask you in this connection if you are able to tell us what dress she had on that morning". Bridget replied, "No sir, I couldn't tell you what dress the girl had on". The attempts by Knowlton to ask what dress Lizzie usually wore in the morning the defence objected to. The court upheld the objection to what appears to be a perfectly relevant question.

Knowlton asked a number of questions relating to the movements of Morse. In his book *Lizzie Borden* Edward D Radin, in his efforts to exonerate Lizzie from guilt attempts to look for an alternative. Morse had an alibi which was thoroughly investigated by the police and proved to be watertight. Bridget accounted for her movements until Andrew Borden's return to the house, by which time Abby Borden was dead upstairs. At the time of Mr Borden's murder, Bridget was in her room in the attic. Neither Morse nor Bridget had the slightest motive for killing the Bordens so far as anyone can tell. Even if there had been a quarrel between Andrew and Morse, for which there is no evidence, Morse had no conceivable reason for butchering Abby. The evidence was that Bridget, unlike Lizzie, had good relations with Mrs Borden. The suggestion that Emma may have committed the crimes has to be absurd, in the light of the admitted fact that she was in Fairhaven on the day of the murders.

As to the theory of an intruder, Radin paints himself into a corner when he writes: "With Lizzie eliminated, this leaves only three logical suspects for the Borden murders, Emma Borden, uncle John Vinnicum Morse and Bridget Sullivan". It is not surprising that in dealing with Morse and Bridget he builds his argument on theorizing about what they "would" or "could" be doing during that fatal day, His entire case against each of them is built on possibilities without any substance or evidence—direct or circumstantial. To this author's knowledge it is unsupported by any serious student of the Borden case.

Lizzie was questioned at the inquest about the relationship of the rooms to one another, before Knowlton moved on to the events of the day of the killings and Lizzie's movements. It was then that Lizzie's evidence becomes a mass of contradictions. It is not surprising that the defence attorneys fought desperately to persuade the court that her replies at the inquest should not be admitted.

She said that her father left to visit the town at some time after nine o'clock. That at the time she was ironing handkerchiefs. She could not say how long she was doing so. Then follows this passage, which it is important to reproduce from the transcript itself.

> **Knowlton:** Where were you when he returned?
> **Lizzie Borden:** I was down in the kitchen.
> **Knowlton:** What doing?
> **Lizzie Borden:** Reading an old magazine that had been left in the cupboard, an old Harpers magazine.
> **Knowlton:** Had you got through ironing?
> **Lizzie Borden:** No sir.
> **Knowlton:** Had you stopped ironing?
> **Lizzie Borden:** Stopped for the flats.
> **Knowlton:** Were you waiting for them to be hot?
> **Lizzie Borden:** Yes sir.
> **Knowlton:** Was there a fire in the stove?
> **Lizzie Borden:** Yes sir.
> **Knowlton:** When your father went away you were ironing them?

Lizzie Borden: I had not commenced, but I was getting the little ironing board and the flannel.

Knowlton: Are you sure you were in the kitchen when your father returned?

Lizzie Borden: I am not sure whether I was there or in the dining room.

Knowlton: Did you go back to your room before your father returned?

Lizzie Borden: I think I did carry up some clean clothes.

Knowlton: Did you stay there?

Lizzie Borden: No sir.

Knowlton: Did you spend any time up the front stairs before your father returned, or after he returned?

Lizzie Borden: No sir, I did stay in my room long enough, when I went up, to sew a little piece of tape on a garment (this was about the time Abby was murdered).

Knowlton: Was that the time when your father came home?

Lizzie Borden: He came home after I came upstairs.

Knowlton: You were not upstairs when he came home?

Lizzie Borden: I was not upstairs when he came home, no sir.

Knowlton: What was Maggie doing when your father came home?

Lizzie Borden: I don't know whether she was there, or whether she had gone upstairs. I can't remember.

Knowlton: Who let your father in?

Lizzie Borden: I think he came to the front door and rang the bell, and I think Maggie let him in, and he said he had forgotten his key, so I think she must have been downstairs.

Knowlton: His key would have been no good if the locks were left as you left them?

Lizzie Borden: But they were always unlocked in the morning.

Knowlton: Who unbolted them that morning?

Lizzie Borden: I don't think they had been unlocked, Maggie can tell you.

Knowlton: If he had not forgotten his key it would have been no good?

Lizzie Borden: No, he had his key and could not get in, I understood Maggie to say he said he had forgotten his key.

Knowlton: You did not hear him say anything about it?

Lizzie Borden: I heard his voice but I don't know what he said.

Knowlton: I understood you to say he had forgotten his key.

Lizzie Borden: No, it was Maggie said he had forgotten his key.

Knowlton: Where was Maggie when the bell rang?

Lizzie Borden: I don't know sir.

Knowlton: Where were you when the bell rang?

Lizzie Borden: I think in my room upstairs.

Knowlton: Then you were upstairs when your father came home?

Lizzie Borden: I don't know sir, but I think I was.

Knowlton: What were you doing?

Lizzie Borden: As I say, I took up these clean clothes and stopped and basted a little piece of tape on a garment.

Knowlton: Did you come down before your father was let in?

Lizzie Borden: I was on the stairs coming down when she let him in.

Knowlton: Then you were upstairs when your father came to the house on his return?

Lizzie Borden: I think I was.

Knowlton: How long had you been there?

Lizzie Borden: I had only been upstairs long enough to take the clothes up, and baste the little loop on the sleeve, I don't think I had been there over five minutes.

Knowlton: Was Maggie still engaged in washing windows when your father got back?

Lizzie Borden: I don't know.

Knowlton: You remember Miss Borden, I will call your attention to it, so as to see if I have any misunderstanding not for the purpose of confusing you. You remember that you told me several times that you were downstairs, and not upstairs when your father came home, you have forgotten perhaps?

Lizzie Borden: I don't know what I have said. I have answered so many questions and I am confused I don't know one thing from another. I am telling you as really as I know.

Knowlton: Calling your attention to what you said about that a few minutes ago, and now again to the circumstance. You have said you were upstairs when the bell rang, and were on the stairs when Maggie let your father in, which is now your recollection of your true statement of the matter, that you were downstairs when the bell rang and your father came in?

Lizzie Borden: I think I was downstairs in the kitchen.

Knowlton: And then you were not upstairs?

Lizzie Borden: I think I was not, because I went up almost immediately, as soon as I went down, and then came down again and stayed down.

Knowlton: What had you in your mind when you said you were on the stairs as Maggie let your father in?

Lizzie Borden: The other day somebody came there and she let them in and I was on the stairs, I don't know the morning before or when it was.

Knowlton: "You understood I was asking you exactly and specifically about this fatal day?

Lizzie Borden: Yes sir.

Knowlton: I now call your attention to the fact that you had specifically told me that you had and that you had been there about five minutes when the bell rang, and were on your way down and were on the stairs when Maggie let your father in that day?

Lizzie Borden: Yes I said that, and then I said I did not know whether I was on the stairs or in the kitchen.

Knowlton: Now how will you have it?

Lizzie Borden: I think as, nearly as I know, think I was in the kitchen.

Knowlton: How long was your father gone?

Lizzie Borden: I don't know sir, not very long.

Knowlton: An hour?

Lizzie Borden: I should not think so.

Lizzie then said she was reading a magazine in the kitchen when her father came back. Knowlton asked Lizzie a number of questions about her movements in relation to her mother. Lizzie's only explanation for the fact that she had been on the upstairs landing when her step-mother was lying butchered and surrounded with blood a few feet away, of which she claimed to be totally unaware, was that she supposed Abby had gone out.

Knowlton: Had you any knowledge of her going out of the house?

Lizzie Borden: She told me she had a note, somebody was sick and she said "I am going to get the dinner on the way" and asked me what I wanted for dinner.

Knowlton: Did you tell her?

Lizzie Borden: Yes, I told her I did not want anything.

Knowlton: Then why did you not suppose she had gone?

Lizzie Borden: I supposed she had gone.

Knowlton: Did you hear her come back?

Lizzie Borden: I did not hear her go or come back, but I supposed she went [according to Bridget Lizzie told her she thought she heard her mother come back].

In the trial the witness Adelaide Churchill gave evidence that when she spoke to Lizzie immediately before the discovery of Mrs Borden's body, she asked Lizzie "where is your mother?" She replied "I don't know she had got a note to go see someone who is sick, but I don't know but she is killed too, for I thought I heard her come in".

Bridget Sullivan gave evidence in the trial that Lizzie had said to her, in respect to Abby Borden, "Maggie, I am almost positive I heard her coming in, won't you go upstairs to see".

Both of these pieces of evidence from two very good witnesses were flatly denied by Lizzie. Why was that? Knowlton turned again to the question of where Lizzie was when Andrew Borden returned from his visit to the town.

Knowlton: Now I call your attention to the fact that twice, yesterday, you told me with some explicitness, that when your father came in you were just coming downstairs?

Lizzie Borden: No I did not, I beg your pardon?

Knowlton: That you were on the stairs when your father was let in, you said with some explicitness (this was the evidence of Bridget at the trial). Do you now say that you did not say so?

Lizzie Borden: I said I thought I was on the stairs, then I remembered I was in the kitchen when he came in.

Knowlton: First you thought you were in the kitchen; afterwards you remembered you were on the stairs?

Lizzie Borden: I said I thought I was on the stairs, then I knew I was in the kitchen. I still say that now, I was in the kitchen.

Knowlton: Did you go into the front part of the house after your father came in?

Lizzie Borden: After he came in from down street I was in the sitting room with him.

Knowlton then proceeded to put a series of questions regarding the fact that only Lizzie herself had the opportunity to murder her father. It is difficult to escape the presumption that Knowlton anticipates the indictment of Lizzie and was laying the foundation of the prosecution case.

Knowlton: You now say after your father went out, you did not go upstairs at all?

Lizzie Borden: No sir, I did not.

Knowlton: When Maggie came in there washing the windows, you did not appear from the front part of the house?

Lizzie Borden: No sir.

Knowlton: When you father was let in, you did not appear from upstairs?

Lizzie Borden: No sir, I was in the kitchen" (at the trial Bridget Sullivan said "I heard Miss Lizzie laughing upstairs).

Knowlton: That is so?

Lizzie Borden: Yes sir, to the best of my knowledge "(the inquest was held only five days after the murders. Would anyone not have the details of such a traumatic day indelibly imprinted upon their memory? Why did Lizzie say "to the best of my knowledge" Why was she so anxious to maintain that she was not upstairs when her father came home and where the butchered body of Abby Borden lay?)

Knowlton: After your father went out, you remained there either in the kitchen or dining room all the time?

Lizzie Borden: I went into the sitting room long enough to direct some paper wrappers.

Knowlton: So it would have been extremely difficult for anybody to have got through the kitchen and dining room, and front hall, without your seeing them?

Lizzie Borden: They could have gone from the kitchen into the sitting room while I was in the dining room, if there was anybody to go (having passed through a locked door).
Knowlton: Then into the front hall?
Lizzie Borden: Yes sir.
Knowlton: You were in the dining room ironing?
Lizzie Borden: Yes sir, part of the time.
Knowlton: You were in all of the three rooms?
Lizzie Borden: Yes sir (Lizzie herself appears to appreciate the absurdity of the intruder theory).

Knowlton concentrated on the intruder issue:

Knowlton: So far as you know you were alone in the lower part of the house a large portion of the time, after your father went away and before he came back?
Lizzie Borden: My father did not go away I think until somewhere about ten, as near as I can remember; he was with me downstairs.
Knowlton: A large portion of the time after your father went away, and before he came back, so far as you know, you were the only person in the house?
Lizzie Borden: Maggie had come in and gone upstairs.
Knowlton: After he went out, and before he came back, a large portion of the time after your father went out, and before he came back, so far as you know you were the only person in the house?
Lizzie Borden: So far as I know I was.
Knowlton: And during that time, so far as you know the front door was locked?
Lizzie Borden: So far as I know.
Knowlton: And never was unlocked at all?
Lizzie Borden: I don't think it was.
Knowlton: Even after your father came home it was locked up again?
Lizzie Borden: I don't know whether she locked it up again after that or not.
Knowlton: It locks itself?

Lizzie Borden: The spring lock opens.

Knowlton: It fastens, so it cannot be opened from the outside?

Lizzie Borden: Sometimes you can push it open.

Knowlton: Have you any reason to suppose the spring lock was left so it could be pushed open from the outside?

Lizzie Borden: I have no reason to suppose so.

Knowlton: Nothing about the lock was changed before the people came?

Lizzie Borden: Nothing that I know of.

Lizzie then said that when her father came in she was eating a pear after having been reading a magazine, She put a piece of wood on the fire to try and heat up the flats but that she did no further ironing at that time. She did not see where Bridget went after she had let Mr Borden into the house.

Then came the issue of Lizzie's alibi of having been in the barn at the time of the murder. We will recall the varying accounts she gave to several different people on the day of the homicides five days before the inquest.

Knowlton: How long was your father in the house before you found him killed?

Lizzie Borden: I don't know exactly because I went out to the barn. I don't know what time he came home. I don't think he had been home more than fifteen or twenty minutes. I am not sure.

Knowlton: When you went out to the barn where did you leave your father?

Lizzie Borden: He had lain down on the sitting room lounge,, taken off his shoes and put on his slippers, and taken off his coat and put on the reefer. I asked him if he wanted the windows left that way (this statement was incorrect since the photograph of Andrew's body shows him still to be wearing his shoes).

Knowlton: Was he asleep?

Lizzie Borden: No sir.

Knowlton: Was he reading?

Lizzie Borden: No sir.

Knowlton: What was the last thing you said to him?

Lizzie Borden: I asked him if he wanted the window left that way. Then I went into the kitchen and from there to the barn.

Knowlton: Whereabouts in the barn did you go?

Lizzie Borden: Upstairs.

Knowlton: To the second story of the barn?

Lizzie Borden: Yes sir.

Knowlton: How long did you remain there?

Lizzie Borden: I don't know fifteen or twenty minutes.

Knowlton: What doing?

Lizzie Borden: Trying to find lead for a sinker.

Knowlton: What made you think there would be lead for a sinker up there?

Lizzie Borden: Because there was some there.

Knowlton: Was there not some by the door?

Lizzie Borden: Some pieces of lead by the open door, but there was a box full of old things upstairs.

Knowlton: Did you bring any sinker back from the barn?

Lizzie Borden: I found no sinkers.

Knowlton: Did you bring any sinker back from the barn?

Lizzie Borden: Nothing but a piece of a chip I picked up in the floor.

Knowlton: Where was that box you say was upstairs containing lead?

Lizzie Borden: There was a kind of workbench.

Knowlton: Is it there now?

Lizzie Borden: I don't know sir.

Knowlton: How long since you have seen it there?

Lizzie Borden: I have not been out there since that day.

Knowlton: Had you been in the barn before?

Knowlton: That day, no sir.

Knowlton: How long since you had been to the barn before?

Lizzie Borden: I don't think I had been into it, I don't know I had, in three months.

Knowlton: When you went out did you unfasten the screen door?

Lizzie Borden: I unhooked it to get out.

Knowlton: It was locked until you went out?

Lizzie Borden: Yes sir.

Knowlton: It had been left locked by Bridget if she was the last one in?

Lizzie's varying accounts of her reason for visiting the barn and her activity when she was there could be explained on the grounds of faulty memory if an appreciable period of time had passed between the events and the time of recalling them. But it had not; in fact the very reverse was the situation. No time at all had passed. One of the questions was put to her on the very same day, and others at the inquest which took place five days later. Furthermore, the accuracy of memory depends very largely upon the importance of the events and their imprint upon the mind of the person concerned.

If someone is questioned about a situation which took place six months ago minor discrepancies in their account may be explicable on the passage of time. Likewise if one is asked about events which took place in a crowded street where, say, an accident had occurred, one's own recollection may differ on some points from that of another observer of the same incident. But neither of these scenarios applies to the situation of Lizzie Borden. All the questions related to the same day or a few days afterwards and the occasion was of an importance and gravity with which no other can compare.

The importance of Lizzie Borden's evidence at the inquest is that she said nothing is in her own defence at the trial, and the only opportunity for the representative of the Commonwealth to test her "alibi" was during the inquest proceedings. Knowlton then put further questions dealing with the contents of the box which Lizzie searched, the length of time for which Lizzie was in the barn, and the possible presence of lines and sinkers at her father's farm.

The extraordinary scenario that Knowlton sought to bring out was that here was Lizzie, who had been the only person in a position to murder her step-mother now, after her father has returned, deciding to absent herself by going to the barn at the very time it so happened a murderer attacked her father. That she decided to do so on the hottest day of the year and that although she found no sinkers for a fishing expedition, which was not due to take place for some days, she remained for 20 minutes in the stifling heat eating pears, having ignored a pile of lead by the door. While she was allegedly eating the pears which she had picked up from the ground and taken in to the barn she agreed she had a good view of the back door and that nobody entered. This would have comprised the greater period of her stay in the barn. The search for lead sinkers would only have taken a few minutes. This was the "window of opportunity" for an intruder to enter the back door!

As if the implausibility of this story was not enough, Lizzie then gave at the inquest an account of her return to the house which completely conflicts with her earlier statements at the time. We recall her accounts of her movements on her return to the house. Summarized they claim that on her return from the barn she was in the yard when she heard a distressing sound like a groan. In response she ran to the house, where in the sitting room she found her father murdered. Compare this story with the evidence given at the inquest:

Knowlton: When you came down from the barn, what did you do then?
Lizzie Borden: I went into the dining room and laid down my hat.
Knowlton: What did you do then?
Lizzie Borden: Opened the sitting room door and went into the sitting room, or pushed it open, it was not latched.
Knowlton: What did you do then?
Lizzie Borden: Found my father, and rushed to the foot of the stairs.
Knowlton: What were you going to the sitting room for?
Lizzie Borden: To go upstairs.
Knowlton: What for.
Lizzie Borden: To sit down.

Here is a completely different account from that of five days earlier. No distressing sound, no anxious hurry into the house. Before finding her father dead there was nothing to give her cause for concern. She had entered the house simply to take a rest.

Knowlton then turned to the murder of Abby. The strength of the case against Lizzie rested in the murder of Abby in addition to that of Andrew. Apart from the almost prohibitive difficulty of gaining access to the house and remaining concealed between the two killings, the question remained of why an enemy of Andrew should want to greatly complicate his task by the pointless murder of Abby.

Knowlton: When did you last see your mother?

Lizzie Borden: I did not see her after when I went down in the morning and she was dusting the dining room.

Knowlton: Where did you or she go then?

Lizzie Borden: I don't know where she went. I know where I was.

Knowlton: Did you or she leave the dining room first?

Lizzie Borden: I think I did. I left her in the dining room.

Knowlton: You never saw or heard of her afterwards?

Lizzie Borden: No sir.

Knowlton: Did she say anything about making the bed?

Lizzie Borden: She said she had been up and made the bed up fresh, and dusted the room and left it all in order. She was going to put some fresh pillow slips on the small pillows at the foot of the bed, and was going to close the room, because she was going to have company Monday and she wanted everything in order.

Knowlton: How long would it take to put on the pillow slips?

Lizzie Borden: About two minutes.

Knowlton: How long to do the rest of the things?

Lizzie Borden: She had done that when I came down.

Knowlton: Can you give me any suggestion as to what occupied her when she was up there and when she was struck dead?

Lizzie Borden: I don't know of anything except that she had some cotton cloth pillowcases up there, and she said that she was going to commence work on them. That is all I know. And the sewing machine was up there.

Knowlton: Did you hear the sewing machine going?

Lizzie Borden: I did not.

Knowlton: If she had remained downstairs you would undoubtedly have seen her?

Lizzie Borden: If she had remained downstairs I should have, if she had remained in her room I should not have.

Knowlton: Where was that?

Lizzie Borden: Over the kitchen.

Knowlton: To get to that room she would have to go through the kitchen?

Lizzie Borden: To get up the back stairs.

Knowlton: That is the way she was in the habit of going?

Lizzie Borden: Yes sir, because the other doors were locked.

Knowlton: Have you any reason to suppose you would not have seen her if she had spent any portion of the time in her own room, or downstairs?

Lizzie Borden: There is no reason why I should not have seen her if she had been down there, except when I first came downstairs, for two or three minutes, I went down to the cellar to the water closet.

Knowlton pressed on with his questions regarding the movements of Abby Borden and Lizzie, bearing in mind that at the crucial time, namely Abby's murder, Lizzie was alone in the house with her, subject to an unknown intruder having gained entry to the premises.

Knowlton: After that you were where you practically commanded the view of the first story the rest of the time?

Lizzie Borden: I think so.

Knowlton: When you went upstairs for a short time, as you say you did, you then went in sight of the sewing machine?

Lizzie Borden: No, I did not see the sewing machine because she had shut that room up.

Knowlton: What do you mean?

Lizzie Borden: I mean the door was closed. She said she wanted it kept closed to keep the heat and everything out.

Knowlton: I ask again, perhaps you have answered all you care to, what explanation can you give, can you suggest, as to what she was doing from the time she said she had got the work all done in the spare room until eleven o'clock?

Lizzie Borden: I suppose she went up and made her own bed.

Knowlton: That would be in the back part?

Lizzie Borden: Yes sir.

Knowlton: She would have had to go by you twice to do that?

Lizzie Borden: Unless she went when I was in my room that few minutes.

Knowlton: That would not be time enough for her to make her own bed and come back again?

Lizzie Borden: Sometimes she stayed up longer and sometimes shorter, I don't know.

Knowlton: Otherwise than that she would have to go in your sight?

Lizzie Borden: I should have had to have seen her once. I don't know that I need to have seen her more than once.

Knowlton: You did not see her at all?

Lizzie Borden: No sir, not after the dining room.

Knowlton: What explanation can you suggest as to the whereabouts of your mother from the time you saw her in the dining room, and she said her work in the spare room was all done, until eleven o'clock?

Lizzie Borden: I don't know. I think she went into the spare room, and whether she came back again I don't know. That has always been a mystery.

Then came the following crucial questions from Knowlton as to where Abby was at the time of her murder.

Knowlton: Can you think of anything she could be doing in the spare room?

Lizzie Borden: Yes sir, I know what she used to do sometimes, she kept her best cape she wore on the street in there, and she used occasionally to go up there to get it, and take it into her room. She kept a great deal in the guest room drawers, she used to go up there and get things and put things, she used those drawers for her own us.

Knowlton: That connects with her own room again, to reach which she had to go downstairs and come up again?

Lizzie Borden: Yes.

Knowlton: Assuming that she did not go into her own room, I understand you to say she could not have gone into her own room without you seeing her?

Lizzie Borden: She could while I was down in the cellar.

Knowlton: You went down immediately you came down, within a few minutes, and you did not see her when you came back?

Lizzie Borden: No sir.

Knowlton: After that time she must have remained in the guest chamber?

Lizzie Borden: I don't know.

Then comes the matter of the alleged and mysterious note. Let us pause here and consider the position. It was of crucial importance to the question of Lizzie's guilt or innocence that Abby Borden was not in the house during the whole period that she and Lizzie were there. If the unknown killer was keeping watch he would have seen Abby both leave and return to the house. Then he would have pursued his prey into the house. Now recall the evidence of Bridget; "I says oh Lizzie, if I knew where Mrs Whitehead was I would go and see if Mrs Borden was there and tell her that Mr Borden was very sick". She says, "Maggie, I am almost positive that I heard her coming in, won't you go upstairs to see". I said, "I am not going upstairs alone".

Now take the evidence, at the time of Adelaide Churchill; I said, "Where is your mother?" She said, "I don't know, she had a note to go out to see someone who is sick, but I don't know but she is killed too, for I thought I heard her come in". Surely the purpose of Lizzie's statements at the time to Bridget and Mrs Churchill was to draw suspicion away from herself which would certainly be strengthened if she were alone with Mrs Borden for the whole period of the run-up to the murder.

Now five days later at the inquest she changes her story. Did she not realise that if she had indeed heard her step-mother return it would have been natural for her to question Abby about her expedition to the sick person and about the details, none of which were ever known. That is if it took place at all.

Let us follow Knowlton's questions:

Knowlton: Had you any knowledge of her going out of the house?
Lizzie Borden: She told me she had had a note, somebody was sick and said "I am going to get the dinner on the way" and asked me what I wanted for dinner.
Knowlton: Did you tell her?
Lizzie Borden: Yes, I told her I did not want anything.
Knowlton: Then why did you suppose she had not gone?
Lizzie Borden: I supposed she had gone.
Knowlton: Did you hear her come back?

Lizzie Borden: I did not hear her go or come back, but I supposed she went.

Knowlton: When you found your father dead you supposed she had gone?

Lizzie Borden: I did not know. I said to the people who came in, "I don't know whether Mrs Borden is out or in, I wish you would see if she is in her room.

Knowlton: Did she tell you where she was going?

Lizzie Borden: No sir.

Knowlton: Did she tell you who the note was from?

Lizzie Borden: No sir.

Knowlton: Did you see the note?

Lizzie Borden: No sir.

Knowlton: Do you know where it is now?

Lizzie Borden: No sir.

Later on Knowlton raised the question of the note again:

Knowlton: You said she had a note?

Lizzie Borden: Yes sir.

Knowlton: You told me yesterday you never saw the note.

Lizzie Borden: No sir, I never did.

Knowlton: You looked for it?

Lizzie Borden: No sir, but the rest have.

Knowlton: She did not say where she was going?

Lizzie Borden: No sir.

Knowlton: Does she usually tell you where she was going?

Lizzie Borden: She does not generally tell me.

Knowlton: Did she say when she was coming back?

Lizzie Borden: No sir.

Knowlton then pressed the most damming argument of the guilt of Lizzie Borden—she was the only person in the house who had the opportunity to murder Abby, and by the same token her father also.

Knowlton: After your father went out, you remained there either in the kitchen or dining room all of the time?

Lizzie Borden: I went in the sitting room long enough to direct some paper wrappers.

Knowlton: "So it would have been extremely difficult for anybody to have gone through the kitchen and dining room and front hall, without you seeing them?

Lizzie Borden: They could have gone from the kitchen into the sitting room while I was in the dining room if there was anybody to go.

Knowlton: You said you thought you heard her come in?

Lizzie Borden: No sir.

Knowlton: Did you say to anybody that you thought she was killed upstairs?

Lizzie Borden: No sir.

Knowlton: To anybody?

Lizzie Borden: No sir.

Knowlton: You made no effort to find your mother at all?

Lizzie Borden: No sir.

These two items of evidence conflict completely with the testimony of Bridget and Mrs Churchill. Small wonder that the defence counsel fought to prevent Lizzie's evidence at the inquest being admitted at the trial. When it was excluded Lizzie broke down in tears. Was this with relief? It is difficult to find any other reason.

Judge Blaisdale, who was presiding at the inquest, took up this point:

Was there any effort made by the witness (Lizzie) to notify Mrs Borden of the fact that Mr Borden was found?

Judge Blaisdale: Did you make any effort to notify Mrs Borden of your father being killed?

Lizzie Borden: No sir, when I found him I rushed right to the foot of the stairs for Maggie. I supposed Mrs Borden was out. I did not think anything about her at the time, I was so …

Judge Blaisdale: At any time did you say anything about her to anybody?

Lizzie Borden: No sir.

The two items of evidence given by Bridget and Adelaide Churchill were potentially extremely dangerous to Lizzie's case. If Lizzie had said "I thought I heard her come in" this puts Lizzie in the house alone with Abby at the time of Abby's murder. It shows that Lizzie knew of Abby's presence and was therefore vulnerable to attack. If Mrs Churchill is to be believed, and she was a very credible witness, why should Lizzie have said, "I don't know but she is killed too, for I thought I heard her come in"? Mrs Churchill corroborates Bridget, but worst of all from Lizzie's point of view, it indicates that Lizzie knew that both Mr and Mrs Borden were killed by the same hand—a disastrous piece of knowledge for the defence to cope with.

Lizzie had had five days to think about her position if the statements were thought to be genuine. She was left with no alternative but to deny them.

Knowlton questions Lizzie on her situation when her father returned. Once again she contradicted her earlier statements. She had said that she was upstairs and was on the stairs coming down when Bridget let him in. Now she corrected that to say that she was downstairs in the kitchen. Her final position was that she could not remember which was correct. She must have realised that being upstairs put her within a few feet of her dead step-mother's body.

Knowlton: Did you ever see the note?
Lizzie Borden: No sir.
Knowlton: Do you know where it is now?
Lizzie Borden: No sir.

The note allegedly received by Abby is of such importance to the case that the known facts bear repetition. In his closing argument at the trial for the defence counsel for Lizzie, George D Robinson said, "The note may have been a part of the scheme in regard to Mrs Borden. It may have got there by foul means and with a criminal purpose. We don't now anything about it. But that a note came there on this evidence you can't question". This proposition is without the slightest foundation.

What the evidence revealed was that the story of the note came from Lizzie and from her alone. Bridget heard it from Lizzie and not from Mrs Borden, therefore Robinson's statement that both Lizzie and Bridget knew from Abby that the note had been received by Abby, is, frankly false. Moreover the absurdity of Robinson's theory that the note may have been part of a plot to murder Mrs Borden is too: why lure her away from the house if the plan is to kill her in the house? She would have been murdered while engaged on her journey responding to the note.

Sometimes an advocate in a plethora of enthusiasm for his client's case flounders into making a reference to the evidence which is plainly inaccurate. Even such an able and experienced trial lawyer as Robinson was not immune from this mistake—if mistake it was. It is suggested that Robinson knew only too well the threat which the note strongly posed to his client. Let's look carefully at the scenario. At 8.50 am Lizzie comes downstairs and eats a meagre breakfast. At approximately 9.15 Andrew Borden leaves to visit the town, and at about 9.30 Abby is murdered in the guest room. These times are on the basis of the medical evidence given at the trial. At 10.45 Andrew returns home. By that time Abby has been lying dead in the guest bedroom for at least an hour.

She and Lizzie have been the only two people in the house. Lizzie Borden—it is clear from the transcript at the inquest—is a highly intelligent person. She knows the very serious position this puts her in. Therefore she provides herself with an alibi. But, unlike the barn story, it is an alibi in reverse. Instead of the usual plea that at the time of the crime the accused person was somewhere else, the plea is that at the time of the murder Lizzie did not, and had no reason to believe the killing had occurred. The story of the note removes Abby from the house during which time, if true, Lizzie cannot have been responsible. But this has a further problem for Lizzie. If the medical experts are correct as to the time gap between the two murders the period when Abby was out of the house was comparatively short, 15 minutes in all. This leaves only 15 minutes if Abby was murdered at 9.30. Another hour at least passes in the house. Lizzie has to strengthen the story that Abby had gone out, and does so by telling Bridget and Mrs Churchill that she thought she heard Abby return. By the time of the inquest Lizzie realised that, by admitting she heard Abby return, she had created a further difficulty for herself. Again in the brief period between Abby's return and her murder what was Lizzie doing? She admitted that if there had been an interloper she would or should have seen him, apart from two or three minutes when she was in the cellar. What were the chances of an interloper using such a small window of opportunity to kill Abby, or is it the case that by that time anyway Abby was dead. Murdered by Lizzie? Hence her denial against the word of two impressive and patently honest witnesses.

The thoroughness of Knowlton's examination, or rather cross examination it may be called, would seem extraordinary for an inquest. Lizzie had not been charged with any offence, yet one suspects that Knowlton was only too aware that she might be and that the answers which he extricated from her now might prove to be valuable ammunition which the prosecution could use at a future trial. He was not to know that Lizzie's failure to give evidence plus the court's refusal to admit evidence of the testimony given at the inquest would remove this weapon from the hand of the Commonwealth.

Knowlton moved on to Lizzie's alibi of the visit to the barn:

> **Knowlton:** Can you give me any information how it happened at that particular time you should go into the chamber of the barn to find a sinker to go to Marion's with, to fish the next Monday?"
>
> **Lizzie Borden:** I was going to finish my ironing, my flats were not hot, I said to myself "I will go and try and find that sinker, perhaps by the time I get back the flats will be hot". That is the only reason.
>
> **Knowlton:** How long had you been reading an old magazine before you went to the barn at all?
>
> **Lizzie Borden:** Perhaps half an hour.
>
> **Knowlton:** Had you got a fish line?
>
> **Lizzie Borden:** Not here, we had some at the farm.
>
> **Knowlton:** Had you got a fish hook?
>
> **Lizzie Borden:** No sir.
>
> **Knowlton:** Had you any apparatus of fishing at all?
>
> **Lizzie Borden:** Yes, over there.
>
> **Knowlton:** Had you any sinkers over there?

Lizzie Borden: I think there were some. It is so long since I have been there. I think there were some.
Knowlton: You had no reason to think you were lacking sinkers?
Lizzie Borden: I don't think there were any on my lines.
Knowlton: Where were your lines?
Lizzie Borden: My fish lines were at the farm.
Knowlton: What made you feel there were no sinkers at the farm on your lines?
Lizzie Borden: Because some time ago when I was there I had none.

The questions put by Knowlton were clearly intended to emphasise the extraordinary coincidence that Lizzie's sudden decision to go looking for lead which might be suitable for fishing lines for some future date occurred at the very time that the murder of her father took place. Secondly, how could she be so sure that there were no suitable lines with sinkers and hooks at the farm from which the apparatus for the ensuing expedition was to take place? Knowlton further pressed Lizzie as to why she had not examined the pile of lead by the door to the barn and why she should have wanted to linger eating pears in the hottest part of the premises, namely the upper floor of the barn.

A weak alibi always rebounds on the person alleging it. Doubtless counsel for Lizzie had this in mind when fighting, during the trial to have the evidence excluded. The court obliged.

Then comes the most remarkable passage of all:

Knowlton: When you came down from the barn, what did you do then?
Lizzie Borden: Came into the kitchen.
Knowlton: What did you do then?
Lizzie Borden: I went into the dining room and laid down my hat.
Knowlton: What did you do then?
Lizzie Borden: Opened the sitting room door and went into the sitting room or pushed it open. It was not locked.
Knowlton: What did you do then?
Lizzie Borden: Found my father and rushed to the foot of the stairs.
Knowlton: What were you going into the sitting room for?

Lizzie Borden: To go upstairs.
Knowlton: What for?
Lizzie Borden: To sit down.

Where does this account square with Lizzie's account at the time? To Bridget: "I was out in the back yard and heard a groan". To Mrs Churchill: "I was out in the barn. I was going for a piece of iron when I heard a distressing noise, and went in and found the door open, and found my father dead". These varying stories, that of hearing a groan and that of the return to the house to lie down, are completely irreconcilable. Why did Lizzie change her story when she was at the inquest? Was it because she realised the weakness of her first account? Andrew was clearly rendered unconscious by the first blow. He couldn't have emitted a groan. And even if he had done so, Lizzie would not have heard it from outside the house.

And what about the strange scraping sound which Lizzie claimed to have heard when she was inside the barn? How could this have been audible to her from the house? And in any event, in the absence of further explanation it has no relevance to the murder of her father.

Lizzie pleaded ignorance of the axe, and the hatchet found at the foot of the stairs in the cellar. Knowlton turned to the question of the skirt. There would be evidence that the silk skirt which Lizzie gave to the police as being the one she had worn on the day of the murders was not on fact that same skirt.

Knowlton: Did you give to the officer the same skirt you had on the day of the tragedy?
Lizzie Borden: Yes sir.
Knowlton: Do you know whether there was any blood on the skirt?
Lizzie Borden: No sir.
Knowlton: Assume that there was. Do you know how it came there?
Lizzie Borden: No sir.
Knowlton: Assume that there was, can you give an explanation of how it came there, on the dress skirt?
Lizzie Borden: No sir.

Knowlton: Have you offered any [explanation]?

Lizzie Borden: No sir.

Knowlton: Have you said it came from flea bites?

Lizzie Borden: On the petticoats I said there was a flea bite. I said it might have been. You said you meant the dress skirt.

Knowlton: I did. Have you offered any explanation how that came there?

Lizzie Borden: I told those men that were at the house that I have had fleas, that is all.

Knowlton: Did you offer that as an explanation?

Lizzie Borden: I said that was the only explanation that I knew of.

Knowlton: Assuming that the blood came from outside, can you give any explanation of how it came there?

Lizzie Borden: No sir.

Lizzie was then questioned regarding her alleged visit to a drugstore in order to obtain prussic acid, only a day before the murder.

Knowlton: Your attention has already been called to the circumstances of going into a drugstore of Smiths on the corner of Columbia and Main Streets, by some officer, has it not, on the day before the tragedy?"

Lizzie Borden: I don't know whether some officer has asked me, somebody has spoken to me of it. I don't know who it was.

Knowlton: Did that take place?

Lizzie Borden: It did not.

Knowlton: Do you know where the drugstore is?

Lizzie Borden: I don't.

Knowlton: Did you go into any drugstore and inquire for prussic acid?

Lizzie Borden: I did not.

Knowlton: Where were you on Wednesday morning that you remember?

Lizzie Borden: At home.

Knowlton: All the time?

Lizzie Borden: All day until Wednesday night.

Knowlton: Nobody there, but your parents, and yourself and the servant?

Lizzie Borden: Why, Mr Morse did come sometime in the afternoon, or at noontide, I suppose, I did not see him.

Knowlton: He did not come to see you?

Lizzie Borden: No sir, I did not see him.

Knowlton: He did not come until afternoon, anyway did he?

Lizzie Borden: I don't think he did, I am not sure.

Knowlton: Did you dine with the family that day?

Lizzie Borden: I was downstairs yes sir, I did not eat any breakfast with them.

Knowlton: Did you go into the drugstore for any purpose whatsoever?

Lizzie Borden: I did not.

How important is the evidence of Lizzie Borden at the inquest? The answer has to be extremely important. It is the only occasion on which she ventures into the witness box and submits to a lengthy and rigorous cross-examination. An inquest is not, of course, a trial but it is all part of the machinery of the law. The purpose of which is a search for the truth. Without the transcript of the inquest we would have no record of what Lizzie had to say regarding her obvious opportunity for accessibility to the murder of both her parents. The defence, having decided not to call her as a witness in her own defence, would be able to say let the prosecutors prove their case; she is not obliged under our law to prove that she is innocent.

In view of the fact that the court ruled against admitting this unique evidence much of this effort was achieved. But those who have, over the years, written and studied this extraordinary case may, and do, ask the question: had the evidence been admitted could Lizzie have survived?

The answer to that question has to be "probably not". The discrepancy between Lizzie's original statements as to her whereabouts at the time of the murders and her testimony at the inquest are irreconcilably different. Then again asked by Alice Russell why she had gone to the barn she said, "I went to get a piece of tin or iron to fix my screen." Yet at the inquest the story had changed. Now the purpose of her visit was to obtain lead for a sinker to fit to her fishing lines which were at the farm and which she had not used for five years. These are but two of the very alarming variations. Why are they important?

When a witness gives testimony on oath which differs substantially from statements made at the time of the offence there are three considerations in deciding whether the divergence is a deliberate lie or merely a mistake of memory. These are:
- firstly the level of intelligence of the witness;
- secondly the time lapse between the first and later utterance; and
- thirdly the surrounding circumstances which might leave no room for such a lapse of memory.

On all of these three counts Lizzie fares badly. First of all she was an extremely intelligent woman. This is clear from the fact that guilty or innocent she withstood the lengthy and thorough interrogation that Knowlton put her through at the inquest. Notwithstanding the intensity of the questioning and the fact of certain inconsistencies in the evidence he never broke her, or indeed effectively cornered her.

Most significantly, the time gap was only five days. Worst of all from the point of view of Lizzie's credibility, could anyone with a normal sense of recall have forgotten precisely what they did during such a traumatic event. During the grilling Lizzie was calm and collected. She never exhibited signs of panic and fluster which might have caused confusion of thought. Some questions she appeared to sidestep and some suggestions she flatly denied, but she never lost her equilibrium.

After the inquest came the preliminary proceedings before Judge Blaisdell. A number of witnesses were called and at the conclusion he gave his decision. His words are quoted by Edmund Pearson in *The Trial of Lizzie Borden*:

> "The long examination is now concluded, and there remains for the magistrate to perform what he believes to be his duty. It would be a pleasure for him, and he would doubtless receive much sympathy, if he could say 'Lizzie I judge you probably not guilty, You may go home. But upon the character of the evidence presented through the witnesses who have been so closely and thoroughly examined, there is but one thing to be done'.

Suppose for a single moment a man was standing there. He was found close by that guest chamber, which to Mrs Borden was a chamber of death. Suppose a man had been found in the vicinity of Mr Borden, was the first to find the body, and the only account he could give of himself was the unreasonable one that he was out in the barn looking for sinkers; then he was out in the yard; then he was out for something else, would there be any question in the minds of men what should be done with such a man?"

The old judge paused; his eyes filled with tears. "So there is only one thing to do, painful as it may be — the judgement of the court is that you are probably guilty, and you are ordered [to be] committed to wait the action of the Superior Court."

CHAPTER SIX

The Scene is Set

On the 2nd December 1892 the Grand Jury indicted Lizzie for both murders. Lizzie Andrew Borden was indicted for the murder of her stepmother, Abby Durfee Borden and her father Andrew Jackson Borden and was placed on trial at the June term of the Superior Court for the County of Bristol, sitting at New Bedford, beginning on Monday the 5th of June 1893. The Honourable Albert Mason, Chief Justice presided, with the Honourable Justice Caleb Bladgett and Honourable Justice Dewey, associate justices.

The Commonwealth was represented by Hosea M Knowlton Esq, District Attorney for the Southern District, and William H Moody Esq District Attorney for the Eastern District. The defendant was represented by her counsel, George D Robinson Esq, Andrew J Jennings Esq and M C Adams Esq.

After due examination a jury of 12 men was selected. So began the murder trial which many lawyers, writers and jurists consider to be the most remarkable and in some ways baffling in the history of American crime.

Let us at this stage stand back somewhat and look firstly at the main figures on the bench and at the bar, and then consider the task confronting the prosecution and defence as they begin to marshal their evidence and their arguments.

It is well worth looking at the judges of this court since they incurred considerable criticism for some of their decisions in the course of the case.

The Superior Court of Massachusetts was a circuit court which sat in all 14 counties of the Commonwealth. It was inferior to the Supreme Judicial Court, but although it had jurisdiction to hear capital cases it was required to do so with three judges presiding. This is in sharp contrast to

English capital trials which had a High Court judge sitting with a jury. Three judges only sit on appeal cases in England and Wales.

This provision gives rise to a question whether vital decisions of the admission or rejection of evidence in the Borden trial were reached unanimously or by a majority. There were 13 justices who were appointed by the governor of the state "For life or good behaviour". These provisions basically still prevail.

Chief Justice Mason was an experienced lawyer who was admitted to the bar in February 1860, fought in the Union army during the Civil War and was appointed associate justice of the Superior Court in 1882. He became Chief Justice in 1890.

Justice Caleb Bladgett graduated from Dartmouth College in 1856, specialised in bankruptcy law and was appointed associate justice of the Superior Court in 1882. He was reputed to have a "genial and unaffected manner".

The third judge was associate Justice Dewey who was admitted to the bar in 1860 and practised law in his home town of Alford, Massachusetts. He was a member of the State Senate and was appointed associate justice of the Superior Court by Governor Robinson in October 1886 — the same George Robinson who successfully defended Lizzie Borden.

Turning now to the counsel in the case. Hosea M Knowlton was the lead advocate for the prosecution. His questioning of Lizzie at the inquest was remarkably thorough and he was not lacking in ability and energy. But he has been criticised for the lack of enthusiasm in this particular murder trial. This would seem to be borne out by a letter which he wrote to the Attorney General H E Pillsbury:

My Dear Sir,

I have thought more about the Lizzie Borden case since I talked with you and think perhaps that it would be well to write to you, as I shall not be able to meet with you probably until Thursday, possibly Wednesday afternoon.

Personally I would like very much to get rid of the trial of the case, and feel that my feeling in that direction may have influenced my better judgement;

I feel this all the more upon you[r] not unexpected announcement that the burden of the trial would come upon me.

Yours truly

Hosea M Knowlton

Knowlton was criticised for his attitude towards the trial by Judge Robert Sullivan in his book *Goodbye Lizzie Borden*: "If this is the pre-trial statement of a courageous public prosecutor then I do not know the meaning of the words".

Although this language is the most specific indication of Knowlton's attitude toward the trial, it is by no means the only one. Beginning with his fastidiously proper but unnecessarily dilatory and protracted proceedings before Judge Blaisdell, and ending with his inappropriate words of congratulations to Lizzie uttered in open court after the jury's verdict of acquittal, there appears a clear pattern of reluctance and lethargy which District Attorney Knowlton pursued yet carefully concealed, throughout the Borden trial. This pattern underlies the entire record.

Why was this? Was Knowlton less than confident in the success of the prosecution? Did he have some private information which has not been revealed? The horror of the crime was unprecedented, and although the evidence was circumstantial there was nothing unusual about this in a murder trial. Indeed it was perfectly normal. Murderers do not as a rule commit their crimes in the presence of witnesses. The answer to this question remains a mystery.

Hosea M Knowlton was born in Durham, Maine in 1847. He graduated in 1867 and studied at the Harvard Law School from 1869 to 1870. He was a representative in the Lower House of the Massachusetts Legislature from 1876 to 1877 and a Senator in 1878 to 1879. He was District Attorney for the Southern District from 1879 to 1893 and Attorney General of Massachusetts from 1894 to 1901. He died in 1902.

The co-prosecutor William H Moody was made of sterner stuff than Knowlton. Of Moody, Sullivan writes:

"In sharp contrast to Knowlton, W H Moody was to hold the prosecution team together, for to the professional in the law it is clear that Moody was easily the most competent lawyer participating in the Borden trial. His professional superiority was apparent in his questioning of the witnesses, and in the sound arguments he advanced when addressing the court concerning questions of admissibility of evidence".

Moody graduated from Harvard College in 1876. Following Harvard Law School he studied for 18 months in the offices of a distinguished lawyer before being admitted to the Bar in 1878. He was District Attorney for the Eastern District in 1890 to 1895 and a member of the Congress in the 54 to 57 Congresses. He served in the legislative, judicial, and executive branches of the US Government and went on to be Secretary of the Navy in Theodore Roosevelt's Cabinet and the United States Attorney General. Finally, from 1906 to 1910 he was an associate justice of the Supreme Court of the United States, retiring in 1910. He died in 1917.

Now let us take a look at the defence team representing Lizzie Borden.

Andrew J Jennings was a Fall River lawyer who had been an attorney for Andrew Borden. After the acquittal of Lizzie he went on to follow Knowlton as District Attorney. He was short with a brusque manner. He graduated from Brown University in 1872 and from Law School at Boston University in 1876. From 1878 to 1879 he was a representative in the Massachusetts State Legislature. He opened the case for the defence in the Borden trial.

George Dexter Robinson, who made the closing speech for the defence is not above criticism for some of his tactics during the case. Like the other advocates involved he was both a representative and a Senator in the Massachusetts Legislature and was a member of Congress. More importantly, he was three times Governor of Massachusetts and as already stated was responsible for appointing Justice Dewey to the Superior Court.

Melvin A Adams graduated from Dartmouth College and studied law at Boston University. He was the United States District Attorney in Massachusetts. Adams was a good looking and very able trial lawyer in the criminal field who had a special gift for jury advocacy. He died in 1923.

Having considered the judges and counsel in the Borden trial, let us now take an overview before making a study of the evidence.

This case, like most cases of murder, was based on circumstantial evidence. There are two varieties of evidence; circumstantial and direct. Direct evidence is where the crime has been seen, heard or otherwise personally experienced by a witness or witnesses. Circumstantial evidence arises when the relevant surrounding circumstances point unmistakably to the guilt of the accused, and where there is no reasonable alternative possibility of anyone but the accused person being the miscreant. As in the case of direct evidence the jury must not convict unless they are sure, beyond all reasonable doubt that the case is proved.

Sometimes circumstantial evidence is spoken of as if it is inferior to direct evidence. One may hear such an expression as, "Of course the evidence was purely circumstantial". This is a fallacy, and has been declared to be so by the highest courts in England and no doubt in the United States as well. It is important to bear this in mind because in his closing speech in the trial Robinson, counsel for Lizzie, came close to enunciating this error.

He compounded this with another serious inaccuracy when he stated that it was the duty of the prosecution to prove guilty motive on the part of the defendant. No such duty exists. In his summing up in the case of William Wallace in 1932 a great English judge defined the nature of circumstantial evidence as follows:

> "This is a most remarkable murder, but there it is. There is no doubt that the woman was murdered and there is no doubt that whoever did it covered up his tracks, and avoided leaving behind any sort of trace. However, there it is. There is certainly no eye witness except the actual murderer, besides the dead woman, and therefore the evidence in this case, and the evidence that can be brought against anybody here, is purely circumstantial. You know, in many cases, especially of murder, the only evidence that is available is circumstantial evidence this may vary in value almost infinitely.
>
> There is some circumstantial evidence which is as good and conclusive as the evidence of the actual eye-witness. In other cases the circumstantial

evidence which anyone can present still leaves loop holes and doubts, and leaves possibilities of other explanations of other persons and still leaves the charge against the accused man little more than a probability and nothing that could be described as reasonably conclusive.

If I might give you an illustration, supposing you have a room with one door and a closed window and a passage leading from that and a man comes up the passage, goes through the door into the room and finds another man standing with a pistol, and on the floor a dead man; the circumstantial evidence there would be almost conclusive, if not conclusive.

If on the other hand, the conditions being much the same, there was an intruder who, hearing the pistol shot went into the room, and there was another door and he went in and found a man holding the pistol, it might be perfectly consistent with his having gone in, and the actual murderer being outside the door. The real test of circumstantial evidence is: does it exclude every other reasonable possibility? I can put it even higher: does it exclude other theories or possibilities?

If you cannot put the evidence against the accused man beyond probability and nothing more, if that is a probability which is not inconsistent with there being other reasonable probabilities, then it is impossible for a jury to say: we are satisfied beyond reasonable doubt that the charge is made out against the accused man. A man cannot be convicted of any crime, least of all murder, merely on probabilities, unless they are so strong as to be reasonable certainty. If you have other possibilities, a jury would not, and I believe ought not, to come to the conclusion that the charge is established."

The highest English judges have, down the years, given helpful guidance as regards circumstantial evidence. The appeal court, in the case of *Ellwood* in 1908 said that facts that tend to prove or negate a person's capacity to do an act into which the court is enquiring may be highly relevant. The accused's knowledge of the effect of certain drugs, his skill in their application and his ability to procure them would be admissible evidence at his trial for murder by means of their use. The absence of these factors would be admissible on his behalf.

In the case of *Taper* in 1952, Lord Norman said:

> "Circumstantial evidence is receivable in criminal as well as civil cases, and indeed the necessity of admitting such evidence is more obvious in the former than in the latter, for in criminal cases the possibility of proving the matter charged by the direct and positive testimony of eye-witnesses or by conclusive documents is much more rare than in civil cases, and where such evidence is not available the jury are permitted to infer from the facts proved other facts necessary to complete the elements of guilt or establish innocence. It must always be narrowly examined, if only because evidence of this kind may be fabricated to cast suspicion on another...it is also necessary before drawing the inference of the accused's guilt from circumstantial evidence to be sure that there are no other co-existing circumstances which would weaken or destroy the inference".

In the case of *Broadhurst* in 1964 a great English judge Lord Denning said:

> "A fact may be relevant to a fact in issue because it throws light on it by reason of proximity in time or circumstance [evidence of Lizzie's attempt to purchase Prussic acid concerned one day only before the murders, yet unbelievably the court ruled it be inadmissible]. This is frequently expressed by the statement that the relevant fact is part of the res gestae (the association of things). This is mainly concerned with the admissibility of statements made contemporaneously with the occurrence of some act or event into which the court is enquiring. As a matter of everyday reasoning the evidence against a man may be greatly strengthened by his failure to give a prompt explanation (or a contradictory explanation?) of conduct proved or alleged against him, or by the inadequacy of his explanation. If on the proved facts, two inferences may be drawn about the accused's conduct or state of mind, untruthfulness is a factor which the jury can properly take into account in strengthening the inference of guilt".

Let us see now how these principles which have been laid down by the courts in England were applied in one of the famous trials in the last century.

Arthur Devereux, a chemist's assistant, was charged with the murder of his wife and their two children. Prior to the birth of the twins a son had been born. Despairing under the financial burden of supporting his family on a small income Devereux bought a tin trunk and poisoned his wife and the twins by means of a bottle of morphine. He placed the bodies in the trunk which was taken to a warehouse. Devereux's mother in law was suspicious by reason of the absence of the wife and children and called the police. When questioned by police, Devereux said, "You are making a mistake I don't know anything about a tin trunk". Up to that point the police had not made any mention of a trunk. This led to his conviction and execution.

CHAPTER SEVEN

The Murder of Abby Borden

The prosecution in the trial of Lizzie Borden enjoyed two distinct advantages, both of which it is hard to see how the defence could get over. The first is the fact that this was a double murder; the second is the admitted certainty that when Abby was killed Lizzie Borden was the only other person in the house. Let us consider the first matter. In her conversation with Alice Russell, Lizzie was very determined to emphasise the threat to her father. She said little or nothing of this in connection with her step-mother.

This was because she knew that Abby was a harmless soul who had no known enemies and lived on peaceful terms with everyone — save

Lizzie who, reluctant as she was to admit it, clearly had no love for her step-mother, to put it mildly. In the setting of this scenario the murder of Abby is inexplicable if Lizzie herself is deleted from the equation. Nor did the defence ever attempt an explanation. What was consensual on both sides was that the murders were committed by the same hand, and that Abby's killing, separated by about an hour and a half from her husband's, was the first in time. That fact was clearly established by the medical evidence.

The second significant feature is the nature of the homicide. In both murders the method was the same. The attack was frenzied. It is said that once the first blow has been struck the blood lust is released and the ferocity of the onslaught follows. But there is generally a difference between one type of murder and another according to the motive behind it and the type of person committing the crime. Feverish, maniacal assault is more common where there is a pre-existing personal relationship between assailant and victim. A betrayal in marriage, or equivalent relationship, is often the scenario for this category of violence. Other motives, such as money or material gain of some kind usually lead the offender to a more planned and sophisticated method of performing the deed. If those who identified Lizzie in the chemist's shop were correct, the failure of Lizzie to complete the planned operation may well explain the series of ferocious blows with an axe.

Whoever killed Andrew killed Abby, and vice versa. Abby was not killed for the purpose of removing a witness because her death came first. The first blow struck Abby from the front. This means that she must have been facing the assassin when he or she entered the spare room. She made no effort to escape, futile as that may have been. Is that because she knew her killer and did not for a moment anticipate the first terrible blow which fell like a streak of lightening? The remaining blows fell in a storm on the head of the already dead Abby.

Now let us look at the movements of the two people alone who can cast any light on the drama which occurred between the departure of Andrew Borden at around 9.15 am and his return at about 10.45 am.

Bridget described how Mrs Borden was dusting with a feather duster in the dining room and that she told her to wash the windows on the first (ground) floor. This was at nine o'clock, which would have been about the time or a little before Mr Borden left to go to town. Bridget worked in the kitchen and dining room preparing breakfast.

Students of the Borden case can become confused by the details of the movements and activities of the various persons involved in the case during Wednesday 3rd August and Thursday 4th August. One can "lose sight of the wood for the trees". It is best to concentrate one's attention on the two vital periods of time. These are between 9.15 am when Andrew Borden left the house and his return at 10.45, and between 10.45 and 11.05 or 11.10 when Lizzie summoned Bridget to come down because her father had been killed. It was between these times that first Abby, then Andrew were brutally murdered. They were both times when Lizzie had the complete run of the house. On the earlier occasion Bridget was engaged on washing the outside windows. On the second she was in her room.

Bridget does not give evidence of seeing Andrew Borden leave, but she gives an account of her movements after the time of his departure:

"I didn't see Miss Lizzie anywhere about. I can't say exactly, but think this was about nine o'clock. Then I cleaned off my stove, went in the dining room and sitting room, shut the windows I was going to wash, and went down into the cellar, and got a pail for to take some water. I didn't see anybody in the rooms. I got a brush in the kitchen closet, filled my pail and took it outdoors.

As I was outside, Lizzie Borden appeared in the back entry (side door) and says 'Maggie are you going to wash the windows?' I say yes. I say you needn't lock the door; I will be out around here, but you can lock it if you want to, I can get water in the barn. I went to the barn to get the handle for the brush.

First I washed the sitting room windows—on the south side of the house—the Kelly side. This was away from the screen door. Before I started washing, Mrs Kelly's girl appeared and I was talking to her at the fence. Then I washed the parlour windows: the two front windows. Between times I went to the barn and got some water. I washed the dining room windows and one parlour window on the side. I went to the barn for water twice while I was on the south side of the house—went round by the rear end went three or four times more while I was working in front or on the other side of the house. Then I went past the screen door to the barn. During all that time I did not see anybody come to the house.

Then I got a dipper from the kitchen and clean water from the barn, and commenced to wash the sitting room windows again by throwing cold water up on them. When I washed these windows, I did not see anyone in the sitting room, and I did not see anyone in the dining room when I washed those windows. I went round the house rinsing the windows with dippers of water. Then I put the brush handle away in the barn and got the hand basin and went into the sitting room to wash these windows inside. I hooked the screen door when I came in [the rear side door].

I began to wash the window next to the front door. I had not seen anyone since I saw Lizzie at the screen door. Then I heard like a person at the door was trying to unlock the door but could not, so I went to the front door and unlocked it. The spring lock was locked. I unlocked the door and it was locked with a key, there were three locks. I said 'oh phshaw' and Miss Lizzie laughed upstairs. Her father was out there on the doorstep. She was upstairs".

Two considerations arise from these passages. The first is the virtual impossibility of any intruder not being seen by Bridget if he or she attempted to enter this house while she worked her way round washing the windows. When she washed the sitting room windows she visited the barn for water more than once. Leaving the barn she would have had a clear view of the north side of the house where the only place of admittance lay. After that she was washing windows at the front and north side where it would have been utterly impossible for an interloper to have entered or left without Bridget seeing him. Add to this her further view of the inside of the premises coupled with the difficulty of negotiating the guest bedroom past so many locked doors, and set against the unlikelihood of Abby having any enemy with such a vicious intent and the theory of a murderer from outside fades considerably.

The second reflection is that if Lizzie's lawyer had not permitted his client to give evidence at the inquest, we should have no knowledge of Lizzie's account of her movements at this very crucial time when Abby was battered to death. Let us take a look then at what Lizzie said during the inquest about this crucial episode:

Hosea M Knowlton: Did your father go down town?
Lizzie Borden: He went down later.
Knowlton: What time did he start away?
Lizzie Borden: I don't know.
Knowlton: What were you doing when he started away?
Lizzie Borden: I was in the dining room, I think, yes I had just commenced to iron. I think to iron.
Knowlton: It may seem a foolish question. How much of an ironing did you have?
Lizzie Borden: I only had about eight or ten of my best handkerchiefs.
Knowlton: Did you let your father out?
Lizzie Borden: No sir, he went out himself.
Knowlton: Did you fasten the door after him?
Lizzie Borden: No sir.
Knowlton: Did Maggie?
Lizzie Borden: I don't know. When she went upstairs she always locked the door, she had charge of the back door.
Knowlton: Did she go out after a brush before your father went away?
Lizzie Borden: I think so.
Knowlton: Did you say anything to Maggie?
Lizzie Borden: I did not.
Knowlton: Did you say anything about washing the windows?
Lizzie Borden: No sir.
Knowlton: Did you speak to her?
Lizzie Borden: I think I told her I did not want any breakfast.
Knowlton: You do not remember talking about washing the windows?
Lizzie Borden: I don't remember whether I did or not. I don't remember it. Yes, I remember; yes I asked her to shut the parlour blinds when she got through, because the sun was so hot.

Knowlton: About what time do you think your father went to town?

Lizzie Borden: I don't know, it must have been after nine o'clock. I don't know what time it was.

Knowlton: You think at that time you had begun to iron your handkerchiefs?

Lizzie Borden: Yes sir.

Knowlton: How long a job was that?

Lizzie Borden: I did not finish them. My flats were not hot enough.

Knowlton: How long a job would it have been if the flats had been right?

Lizzie Borden: If they had been hot, not more than twenty minutes, perhaps.

Knowlton: How long did you work on the job?

Lizzie Borden: I don't know sir.

Knowlton: How long was your father gone?

Lizzie Borden: I don't know that.

Knowlton: Where were you when he returned?

Lizzie Borden: I was down in the kitchen.

To pause here, this passage concludes with the first of those contradictory accounts which Lizzie gave at the inquest regarding her whereabouts in the house when her father returned. She variously stated that she was in the kitchen reading an old *Harpers* magazine; in the dining room; definitely not upstairs; in her room upstairs; on the stairs coming down; again downstairs in the kitchen; in the kitchen but not reading the magazine. Bridget's evidence is clear that when Mr Borden arrived home, "Lizzie laughed upstairs. Her father was out there on the doorstep, she was upstairs".

Here we have Bridget a sound and reliable witness placing Lizzie at the crucial moment upstairs where the mutilated body of Abby Borden lay as against the prevarication and contradictions of a Lizzie Borden who knew full well that for her to have been the only person in the house besides Abby and in close proximity to her for a period which would leave ample opportunity and time for the murder would be fatal to her chances of escaping the criminal law.

How serious for a person's veracity should it be that they give contradictory evidence on oath regarding an important matter? This depends on several features: the importance of the occasion; the distance in time between the events and the evidence given about them; the intelligence level of the witness and his or her powers of recall. How does Lizzie's account look in the light of these tests?

Firstly let us note the dates of the relevant events. The murders were on the 4th August; the funeral of Mr and Mrs Borden was on the 6th August, which was the day on which Lizzie was put on notice that she was under suspicion; the inquest was on the 9th August. The importance of the events, the murder of her parents could not have been greater; Lizzie Borden was a highly intelligent woman. Could she really have been so confused?

Judge Robert Sullivan in his book *Goodbye Lizzie Borden* says:

> "[I]t was clear that the testimony of Bridget Sullivan supported all three of the basic propositions of proof of guilt as outlined by Moody in his opening. Firstly there was evidence of at least incompatibility between Lizzie and her step-mother for some time prior to the murders. Second, there was evidence which if believed, showed that Lizzie had exclusive opportunity to commit the crimes. And third, there was consciousness of guilt in the testimony concerning the note from a sick friend which Mrs Borden was supposed to have received".

Knowlton questioned Lizzie at the inquest regarding her movements during that crucial one-and-a-half hours when she was alone in the house with Abby.

> **Knowlton:** When did you last see your mother?
> **Lizzie Borden:** I did not see her after when I went down in the morning and she was dusting the dining room.
> **Knowlton:** Where did you or she go then?
> **Lizzie Borden:** I don't know where she went. I know where I was.
> **Knowlton:** Did you or she leave the dining room first?
> **Lizzie Borden:** I think I did. I left her in the dining room.
> **Knowlton:** You never saw her or heard her afterwards?
> **Lizzie Borden:** No sir.

Knowlton: Did she say anything about making the bed?

Lizzie Borden: She said she had been up and made the bed up fresh, and had dusted the room and left it all in order. She was going to put some fresh pillow slips on the small pillows at the foot of the bed, and was going to close the room because she was going to have company Monday and she wanted everything in order.

Knowlton: How long would it take to put on the pillow slips?

Lizzie Borden: About two minutes.

Knowlton: How long to do the rest of the things?

Lizzie Borden: She had done that when I came down.

Knowlton: Can you give me any suggestion as to what occupied her when she was up there, when she was struck dead?

Lizzie Borden: I don't know of anything except she had some cotton cloth pillow cases up there, and she said she was going to commence work on them. That is all I know. And the sewing machine was up there.

Knowlton: Did you hear the sewing machine?

Lizzie Borden: I did not.

Knowlton: If she had remained downstairs, you would undoubtedly have seen her?

Lizzie Borden: If she had remained downstairs, I should have, if she had remained in her room, I should not have.

Knowlton: Where was that?

Lizzie Borden: Over the kitchen.

Knowlton: To get to that room, she would have to go through the kitchen?

Lizzie Borden: To get up the back stairs.

Knowlton: That is the way she was in the habit of going?

Lizzie Borden: Yes sir. Because the other doors were locked.

Knowlton: Have you any reason to suppose you would not have seen her if she had spent any portion of the time in her room or downstairs?

Lizzie Borden: There is no reason why I should not have seen her if she had been down there, except when I first came downstairs, for two or three minutes I went down cellar to the water closet.

Knowlton: After that you were where you practically commanded the view of the first story the rest of the time?

Lizzie Borden: I think so.

Knowlton: When you went upstairs for a short time, as you say did you then went [sic] in sight of the sewing machine?

Lizzie Borden: No I did not see the sewing machine because she had shut that room up.

Knowlton: What do you mean?

Lizzie Borden: I mean the door was closed. She said she wanted it kept closed to keep the dust and everything out.

Knowlton: I ask again, perhaps you have answered all you care to, what explanation can you give, can you suggest, as to what she was doing from the time she said she had got the work all done in the spare room until eleven o'clock?

Lizzie Borden: I suppose she went up and made her own bed.

Knowlton: That would be in the back part?

Lizzie Borden: Yes sir.

Knowlton: She would have to go by you twice to do that?

Lizzie Borden: Unless she went when I was in my room that few minutes.

Knowlton: That would not be time enough for her to go and make her own bed and come back again?

Lizzie Borden: Sometimes she stayed up longer and sometimes shorter. I don't know.

Knowlton: Otherwise other than that she would have to go in your sight?

Lizzie Borden: I would have had to have seen her once. I don't know that I need to have seen her more than once.

Knowlton: You did not see her at all?

Lizzie Borden: No sir, not after the dining room.

Knowlton: What explanation can you offer as to the whereabouts of your mother from the time you saw her in the dining room and she said her work in the spare room was all done, until eleven o'clock?

Lizzie Borden: I don't know. I think she went back into the spare room, and whether she came back again or not I don't know; that has always been a mystery.

Knowlton: Can you think of anything she could be doing in the spare room?

Lizzie Borden: Yes sir. I know what she used to do sometimes. She kept her best cape on the street in there, and she used occasionally to go up there

> to get it and take it into her room, She kept a great deal in the guest room drawers; she used to go up there and get things and put things; she used those drawers for her own use.
>
> **Knowlton:** That connects her with her own room again to reach which she had to go downstairs and come up again?
>
> **Lizzie Borden:** Yes.
>
> **Knowlton:** Assuming that she did not go into her own room, I understand you to say she could not have gone into her own room without your seeing her?
>
> **Lizzie Borden:** She could while I was down [the] cellar (for a few minutes).
>
> **Knowlton:** You went down immediately you came down, within a few minutes, and you did not see her when you came back?
>
> **Lizzie Borden:** No sir.
>
> **Knowlton:** After that time she must have remained in the guest chamber?
>
> **Lizzie Borden:** I don't know.
>
> **Knowlton:** Have you had any knowledge of her going out of the house?
>
> **Lizzie Borden:** She told me she had had a note somebody was sick and said "I am going to get the dinner on the way" and asked me what I wanted for dinner.

This story was Lizzie's alone, and was completely uncorroborated. Contrary to the false impression given by Robinson in his address to the jury, Bridget's only knowledge of the matter came from Lizzie. When Abby was supposed to be out of the house responding to the note and getting the dinner she was in fact lying in the guest room battered to death.

> **Knowlton:** Did you tell her?
>
> **Lizzie Borden:** Yes. I told her I did not want anything.
>
> **Knowlton:** Then why did you suppose she had gone?
>
> **Lizzie Borden:** I supposed she had gone.
>
> **Knowlton:** Did you hear her come back?
>
> **Lizzie Borden:** I did not hear her go or come back, but I supposed she went.

Contrast with Bridget's evidence, she [Lizzie] said "Maggie, I am almost positive I heard her [Abby] coming in".

Knowlton: When you found your father dead you supposed your mother had gone?

Lizzie Borden: I did not know. I said to the people who came in "I don't know whether Mrs Borden is out or in. I wish you would see if she is in her room".

Knowlton: Did she tell you where she was going?

Lizzie Borden: No sir.

Knowlton: Did she tell you who the note was from?

Lizzie Borden: No sir.

Knowlton: Did you ever see the note?

Lizzie Borden: No sir.

Knowlton: Do you know where it is now?

Lizzie Borden: No sir.

Knowlton: Did she tell you who the note was from?

Lizzie Borden: No sir.

Knowlton: Did you ever see the note?

Lizzie Borden: No sir.

Knowlton: Do you know where it is now?

Lizzie Borden: No sir.

Knowlton: I shall have to ask you once more about that morning. Do you know what the family ate for breakfast?

Lizzie Borden: No sir.

Knowlton: Had the breakfast all been cleared away when you got down?

Lizzie Borden: Yes sir.

Knowlton: I want you to tell me just where you found the people when you got down?

Lizzie Borden: I found Mrs Borden in the dining room. I found my father in the sitting room.

Knowlton: And Maggie?

Lizzie Borden: Maggie was coming in the back door with her pail and brush.

Knowlton: Tell me what talk you had with your mother at that time?

Lizzie Borden: She asked me how I felt. I said I felt better than I did Tuesday but I did not want any breakfast. She asked me what I wanted for dinner; I told her I did not want anything. She said she was going out and would get the dinner. That is the last I saw her or said anything to her.

Knowlton: Where did you go then?

Lizzie Borden: Into the kitchen.

Knowlton: Where then?

Lizzie Borden: Down cellar.

Knowlton: Gone perhaps five minutes?

Lizzie Borden: Perhaps. Not more than that. Possibly a little more.

Knowlton: When you came back did you see your mother?

Lizzie Borden: I did not. I supposed she had gone out.

Knowlton: When you came back was your father there?

Lizzie Borden: Yes sir.

Knowlton: What was he doing?

Lizzie Borden: Reading the paper.

Knowlton: Was it usual for your mother to go out?

Lizzie Borden: Yes sir, she went out every morning nearly and did the marketing.

The above passages quoted from the transcript at the inquest are not, of course, part of the trial. Evidence of them was excluded by the judge. Consequently the jury never heard the prevarications and contradictions made by Lizzie. They were denied the opportunity of deciding whether or not her word was to be trusted. Whether she was a truthful witness, or wrongfully charged as a liar and a murderer.

Lizzie did not give evidence in her own defence at her trial. She had doubtless been advised by her counsel not to. Her performance at the inquest ensured that. Robinson may well have regretted that she was subjected to Knowlton's cross-examination which was lengthy and searching. If the same thing had taken place at the trial she would almost certainly have greatly reduced her chances of an acquittal.

In the English case of *Thompson and Bywaters*, where both were charged with the murder of Mr Thompson, Edith Thompson, the victim's wife, insisted on going into the witness box against the strong advice of her lawyers. Her performance was so poor that she alienated the jury, who convicted her. She was executed.[1]

Continuing Knowlton's cross-examination:

> **Knowlton:** Was it usual for your mother to go out?
>
> **Lizzie Borden:** Yes sir. She went out every morning nearly and did the marketing.
>
> **Knowlton:** Was it usual for her to be gone away for dinner?
>
> **Lizzie Borden:** Yes sir. Sometimes. Not very often.
>
> **Knowlton:** How often say?
>
> **Lizzie Borden:** Oh. I should not think more than, well I don't know — more than once in three months perhaps.
>
> **Knowlton:** Now I call your attention to the fact that twice, yesterday you told me with some explicitness, that when your father came in, you were just coming downstairs?
>
> **Lizzie Borden:** No I did not, I beg your pardon?
>
> **Knowlton:** That you were on the stairs at the time your father was let in, you said with some explicitness. Do you now say you did not say so?
>
> **Lizzie Borden:** I said I thought I was on the stairs, then I remembered I was in the kitchen when he came in.
>
> **Knowlton:** First you thought you were in the kitchen; afterwards you remembered you were on the stairs?
>
> **Lizzie Borden:** I said I thought I was on the stairs; then I said I knew I was in the kitchen. I still say now I was in the kitchen [contrary to the plain evidence of Bridget].
>
> **Knowlton:** Did you go into the front part of the house after your father came in?
>
> **Lizzie Borden:** After he came in from downstreet I was in the sitting room with him.
>
> **Knowlton:** Did you go into the front hall afterwards?
>
> **Lizzie Borden:** No sir.

---

1. The case is described more fully in *Chapter 16*.

Knowlton then directed his questions to the fact that Lizzie was alone in the house at the time of Abby's murder, and that nobody else was seen to be on the premises at that time.

> **Knowlton:** Excepting the two or three minutes you were down in the cellar, were you away from the house until your father came in?
> **Lizzie Borden:** No sir.
> **Knowlton:** You were always in the kitchen or dining room, excepting when you went upstairs?
> **Lizzie Borden:** I went upstairs before he went out.
> **Knowlton:** You mean you went up there to sew a button on?
> **Lizzie Borden:** I basted a piece of tape on.
> **Knowlton:** Do you remember you did not say that yesterday?
> **Lizzie Borden:** I don't think you asked me. I told you yesterday I went upstairs directly after I came up from the cellar, with clean clothes.
> **Knowlton:** You now say after your father went out, you did not go upstairs at all?
> **Lizzie Borden:** No sir, I did not.
> **Knowlton:** When Maggie came in there washing the windows, you did not appear from the front part of the house?
> **Lizzie Borden:** No sir.
> **Knowlton:** When your father was let in, you did not appear from upstairs?
> **Lizzie Borden:** No sir, I was in the kitchen.
> **Knowlton:** That is so?
> **Lizzie Borden:** Upstairs, to the best of my knowledge.

After having contradicted herself several times on this point Lizzie still adds 'to the best of my knowledge'.

> **Knowlton:** After your father went out, you remained there, either in the kitchen or dining room all the time?
> **Lizzie Borden:** I went in the sitting room long enough to direct some paper wrappers.

Knowlton: So it would have been extremely difficult for anybody to have gone through the kitchen and dining room and front hall without your seeing them?

Lizzie Borden: They could have gone from the kitchen into the sitting room while I was in the dining room if there was anybody to go [an interesting concession by Lizzie].

Knowlton: Then into the front hall?

Lizzie Borden: Yes sir.

This leaves the question of how someone could have got into the kitchen via the cellar entry without being seen by Lizzie or via the side entry without being seen or heard by Bridget.

Knowlton: You were in the dining room ironing?

Lizzie Borden: Yes sir, part of the time.

Knowlton: You were in all three of the rooms? So far as you know you were alone in the lower part of the house, a large portion of the time, after your father went away, and before he came back?

Lizzie Borden: My father did not go away I think until somewhere about ten, as near as I can remember; he was with me downstairs.

Knowlton: A large portion of the time after your father went away, and before he came back, so far as you know, you were the only person in the house?

Lizzie Borden: So far as I know.

Knowlton: And during that time, so far as you know the front door was locked?

Lizzie Borden: So far as I know.

Knowlton: And was never unlocked at all?

Lizzie Borden: I don't think it was.

Knowlton: Even after your father came home, it was locked up again?

Lizzie Borden: I don't know whether she locked it up again after that or not.

Knowlton: It locks itself?

Lizzie Borden: The spring lock opens.

Knowlton: It fastens it so it cannot be opened from the outside?

Lizzie Borden: Sometimes you can press it open.

Knowlton: Have you any reason to suppose the spring lock was left so it could be pressed open from the outside?

Lizzie Borden: I have no reason to suppose so.

Knowlton: Nothing about the lock was changed before the people came?

Lizzie Borden: Nothing that I know of.

Knowlton: What were you doing in the kitchen when your father came home?

Lizzie Borden: I think I was eating a pear when he came home.

Knowlton: What had you been doing before that?

Lizzie Borden: Been reading a magazine.

Knowlton: Were you making preparations to iron again?

Lizzie Borden: I had sprinkled my clothes and was waiting for the flat. I sprinkled the clothes before I went out.

Knowlton: Had you built up the fire again?

Lizzie Borden: I put on a stick of wood. There was a few sparks. I put in a stick of wood to try and heat the flat.

Knowlton then went on to question Lizzie on the circumstances of Andrew's murder, with particular reference to the barn "alibi". We shall dwell upon this in due course.

The principal factor in the crimes is that by common consent the same hand slew both husband and wife. The same barbaric method was employed, and common sense dictates that it had to be someone who had immediate access to both victims. Common sense again dictates that there are only two likely candidates for this gruesome role, an intruder from the street outside the house—or Lizzie herself. Uncle John Morse was not even present in the premises. Bridget was busy washing the windows at the time of Abby's death and resting in her attic room when Andrew was killed. We are then left with two and two only possible scenarios.

The first of these is that the assailant gained entry by the side door in full view of a busy street and unobserved by Bridget who while washing the windows on that side of the house and making frequent visits to the barn for water had the whole site in her view. He or she then, without being seen by Lizzie, who at various times was present in the ground floor rooms, and at times the first floor, and without any knowledge of the geography of the interior of the building retrieved from the cellar an axe, of whose whereabouts he or she was ignorant. He or she then crossed the kitchen entry, mounted the stairs, passed several locked doors to reach the guest room. They then had to conceal themself, presumably in the dress closet for and hour-and-a-half, clutching the bloodstained axe before descending the front stairs then entering the parlour and the dining room and striking at Mr Borden who was lying, probably asleep, on the couch. If Lizzie had opportunely left to go to the barn this would have been a fortunate event for him or her of which he or she could not have had any foreknowledge. Nor could he or she have known the time of her departure for the barn, or of her return.

Then there is another scenario. The unsuspecting Abby goes to the guest room to change the pillow cases pending the arrival of Uncle Morse. Lizzie, having retrieved the axe from the cellar crosses the kitchen and the kitchen entry and mounts the back stairs. She passes the locked bedroom door of Mr and Mrs Borden, enters her own room via the door adjacent to Emma's room and then moves from her own room into the guest room. Abby looks querulously at her step-daughter, a look which turns to fear as she is transfixed by the hatred in Lizzie's eyes. Perhaps in those moments between life and death Abby realised that she had no hope of defence or survival. Lizzie's hand moved forward from behind her back where she had concealed the axe. The deadly blow fell with lightning speed. Death was instant. Lizzie, the blood lust with which forensic experts are familiar, fully aroused stands over the now dead body and rains further blow upon blow on the defenceless head of Abby. Lizzie, her butchery complete, crosses the front landing, descends the front stairs. She crosses the front entry, the sitting room, the kitchen and goes down to the cellar where water is available. She then washes the blood from the axe and places it out of sight, but available for the future use for which she intends it. Any spots of blood on her clothing are also removed with the water. Lizzie has no time problem. It is an hour to an hour-and-a-half before Andrew will return. Before leaving the subject of Abby Borden's murder let us consider the much discussed matter of the sick note.

The Sick Note

If Lizzie was guilty of the crimes the only discernible reason for the story about the sick note is that Lizzie wanted to disassociate herself from the murder of Abby as far as she could. She couldn't be guilty if at the time when Abby lay dead in the guest room, she, Lizzie, believed that her step-mother was visiting a sick friend in the town. But this account proved difficult to maintain and required some alteration by Lizzie as we shall see.

One thing is certain. The story of the note came from Lizzie, and from Lizzie alone. Bridget heard it from Lizzie and not from Mrs Borden. This is clear from Bridget's evidence at the trial:

> "While I was washing the dining room windows Lizzie came down. She came to me and said: 'Maggie, are you going out this ,afternoon?' I said, 'I don't know, I might and I might not. I don't feel very well'. And she said, 'Well be sure and lock the doors, for Mrs Borden has gone out on a sick call, and I might go out too. I said 'Miss Lizzie, who is sick?'" She said 'I don't know she had a note this morning. It must be in town'".

Cross-examined by Robinson for Lizzie Borden about the return of Mr Borden:

> **George Dexter Robinson:** And there was talk with her father about the mail?
> **Bridget Sullivan:** Yes sir.
> **Robinson:** And what did he say?
> **Bridget Sullivan:** I don't know.
> **Robinson:** You don't know what was said?
> **Bridget Sullivan:** I only heard her tell her father her mother had a note and had gone out.
> **Robinson:** Did you hear what she said about that?
> **Bridget Sullivan:** No sir.
> **Robinson:** You simply say you didn't see anybody come with a note?
> **Bridget Sullivan:** No sir, I did not.

Robinson: Easy enough for somebody to come with a note to the house, and you not know wasn't it?
Bridget Sullivan: Well, I don't know if a note came to the back door that I wouldn't know.
Robinson: But they wouldn't necessarily go to the back door would they?
Bridget Sullivan: No. I never heard anything about a note, whether they got it or not, I don't know.

When Adelaide Churchill was questioned by Robinson about the note she was asked:

Robinson: Did Bridget tell you about Mrs Borden having a note?
Mrs Adelaide Churchill: She said Mrs Borden had a note to go and see someone who was sick, and she was dusting the sitting room and she hurried off, and she [Lizzie] said "She didn't tell me where she was going she generally does".
Robinson: Bridget said that?
Mrs Churchill: Yes sir.
Robinson: That was not what Lizzie said?
Mrs Churchill: No sir.

Moody correctly re-examined on this point:

William H Moody: Lest there be any mistake Mrs Churchill, you don't speak of this talk with Bridget with reference to the note as in substitution, but in addition to what Miss Lizzie Borden told you?
Mrs Churchill: It was after Lizzie had told me.
Moody: Then Bridget told you what you have told us?
Mrs Churchill: Yes, after that.

In fact the whole story of the sick note is extraordinary. Firstly it is completely uncorroborated. The only witness to it was Lizzie. There was nobody who said they had delivered it, nobody has admitted being sick or having been attended by Abby. No person saw Abby leave or return to the house. The note was never discovered, and widespread publicity brought no-one forward who could shed any light on the matter. There is an underlying absurdity to the tale. If the note really came, and was sent under some false pretence, what could have been the point? Abby was murdered in her home, not elsewhere. To decoy a victim away from their home and then slay them in their abode after their return makes no sense at all.

On the other hand if the note was delivered and was genuine, how could it be true that Abby was tending to a sick friend at the very time when she was lying battered to death in the Borden's house?

The evidence of Mrs Churchill is interesting on this issue:

> "Miss Lizzie Borden was standing outside their screen door, at the side of their house. I opened the window and said 'Lizzie, what is the matter'. She replied 'Oh Mrs Churchill, do come over. Someone has killed father'. I went over and stepped inside the screen door. She was sitting on the stair. I put my hand on her arm and said 'Oh Lizzie…Then I said 'where is your father?' She said 'in the sitting room', and I said 'Where were you when it happened?' And, she said 'I went to the barn to get a piece of iron'. I said 'where is your mother?' She said 'I don't know. She had got a note to go see someone who is sick, but I don't know but she is killed too, for I thought I heard her come in.'"

Let us pause at this point and consider Lizzie's words. Firstly, why had she made no effort to find where her step-mother was? It might be thought that this was the first thing she would want to do. Secondly, is there considerable significance in her remark, "… but I don't know but she is killed too, for I thought I heard her come in"? Why should Lizzie assume that her step-mother had also been murdered? Had she added to the embellishment to the note story because the tale itself was absurd without the return of Abby to the home? She then speaks again of her father having an enemy. But why should she assume he would also target her step-mother.

Questioned at the inquest Lizzie again modified the story regarding the note:

Knowlton: Had you any knowledge of her going out of the house?

Lizzie Borden: She told me she had a note. Somebody was sick, and said I am going to get the dinner on the way, and asked me what I wanted for dinner.

Knowlton: Did you tell her?

Lizzie Borden: Yes. I told her I did not want anything.

Knowlton: Then why did you suppose she had gone?

Lizzie Borden: I supposed she had gone.

Knowlton: Did you hear her come back?

Lizzie Borden: I did not hear her go or come back, but I suppose she went.

Knowlton: When you found your father dead you supposed your mother had gone?

Lizzie Borden: I did not know. I said to the people who came in, "I don't know if Mrs Borden is in or out. I wish you would see if she is in her room".

Knowlton: Did she tell you where she was going?

Lizzie Borden: No sir.

Knowlton: Did she tell you who the note was from?

Lizzie Borden: No sir.

Knowlton: Did you ever see the note?

Lizzie Borden: No sir.

Knowlton: Do you know where it is now?

Lizzie Borden: No sir.

The sick note is a mysterious element in the Borden saga. If Lizzie was lying about the existence of the note her credibility is in shreds—but her motive is difficult to see. If she told the truth the motive of the sender is impossible to understand. Either way it does not seem to carry the case very far one way or the other.

Lizzie Borden and the Massachusetts Axe Murders

CHAPTER EIGHT

The Murder of Andrew Borden

The death of Andrew Borden mirrored that of his wife. The same wild butchery, the same remorseless blows to the head; in her case 19 in his case ten. It was agreed on all sides that both of them had died by the same hand. That fact, and the medical evidence which proved that Abby had died at least, but no more than, one-and-a-half hours before her husband, should have been a fatal disadvantage to the defence. The fact that it was not is no adverse judgement upon the prosecution, which was conducted with both competence and fairness. It is, in the view of this author, due to the wrongful exclusion by the judges of the evidence in relation to the inquest and the attempted purchase of the Prussic acid. Those two decisions, coupled with the wholly unreasonable wave of sentimental sympathy which infected the all-male jury, together with the horrific consequence of a conviction for Lizzie were the main factors which saved Lizzie Borden from the just process of the law.

Lizzie persisted in her expressed view that it was an enemy of her father who was the assassin, This was expressed by her to Alice Russell on the night before the killings:

> "'I don't know' she [Lizzie] says, 'I feel afraid sometimes that father has got an enemy'. For she said, 'He has so much trouble with his men that come to see him'. She told me of a man that came to see him and she heard him say—she didn't see him, but heard her father say, 'I don't care to let my property, for such business' and she said the man answered sneeringly, 'I shouldn't think you would care what you let your property for', and she said 'father was mad and ordered him out of the house.'"

Lizzie repeated her suspicions in the presence of Assistant City Marshall, John Fleet who said in his evidence:

> "I then asked her if she had any idea who could have killed her father and mother. Then she said, 'She is not my mother sir, she is my step-mother; my mother died when I was a child'. I then asked her if there had been anyone around this morning whom she would suspect of having done the killing of these people, and she said that she had not seen anyone, but, about nine o'clock that morning, a man came to the door and was talking with her father. I asked her what they were talking about, and she said she thought they were talking about a store, and he spoke like an Englishman. I think about all the conversation I had with her at that time—oh no. Miss Russell was in the room and Lizzie looked at Miss Russell, and she said to Lizzie, 'tell him all, tell him what you was telling me'. And she looked at Miss Russell and then she says 'about two weeks ago a man came to the house, to the front door, and had some talk with father, and talked as though he was angry', I asked her what he was talking about. She said he was talking about

a store, and father said to him 'I cannot have the store for that purpose'. The man seemed to be angry. I then came downstairs."

Mrs Churchill reported Lizzie as saying to her: "Father must have an enemy, for we have all been sick, and we think the milk has been poisoned…". Dr Bowen had already assured Abby that this was most unlikely.

To Captain Philip Harrington of the Fall River Police Lizzie said, "A few weeks ago father had angry words with a man about something". Asked, "What was it?" Lizzie replied "I don't know but they were very angry at the time, and the stranger went away". Asked, "Did you see him at all?" she replied, "No sir, they were in another room, but from the tone of their voices I know everything wasn't pleasant between them". "Did you hear your father saying anything about him?" "No sir, about two weeks ago he came again. They had a very animated conversation during which they got angry again, and I heard father say, 'No sir, I will not let my store for any such business!' But before they separated I heard father say, 'When you are in town come again and I will let you know about it.'"

Lizzie was unable to give any details at all about the man in question. None of the men referred to by Lizzie had any reason for murdering Abby.

Doctor Seabury Bowen described the state of Andrew Borden's body when he conducted his first brief examination:

> "I saw the form of Mr Borden lying on the lounge (sofa) at the left of the sitting room door. His face was very badly cut, apparently with a sharp instrument; his face was covered with blood. I felt his pulse and satisfied myself he was dead. Glanced about the room and saw that there was nothing disturbed; neither the furniture not anything at all. Mr Borden was lying with his face towards the south on his right side, and apparently at ease as if asleep. His face was hardly to be recognised by one who knew him. I made no other examination at the time except to feel his pulse."

Dr William Dolan gave evidence of his fuller examination of the bodies of Mr and Mrs Borden:

"When I entered the house, I went into the kitchen and then to the sitting room. The body of Mr Borden was lying on the sofa. Sofa was against the north wall of the room, running east and west, with the head towards the parlour and the feet towards the kitchen, that is towards the east. The sofa was against the jamb of the dining room door. The body was covered with a sheet. Dr Bowen was with me. I found that Mr Borden's hand was warm; the blood was oozing from his wounds and was bright red in colour. The head was resting on a sofa cushion that had a little white tidy on it. The cushion I think rested in his coat, which had been doubled up and put under there. And the coat in turn rested on an afghan or sofa cover. I made no particular examination of the wounds then; only stayed two or three minutes.

I went upstairs to see Mrs Borden. She was lying between the dressing case and the bed. I touched the body, noted the wounds on the back of her head, noted that her blood was coagulated and as of a dark colour. She was lying with her back exposed; her hands were nearer the wall than her head; they were not clasped. The upper part of her dress, the waist, was bloody. I found an old silk handkerchief there and took it with me. It was nearer the wall than the head. It was not cut, but it was blood-stained. I was there examining the body for only two or three minutes. When I saw Mr Borden I had a clinical thermometer with me, but I did not use it. At Mr Borden's head, the blood was dripping on the carpet underneath. There were two spots in the carpet, about eight or ten inches in diameter.

Turning back to Mrs Borden's body, I felt that with my hand; touched her head and hand; it was much colder than that of Mr Borden. Did not use thermometer. Her blood on the head was matted and practically dry. There was no oozing from it, as in Mr Borden's."

At the inquest Lizzie was questioned about her movements when her father got home after his visit to the town:

Hosea M Knowlton: Have you any idea what time it was that your father came home?

Lizzie Borden: I am not sure, but I think it must have been after ten, because I think he told me he did not think he should go out until about ten. When he went out I did not look at the clock to see what time it was. I think he did not go out until ten or a little after. He was not gone so very long.

Knowlton: Will you give me the best judgement you can as to the time your father got back? If you have not any, it is sufficient to say so.

Lizzie Borden: No sir, I have not any.

Knowlton: Can you give me any judgment as to the length of time that elapsed after he came back, and before you went to the barn?

Lizzie Borden: I went right out to the barn.

Knowlton: How soon after he came back?

Lizzie Borden: I should think not less than five minutes. I saw him taking off his shoes and lying down; it only took him two or three minutes to do it. I went right out.

Knowlton: When he came into the house did he not go into the dining room first?

Lizzie Borden: I don't know.

Knowlton: And then sit down?

Lizzie Borden: I don't know.

Knowlton: Why don't you know?

Lizzie Borden: Because I was in the kitchen.

Knowlton: It might have happened and you might not have known it?

Lizzie Borden: Yes sir.

Knowlton: You heard the bell ring?

Lizzie Borden: Yes sir.

Knowlton: And you knew when he came in?

Lizzie Borden: Yes sir.

Knowlton: You did not see him?

Lizzie Borden: No sir.

Knowlton: When did you first see him?

Lizzie Borden: I went into the sitting room and he was there. I don't know whether he had been in the dining room before or not.

Knowlton: What made you go into the sitting room?

Lizzie Borden: Because I wanted to ask him a question.

Knowlton: What question?

Lizzie Borden: Was there any mail for me.

Knowlton: Did you not ask him that question in the dining room?

Lizzie Borden: No sir. I think not.

Knowlton: Was he not in the dining room sitting down?

Lizzie Borden: I don't remember him being in the dining room sitting down.

Knowlton: At that time was not Maggie washing the windows in the sitting room?

Lizzie Borden: I thought I asked him for the mail in the sitting room. I am not sure.

Knowlton: Was not the reason he went in the dining room because she was in the sitting room washing windows?

Lizzie Borden: I don't know.

Knowlton: Did he not go upstairs to his own room before he sat down in the sitting room?

Lizzie Borden: I did not see him go.

Knowlton: He had the key to his room down there?

Lizzie Borden: I don't know whether he had it, it was kept on a shelf.

Knowlton: When you did go into the sitting room to ask him a question, if it was the sitting room, what took place then?

Lizzie Borden: I asked him if he had any mail. He said "none for you". He had a letter in his hand. I supposed it was for himself. I asked him how he felt. He said "about the same". He said he should lie down. I asked him if he thought he should have a nap. He said he should try to. I asked him if he wanted the window left the way it was or if he felt a draft, he said "no". That is all.

Knowlton: Did you help him about lying down?

Lizzie Borden: No sir.

Knowlton: Fix his pillows or head?

Lizzie Borden: No sir. I did not touch the sofa.

Knowlton: Did he lie down before you left the room?

Lizzie Borden: Yes sir.

Knowlton: Did anything else take place?

Lizzie Borden: Not that I remember of.

Knowlton: Was he then under medical treatment?

Lizzie Borden: No sir.

Knowlton: The doctor had not given him any medicine that you know of?

Lizzie Borden: No sir. He took some medicine, it was not doctors medicine. It was what we gave him.

Knowlton: What was it?

Lizzie Borden: We gave him castor oil first, and then the Garfield Tea.

Knowlton: When was that?

Lizzie Borden: He took the castor oil sometime Wednesday, I think sometime Wednesday noon, and I think the tea Wednesday night. Mrs Borden gave it to him. She went over to the doctor.

Knowlton: When did you first consult Mr Jennings?

Lizzie Borden: I can't tell you that; I think my sister sent for him; I don't know.

Knowlton: Was it you or your sister?

Lizzie Borden: My sister.

Knowlton: You did not send for him?

Lizzie Borden: I did not send for him. She said did we think we ought to have him. I said do as she thought best. I don't know when he came first.

The questioning then turned to the dispute over property four or five years previously.

If Lizzie's behaviour towards her step-mother prior to the first murder has a number of question marks, the same can be said in the case of her father's demise.

In her first account of the homecoming of Andrew Borden after his various visitations in the town she appeared to be trying to give the impression that she had been very solicitous for his welfare. Yet later, at the inquest she seems to distance herself. The whole scenario of the second murder contains a number of remarkable coincidences.

Was it coincidence that at the time of these terrifying events the house was effectively empty except for the victim? Uncle John Morse and sister Emma were both away from the house, Abby was lying dead in the guest room, Bridget was in her attic room and Lizzie was allegedly in the barn. Was it coincidence that Lizzie suddenly broke off her ironing in search of lead sinkers which could be had for next to nothing in the town at any time? Was it coincidence that Lizzie was away in the barn at the precise period and at the precise time that these terrible events took place? And why, if Bridget is right when she says that Lizzie said she had heard her step-mother return to the house, was it that Lizzie never ascended the few steps on the staircase to look for her step-mother, but sent someone else instead.

Or was it because she could not face the dreadful sight which she knew awaited in the guest room? And why was it that, if Lizzie held her father in such affection there was no scream or cry of anguish when she found his body and that she maintained such composure throughout what must have been a terrible ordeal for her? And why did she send for a doctor when Andrew was plainly beyond medical help? It was plainly a matter for the police not for doctors.

CHAPTER NINE

The Evidence of Hannah Reagan

The testimony of Mrs Reagan, like the Borden case itself, was something of a mystery. Here was a story which was not central to the trial, but nevertheless had great potential to influence the result if accepted at its face value. This is what she told the court:

"I am the matron at the Fall River Police Station. The prisoner was in my charge for nine or ten days; she occupied my own room. On August 24th Miss Emma Borden came to see her sister, it was about twenty minutes to nine in the morning, and I was tidying up the room.

I let her in and she spoke to her sister Lizzie, and I left the two women talking together, and I went into the toilet room about four feet from where Miss Lizzie Borden was lying on a couch, and I heard very loud talk and I came to my door and it was Miss Lizzie Borden; she was lying on her left side and her sister Emma was talking to her and bending right over her, and Lizzie says, 'Emma you have gave me away, haven't you?' She says 'No Lizzie I have not,' 'you have,' she says 'and I will let you see I wont give in one inch' and she sat right up and put up her finger, and I stood in the doorway looking at both of them.

Lizzie Borden lay right down on the couch on her left side and faced out the window and closed her eyes, and Miss Emma got a chair, I gave her a chair, and she sat right down beside her sister. They sat there till Mr Jennings came to my door, somewhere about eleven o'clock. Miss Lizzie didn't speak to her sister, nor turn her face to her any more that afternoon."

Mrs Reagan after this episode let Mr Jennings in, and according to Mrs Reagan Jennings said to Emma, "Have you told her all?" To which Emma replied, "Yes all." Porter, a reporter from the *Globe*, who questioned Mrs Reagan gave a slightly different story. According to him, when Lizzie made her accusation Emma said, "I only told Mr Jennings what I thought he ought to know". Another newspaper recorded the words as, "What he ought to know for your defence". If these words are to be believed the statement made by Emma to Mr Jennings, the defence lawyer, cannot have implicated Lizzie in the crime, otherwise Jennings would have been concealing the truth from the court throughout the trial. There is no reason to think that an honourable family solicitor such as Jennings would do such a thing, nor is it likely that Emma, although keen to protect her sister, knew that she was guilty.

At the trial Hannah Reagan was cross-examined by Jennings:

Andrew J Jennings: How long did Miss Emma remain that morning in the room?

Hannah Reagan: She remained sir, from twenty minutes of nine o'clock until you came to the door.

Jennings: Did Miss Emma come again that day?

Hannah Reagan: In the afternoon sir.

Jennings: What time did she come in the afternoon?

Hannah Reagan: I never kept the time of when she came. She came at all hours of the day.

Jennings: How came you to keep the time she came in the morning?

Hannah Reagan: Well I was cleaning up that morning, and it was rather early.

Jennings: Did anybody else come in the afternoon?

Hannah Reagan: Let me see. Why yes there was lots of visitors come in the afternoon.

Jennings: Who were they?

Hannah Reagan: Mr Buck came in the afternoon.

Jennings: Are you sure he came that afternoon?

Hannah Reagan: Well I know we had visitors that afternoon, I think Mr Buck came. I don't remember when Miss Emma came in the afternoon; I can't give you any idea, I am sure there was no-one there in the morning but her sister and you [Mr Jennings]. I don't remember Mrs Holmes in the afternoon.

Jennings: Now let me go a little further and see if I can refresh your recollection [by which Jennings meant; persuade you to go back on your story]. Do you remember that Mrs Holmes was there that afternoon and you had some conversation about an egg?

Hannah Reagan: About what?

Jennings: About an egg?

Hannah Reagan: I remember about the eggs, but I couldn't tell you whether it was that afternoon or not, sir.

Jennings: What was it about the egg?

Hannah Reagan: The breaking of the egg.

Jennings: Well. What was said or done?

Hannah Reagan: We were talking in the afternoon, me and Lizzie Borden, and I says "I can tell you one thing you can't do" and she says "Tell me what it is Mrs Reagan". I says "break an egg Miss Borden". And she says "break an egg?". I says "yes" "well" she says, "I can break an egg". I says "not the way I would tell you to break it", she says "well, what way is it Mrs Reagan?". So I told her that she couldn't break it the way I wanted her to break it, and I said I would give her a dollar that she couldn't, and she said she would bet me a quarter, and in the afternoon someone fetched Lizzie an egg, and Miss Emma Borden was sitting down beside her, and I told Miss Emma Borden to get a little way away. "Because I said she will break the egg the wrong way it will destroy your dress" and she did get the egg, and she got it in her hands and she couldn't break it and she says. "There" she says "that is the first thing that I undertook to do that I never could."

Yes I did speak of the talk between the two sisters as a quarrel. I don't remember the day of the week, it was August 24th. I didn't see about it in the papers; I heard of it from Mr Buck. I was asked about it by the reporter. I did not tell the reporters it was all a lie. I didn't tell Mr Buck it wasn't true.

Jennings: Subsequent to that was a paper drawn up for you to sign?

Hannah Reagan: Yes sir.

Jennings: Was it read to you?
Hannah Reagan: Yes sir.
Jennings: Can you tell us what it was?
Hannah Reagan: No sir, I can't.
Jennings: Who brought it to you?
Hannah Reagan: Mr Buck.
Jennings: And you say you can't recall any part of it?
Hannah Reagan: No sir.
Jennings: Will you listen to this and see if this sounds anything like it:

"This is [to] certify that my attention has been called to a report said to have been made by me in regard to a quarrel between Lizzie and her sister Emma, in which Lizzie said to Emma 'you have given me away', and that I expressly and positively deny any such conversation took place, and I further deny that I ever heard anything that could be construed as a quarrel between the sisters".

Jennings: Does that sound anything like it?
Hannah Reagan: No sir. I don't remember one word that Mr Buck said to me that evening.
Jennings: Will you say that that was not the substance of the paper that was presented to you?
Hannah Reagan: I couldn't tell you sir.

Re-examination by Moody:

William H Moody: Mrs Reagan, you told Mr Jennings that you told this story to some reporter on the afternoon it occurred. What reporter was that?
Hannah Reagan: The reporter of the Fall River Globe.
Moody: Do you see him now?
Hannah Reagan: Mr Porter. Yes sir.
Moody: Was anyone with you when Mr Buck came in with the paper?
Hannah Reagan: No sir.
Moody: Just say what he said to you when he brought the paper.

Hannah Reagan: The court was going on in the afternoon and Mr Buck came in and said "Mrs Reagan there is a report going round that there has been trouble between Miss Emma Borden and her sister". I said "Where did you hear it?" He said "It has come from the papers". I said "you can't believe all you read in the papers". He went away and came back again and called me out of my room into the landing, and all the reporters were standing there, and he turned round and says "Mrs Reagan, I want you to sign this paper". Said I "for what sir?" He says "If you will sign this paper it will make everything all right between Miss Lizzie Borden and her sister", I said "Will you give me that paper and I will take it to Marshall Hilliard?" He says "No, I can't give it to you, but I will go downstairs with you" and I went downstairs with him.

Moody: Now tell us all that was said or done in the Marshall's office.

Hannah Reagan: Mr Buck went in and showed this paper to Marshall Hilliard and I stood outside the rail. Marshall Hilliard said "you go to your room and I will attend to this business and you Mr Buck attend to yours".

One thing which emerges from the story is the outrageous behaviour of the Reverend Buck. To interfere in the evidence in the way in which he did comes very near to attempting to pervert the course of justice. The revered gentleman might well have found himself in prison. He was very properly told by Hilliard to go away and mind his own business.

There are numerous reasons for asking why Hannah Reagan should lie. Firstly, she would have had to construct a completely false story. What could have been her motive for doing such a grossly dishonest thing? Why should she be so biased against Lizzie as to do that? Was the result of the trial so important to her personally that she, a prison officer, should fabricate vital evidence? Her good character was crucially important to her in her particular profession. She would clearly appreciate that if her account of events was disbelieved it would rebound on her and her good name would suffer irreparable harm. Moreover she would be well aware that the prosecution would want her to give evidence at the trial and she would be subjected to rigorous cross-examination. There would be no room for mistake, either she was a truthful witness or a liar, the defence would be uncompromising that she was the latter.

There is no evidence that she had been on bad terms with Lizzie, or certainly that feelings between them were such that Mrs Reagan would wish to hasten Lizzie towards the hangman's rope. Mrs Reagan was mistaken in speaking to the press about what she claims to have heard, even in a country where there is a looser reign kept on contact between potential witnesses and the media than is the case in England and Wales. Nevertheless her story remained consistent throughout, she could never be said to have embellished it, Nor could it be said that whatever inducement may have been held out she ever came close to putting her signature to the document retracting the statement.

Yet these matters notwithstanding, an aura of doubt hangs about Hannah Reagan's version of events. It is clear that the jury would give Lizzie the benefit of the doubt if there was any room for doubt at all, No fewer than five witnesses were ready to refute Hannah Reagan's evidence. It could be said that Mrs Reagan was consulting Marshall Hilliard concerning putting her signature to the document — otherwise she would have rejected putting her signature to it out of hand. A reporter who represented the associated press John J Manning was sworn and testified that he was at 92 Second Street at 11.25 am on the 24th August 1892. John Manning was asked:

> **Jennings:** Do you recall the publication of a story told by Mrs Reagan about a quarrel between Lizzie Borden and her sister Emma?
> **John Manning:** Yes, it was published in the Boston Globe that night, however I talked to Mrs Reagan and she said "there was nothing in it". I asked her if the story was true, and she said again "there was nothing in it".

Under cross-examination by Knowlton Manning somewhat qualified his evidence by admitting that Mrs Reagan said "what I have to say about the quarrel I will say on the witness stand".

Thomas F Hickey, a reporter for the *Boston Herald* gave evidence about an interview with Mrs Reagan in her room:

Knowlton: What did you do?

John Manning: I remember going into Mrs Reagan's room and making a remark something like this "I see that you are getting yourself into the paper Mrs Reagan". She laughed and said "yes, but they have got to take that all back". After some questions which I have forgotten now, I asked her again abut the alleged quarrel between Lizzie and Emma Borden, Mrs Reagan said to me "there is no truth at all in the story that was printed".

Mrs Holmes gave evidence and was asked:

Jennings: Mrs Holmes do you remember the publication of a story about a quarrel between Lizzie and her sister Emma Borden?
Mrs Holmes: I do.
Jennings: Did you later speak to Mrs Reagan?
Mrs Holmes: Yes, Mrs Reagan said "No Mrs Holmes, it isn't so , for that was the afternoon we were talking about the eggs.
Jennings: Do you remember a time when there was talk about Mrs Reagan signing a paper?
Mrs Holmes: Yes but the conversation was not to me.

Charles J Holmes, the husband of the last witness, gave evidence and said that after the Reverend Buck had read the affidavit to Mrs Reagan, she said that the contents of the affidavit were true:

Jennings: The affidavit was trying to get a denial of something that was published in a newspaper?
Charles J Holmes: It was to prove that no such statement has been made by Mrs Reagan.
Jennings: Did Mrs Reagan sign the affidavit?
Charles J Holmes: She did not.
Jennings: And never has signed it as far as you know?
Charles J Holmes: Not as far as I know.

A reporter named John R Caldwell said that he had heard Marshall Hilliard expressly order Mrs Reagan not to sign the statement. An old friend of Lizzie Borden, Mary Brigham, testified that Mrs Reagan said in her presence, "It is all a lie from beginning to end. I was willing to sign that paper, but the Marshall wouldn't let me do it. He told me to go to my room and obey orders".

Taken all in all the evidence of Mrs Reagan could not expect to stand up before a jury.

CHAPTER TEN

The Blood Mystery

There can be little doubt that the strongest argument for the defence in the Borden trial was the absence of any trace of blood on the person of Lizzie—shoes, stockings, dress, skirt or hair. On the basis of evidence from witnesses who attended to her, the prosecution had no alternative but to accept their testimony.

Knowlton and Moody were wise enough not to invite the jury to consider theories which might stretch their imagination in order to get around an uncomfortable obstacle. Moody made this clear in his opening address:

> "Now gentlemen, it will appear that in about two rooms in which the homicides were committed there was blood spattered in various directions, so that would make it probable that one or more splatters of blood would be upon the person or upon the clothing of the assailant. And there has been produced for the inspection of the Commonwealth—it was produced a good many days after the homicide the clothing said to have been worn by the prisoner on the morning of August 4th—the shoes, stockings, dress, skirt.
>
> The most rigid examination by the most competent expert in this country fails to disclose any marks of blood upon the dress which is produced as the one which she wore on the morning of the homicide, and the skirt which she is said to have worn upon that morning produces one minute spot of blood, which I do not think worth while to call to your attention at the present time".

This was a fair and sensible concession made at the very start of the case, particularly since it was a matter which could weigh heavily with the jury. Yet the matter does not end there. Other questions arise: Did Lizzie have time and opportunity to erase any blood stains before the crimes were discovered? Were the clothes produced at the trial the same ones as those she was wearing on the morning of the killings? Why were the clothes not examined by an expert as soon as possible instead of some days later? Did Lizzie destroy the guilty bloodstains when she burnt a dress on August 7th? How could an intruder escape after committing a double murder while his or her clothes were covered with the blood of the victims? It was plain from the evidence of both doctors Seabury Bowen and William Dolan that there must have been an amount of blood splashed in the area of both bodies. Yet the testimony of two powerful witnesses of truth Adelaide Churchill and Alice Russell is favourable to Lizzie. Mrs Churchill on the period when she was comforting Lizzie on her father's death was cross-examined by Robinson:

George Dexter Robinson: You had been there with Miss Lizzie all the time?
Mrs Adelaide Churchill: Yes sir.
Robinson: Did you see any blood on her dress?
Mrs Churchill: No sir.
Robinson: On a dress as light as that, if there had been any blood you would have seen it, wouldn't you?
Mrs Churchill: I don't know. I should think if it was in front I might have seen it. If I was right side of her then I couldn't help it, I don't think.
Robinson: You were right over her, fanning her?
Mrs Churchill: Yes sir, stood right in front of her.
Robinson: Rubbing both her hands, as she was lying on the lounge?
Mrs Churchill: She wasn't on the lounge when I fanned. She was in the kitchen when I fanned her.
Robinson: You afterwards saw her with Miss Russell, and she was lying on the lounge [sofa]?
Mrs Churchill: Yes sir.
Robinson: At that time did you see a single particle of blood on her dress?

Mrs Churchill: No sir.
Robinson: On her hands?
Mrs Churchill: No sir.
Robinson: On her face?
Mrs Churchill: No sir.
Robinson: Or any disarrangement of her hair?
Mrs Churchill: No sir.
Robinson: Or anything about her shoes?
Mrs Churchill: I didn't notice her shoes at all.

However Mrs Churchill's evidence on the question of the dress which was produced to the court was anything but helpful to Lizzie:

Robinson: Will you describe the dress that she had on while you were there (at the house on the murder day).
Mrs Churchill: It looked like a light-blue—and white ground work with a dark navy—blue diamond printed on it.
Robinson: Was the whole dress alike, the skirt and waist?
Mrs Churchill: It looked so to me.
Robinson: Was that the dress she had on this morning? (showing a dark-blue dress produced to the court).
Mrs Churchill: That is not the dress I have described.
Robinson: Was it the dress she had on?
Mrs Churchill: I did not see her with that on that morning.
Robinson: Didn't see her with it on that morning?
Mrs Churchill: No sir.

Alice Russell cross-examined by Robinson:

Robinson: Now, Miss Russell did you see any blood upon her clothing?
Alice Russell: No sir.
Robinson: A speck of it?
Alice Russell: No sir.
Robinson: Or was her hair disturbed?

Alice Russell: I don't think it was. I think I should have noticed if it was disordered.
Robinson: Saw nothing out of the way did you?
Alice Russell: No sir.
Robinson: About any of her clothing or about her person?
Alice Russell: No sir.
Robinson: Everything look alright did it?
Alice Russell: As far as I saw.

Dr William A Dolan examined both the bodies. He gave his opinion regarding the angle of attack. Cross-examined by Robinson:

Robinson: Have you any opinion as to where the assailant of Mr Borden stood, taking into account the spots (of blood) which you saw?
Dr William A Dolan: I have.
Robinson: From the appearance of things where did the assailant stand?
Dr Dolan: Stood close behind the head of the lounge [sofa] that is, between the parlour door and the head of the lounge.
Robinson: You no longer, if you have ever put him there, make him stand in the dining room door?
Dr Dolan: I never put him there.
Robinson: Did you ever have an opinion that one or more of these blows might have been given by a person reaching around the jamb of the dining room door and striking the head?
Dr Dolan: Well to stand even behind the dining room door you would not have to reach around.
Robinson: You think the assailant swung the instrument from left to right don't you?
Dr Dolan: Yes sir.
Robinson: And all those wounds can be fairly accounted for by blows from left to right?
Dr Dolan: Yes sir.
Robinson: That is to say it is a left handed blow?
Dr Dolan: In what sense left handed, delivered by the left hand?

Robinson: That it strikes the body in a left handed direction—from left to right?

Dr Dolan: Yes sir, to a certain extent. Those that are most markedly from left to right are those that would come down directly as the head lies there now, and give the direction of a left handed blow.

Robinson: And those blows made quite as severe injuries as any?

Dr Dolan: Yes sir.

Robinson: And the strongest left handed blow, in your opinion was the blow upon the eyebrow where that bone was chipped out?

Dr Dolan: Yes sir.

Robinson: In your opinion, would a strong and crushing blow not have been necessary to have made that?

Dr Dolan: No sir.

Robinson: A light blow in your opinion could have done that?

Dr Dolan: Not a light blow, no sir.

Robinson: A fairly strong blow?

Dr Dolan: Yes sir.

Robinson: Was it a one handed or a two handed blow in your opinion?

Dr Dolan: I could not tell you.

Robinson: Have you any opinion about that?

Dr Dolan: I think one handed could do it.

Robinson: Assuming that the carotid artery [that running up through the neck and under the angle of the jaw) had been cut, would there be a large flow of blood?

Dr Dolan: It depends on where it was cut, sir.

Robinson: Suppose it was the interior one, there are two of them, I believe or two branches.

Dr Dolan: Even then it would depend upon where.

Robinson: Well supposing it was cut near the angle of the jaw, would there be a large flow of blood immediately?

Dr Dolan: There would immediately, a very large flow of blood.

Robinson: And if the assailant using the instrument which you have described, or a similar one had cut that would it not have been natural that the assailant would have been covered in blood or would have been spattered or sprinkled with blood?

Dr Dolan: Not necessarily.

Robinson: How do you explain that they would have not been?

Dr Dolan: Because it would not spurt in that direction.

Robinson: In what direction?

Dr Dolan: In the direction of the assailant.

Robinson: But when the hatchet goes into the wound doesn't it get covered with blood, particularly the edge of it?

Dr Dolan: Yes sir.

Robinson: And when it is covered with blood which is fresh and warm isn't it liable to come off in a swinging blow?

Dr Dolan: Yes sir.

Robinson: And isn't it liable to strike the assailant somewhere as he swings his blow from front to rear and from rear to front?

Dr Dolan: Yes sir.

Robinson: And wouldn't you say it would be probable that the assailant would be covered with blood or have splatters on him?

Dr Dolan: He would have splatters, yes sir.

Robinson: And in what part of the body in the case of Mr Borden would these spatters come?

Dr Dolan: The upper part.

Robinson: That is the head, the breast?

Dr Dolan: Yes sir.

Robinson: Would the hands be liable to be spotted or spattered?

Dr Dolan: They might.

Robinson: Would it not be probable?

Dr Dolan: Probable.

Dr Dolan then went on to say that the attacker of Abby Borden would have stood astride her prostrate body and swung the axe from left to right and back. He then gave the approximate time between the two deaths at around one-and-a-half-hours which he estimated from the respective condition of the blood and stomach of the two victims.

Professor Edward Wood said he was a physician and chemist at the Harvard Medical School. He had given special attention to medico-legal cases involving poisons and bloodstains and had given evidence in several hundred trials, including a large number of capital cases.

He was questioned regarding the tiny spot of blood on Lizzie's shirt:

> **Robinson:** The white skirt to which your attention was called had upon it, you have stated, I believe, a spot of blood appearing as large as the size of the head of a small pin?
> **Professor Edward Wood:** Yes sir — the diameter, not the size.
> **Robinson:** Are you able to say that that was not a spot of blood, which might have gotten on from the menstrual flow of the woman?
> **Professor Wood:** No sir, I am not.
> **Robinson:** It would be consistent with that would it?
> **Professor Wood:** Yes sir, it may have been menstrual blood, or may not, so far as I can determine.

This was long before DNA which would have solved the problem. Dr Frank Draper was well qualified in giving evidence in cases of homicide when murder was suspected:

> "I believe that Mrs Borden's assailant stood astride the prostrate body. This is my opinion but it is an open question. As to the flap wound in the scalp at the left side of the head. That was delivered while Mrs Borden was standing and facing the assailant.
>
> In my opinion Mr Borden's assailant stood at the head of the sofa, over the head of the victim. Mr Borden, at the time, was lying on his right side, his face well turned to the right, and his right cheek concealed in the pillow — I think all the blows could have been received with the body lying as shown in the photograph. To speak as to the spattering of blood from his wounds its mere guesswork as to whether the assailant would be spattered with blood, I have no opinion".

Dr Draper did say however:

"Taking into consideration the spots of blood in the guest chamber, the number of injuries received by Mrs Borden and the appearance of the flowing of blood, I should think the assailant would of necessity be spattered with blood.

I think that blood could be so effectively removed from a metal instrument that a subsequent chemical test would find no trace of it. It could not easily be done".

CHAPTER ELEVEN

The Murder Weapon

In every murder enquiry an important element is the weapon used in committing the crime. There are several reasons for this. Firstly if there is blood on the weapon this may be traced to the killer should blood of the same type be found on this person or his or her clothes or his or her possessions. Secondly, it may be possible to "marry up" the type of instrument with the particular wounds on the body. Thirdly, the whereabouts of the murder weapon may indicate where the crime was committed — that is to say whether it was carried into the premises in question or whether it was already there.

This was an extremely important issue in the Borden case because the only individual who had an intimate knowledge of the contents of the cellar, where the suspect object was found, apart from Bridget, was Lizzie herself. What would-be murderer would gain access to a house without having the slightest idea of where a suitable implement for his purposes was to be found? And having completed his or her foul purpose who spends precious minutes washing and replacing it in the place where he or she found it while delaying their exit.

These points would seem to weigh against the defence. Yet by cleverly clouding the issue of which was the fatal implement Robinson drew the sting of the prosecution and created an air of mystery about the whole situation. In Moody's opening address he dealt with the question of the murder weapon:

> "You have noticed Mr Foreman and gentlemen that this indictment states that these homicides were committed with 'a sharp cutting instrument a more particular description of which is to the jurors unknown'. It is the duty of the government to bring forward all its information upon this subject, and I propose to open it all to you at the present time.
>
> Upon the premises was found two axes and two hatchets. Upon one of these hatchets spots were discovered which upon view were thought to be blood. It is extremely difficult, impossible in fact—Dr Wood, the highest authority on the subject in this country if not in the world, will say, to distinguish between blood and some other substances."

Moody then held up two axes, neither of which could have been the murder weapon. He then said, "Upon the day of the homicides another weapon or part of a weapon was found, after what was thought to be a bloody hatchet was discovered, and it attracted little attention. It was seen by one officer and left where it was. At that time this fragment of the handle was in its appropriate place in the helve, if that is its proper name, of the hatchet in the place fitted in the tread. It was covered with an adhesion of ashes. Not the fine dust which floats about the room when ashes are emptied, but a coarse dust of ashes adhering more or less to all sides of the hatchet. Upon the Monday morning this hatchet was taken away and its custody from that time to the present will be traced."

Moody then said that the break in the handle was fresh and the blade covered with a coarse dust. He pointed out that the blade of the weapon that killed Mr Borden was three-and-a-half inches, the exact size of this handless hatchet. Moody:

> "Let there be no mistake Mr Foreman and gentlemen, about my meaning. The government does not insist that these homicides were committed by this handless hatchet. It may have been the weapon. It may well have been the weapon. The one significant fact which in this respect is emphasised is that the bloody weapon was not found by the side of the victims upon the premises or near them. Doubtless you will consider that fact well when you come to consider whether the homicides were the act of an intruder or stranger flying from his crimes with the bloody weapon in his possession through the streets of Fall River at noon day, or the acts of an inmate of the house familiar with its recourse for destruction, obliteration and concealment".

Referring in the course of his address to the pending evidence of Professor Wood, Moody said:

> "Professor Wood will say to you—he saw this hatchet soon after it was found—that while there were ragged fragments of wood which would retain absolutely no indication of blood on these other weapons, that of the weapon had had on it the remainder of its handle and was as smooth as he saw it. By the application of water soon after the homicide, blood could be readily, effectively and completely removed".

It was clear that the case for the prosecutor was that the broken hatchet was the murder weapon and that Lizzie had broken it, washed it, then rolled the blade in ashes to obliterate the traces of blood. Now let us see how much of the evidence supported Moody's opening speech.

John Fleet was assistant City Marshall of Fall River. He was questioned by Moody and described how he went down into the cellar and spoke to officer Mullaly:

> **William H Moody:** What did you do after you said something to Officer Mullaly?

John Fleet: In the consequence of my asking him, I found a box in the middle cellar. As I recall it, on a shelf or a jag of a chimney—an old fashioned chimney—was the head of the hatchet.

Moody: What sort of box was it in which this head of the hatchet was?

John Fleet: Well, it was a box, I should say, about a foot or fourteen inches long. Perhaps eight or ten inches wide. It might have been a little larger, and I should say about four inches deep.

Moody: Was there anything else in the box except the head of the hatchet?

John Fleet: Yes—there were other tools—I can't think just what there were now, but there were other small tools in there, pieces of iron.

Moody: At the time you found that hatchet, was the wood, and iron or steel separate?

John Fleet: Let me see if that is the one.

Moody: Yes, I will withdraw that question and ask you if that is the hatchet you found.

John Fleet: This looks like the hatchet that I found there, pretty sure that is the one. This piece of wood was in the head of the hatchet, broken off close.

Moody: Mr Fleet, will you describe everything in respect of that hatchet if you can?

George Dexter Robinson: Don't want anything but what the hatchet was at that time, don't want any inferences.

Moody: I think he will be careful.

Moody: Any appearances that you noticed about the hatchet, you may describe?

John Fleet: Yes sir, I don't want to do anything else, Mr Attorney. The hatchet was covered with a heavy dust or ashes.

Moody: Describe those ashes as well as you can.

John Fleet: It was covered with a white ash, I should say, upon the blade of the hatchet—not upon one side but upon both.

Moody: Could you tell anything about whether there was ashes upon he head of the hatchet?

Robinson: I don't think you ought to make suggestions. I object to that style of question.

Moody: Well describe further.

John Fleet: I should say that upon this hatchet was dust or ashes as though the head—

Robinson: Wait a moment. I object to that.

Moody: Describe on what parts of the hatchet.

John Fleet: On both faces, and all over the hatchet was covered with dust or ashes.

Moody: Was that fine dust?

Robinson: Wait a moment. The witness did not say fine dust. We object to that.

Moody: Describe the dust there.

John Fleet: The dust in my opinion was ashes.

Moody: According to you[r] observation what did it look like?

Robinson: I object to it.

The Chief Justice: Describe it. Whether he recognised it as ashes of any particular substance. He may say.

John Fleet: I recognised it as ashes.

Moody: Can you tell me how fine or coarse the ashes were?

John Fleet: They were fine.

Moody: Did you notice anything with reference to the other tools in the box at that time?

John Fleet: Yes sir.

Moody: Did you notice anything with reference to their condition in respect of the ashes?

John Fleet: I did.

Moody: Will you tell us what it was?

John Fleet: There was dust upon them.

Moody: The same as upon this?

John Fleet: No sir.

Moody: What difference was there if any?

John Fleet: The other was a kind of a dust, and there might be the dust of ashes. It was a light dust.

Moody: How in appearance did it differ from the covering of this hatchet?

Robinson: Wait a moment: I object.

The Chief Justice: He may describe the difference, if there was any.

John Fleet: That is, the dust on the other tools was lighter and finer than the dust upon that hatchet.

Moody: At that time Mr Fleet, did you observe anything with reference to the point of breaking of the hatchet?

John Fleet: The only thing that I recognised at the time was that this was apparently a new break.

Robinson: I object to that answer, that this was a new break.

Moody: At that time did you observe anything with reference to the ashes upon the point of the break of the handle, upon the wood where it was broken?

John Fleet: There seemed to be ashes there like the other.

Moody: What did you do with that hatchet, Mr Fleet?

John Fleet: I put it back in the box.

Moody: That was after you had sequestered, separated this hatchet [i.e. claw hammer].

John Fleet: Yes sir.

Moody: After you had seen this hatchet, Mr Fleet, what did you do?

John Fleet: I put it back in the box.

After Fleet had completed his evidence he was followed by Police Officer Mullaly. Mullaly was the other police officer of Fall River who gave evidence relating to the hatchet. He had a discussion with Lizzie Borden regarding the items which were found on Mr Borden after his murder. Lizzie told Mullahy that she knew there were axes in the cellar and that Bridget the maid would show him where they were.

Mullaly:

Moody: When you came downstairs where did you go?

Officer Mullaly: I went from there down to the cellar.

Moody: What did you do down there Mr Mullaly?

Officer Mullaly: Bridget went with us. We went looking for the hatchet and the axe. Bridget led the way, she went in the cellar there, and she took from a box two axes.

Moody: Can you tell us what room that was?

Officer Mullaly: Well, that was in the east end of the house, in the cellar, in the cellar toward the east end.
Moody: Could you tell those hatchets if you should see them again?
Officer Mullaly: I think I could.
Moody: (Presenting the claw hammer and another) What do you say to those?
Officer Mullaly: That (not the claw hammer) looks very much like one of them which she took out. There was a spot on this large hatchet (claw hatchet) a little round spot, a rusty spot.
Moody: What did you do with the hatchet?
Officer Mullaly: I took them out into what I call the wash room and laid them on the floor, and I stayed there with them until Mr Fleet came in.
Moody: Now then. Mr Fleet came you say. After he came was anything done?
Officer Mullaly: I gave him — called his attention to the hatchets and axes.
Moody: What did you do?
Officer Mullaly: I looked around there, and from there I went up the stairs again and went to the room — no I didn't. I went into the yard and into the barn and made a search of the premises all around.
Moody: Did you find any weapon or any indicator of blood on any part of the premises on the outside of the house?
Officer Mullaly: We did not.

Mullaly was cross-examined by Robinson but Edmund Pearson's report of the transcript does not appear complete on the question of the handleless hatchet. In his book *Goodbye Lizzie Borden* Robert Sullivan writes:

"In cross-examination Robinson again took Mullaly over the same territory as had been covered in direct examination. The witness describes seeing a pile of ashes in the cellar. He testified that there was another piece of the handle of the hatchet which was broken, which he saw but he did not know where it was now — it was a piece that corresponded with the rest of the handle, and it had a fresh break in it and the other piece [the piece fixed to the head of the hatchet] did too."

Robinson: Was it the handle to a hatchet?
Officer Mullaly: It was what I call a hatchet handle. It was somewhat shorter than the handles of the other hatchets.

This was something of a bombshell. Both counsel were apparently taken by surprise. Knowlton, asked by Robinson to produce the detached part of the handle, denied any knowledge of it or its whereabouts.

In answer to Robinson, Mullaly said that he had never told anyone of this before. Moody, for the government put further questions to Mullaly in re-direct examination:

Moody: Do you say it fitted into these breaks?
Officer Mullaly: I did not try to fit it in.
Moody: Did you notice anything in reference to the handle of the hatchet?
Officer Mullaly: They were fresh broken.
Moody: Did you notice anything with respect to the ashes on the handle?
Officer Mullaly: Ashes were on both sides of it.
Moody: On the handle of the hatchet?
Officer Mullaly: Oh, the handle. I did not notice no ashes on the handle.

John Fleet, the deputy marshall was recalled. He denied seeing the broken handle of the hatchet. This was totally at variance with what Mullaly had said.

The strongest argument for the handless hatchet being the murder weapon is the fact that it fitted perfectly into the wounds on the head of Mr Borden.

Frank W Draper was another medical witness. Dr Draper had a formidable list of qualifications; a physician, educated at Harvard Medical School; in practice for 24 years; medical examiner for Suffolk County; called upon in 3,500 cases of death where homicide is suspected or charged; and a professor of legal medicine in the Harvard Medical School.

Dr Draper described how Dr Dolan had conducted the autopsy. Dr Draper described the head wounds to Mr and Mrs Borden. The skull of Mr Borden was brought into the courtroom.

Dr Frank W Draper: I believe that the cutting edge of the weapon was 3 1/2 inches long. I determine that by this metallic plate of stiff tin which I now hold in my hand and which is 3½ inches on its longer edge. Adjusting it thus it fits in the wound in the base of the skull which I have described as cutting across the large arteries supplying the brain. It also rests against and cuts the surface of the upper portion, but takes in this is edge, and no more.

Moody: Are you able to say whether that hatchet head (showing the witness the handless hatchet head) is capable of making these wounds?

Dr Draper: I believe it is.

Moody: Have you attempted to fit that in the wounds?

Dr Draper: I have seen the attempt made.

Draper then illustrated the fitting of the hatchet into various wounds.

Moody: Now, having shown what you desire to call attention to the jury, what do you say the cutting edge was of the instrument that caused the wounds that you have described the borders of?

Dr Draper: Three and a half inches…A hatchet is consistent with these wounds. In my opinion the wounds could have been caused by the use of an ordinary hatchet in the hand of a woman of ordinary strength.

David W Beecher came next. In the Harvard Medical School a Professor of Surgery, he said: "The injuries to the skull indicate a heavy metallic weapon with an edge not over 3½ inches in length. This hatchet (indicating the handleless hatchet) could have caused the wounds."

Dr William Dolan, a general practitioner for eleven years in Fall River gave evidence. During his evidence he agreed that the wounds found upon the skull of Mr Borden were such as could have been inflicted with a hatchet by a woman of ordinary strength. He said that in the case of both murders there would be some splattering of blood on the assailant, in the case of Mr Borden as on the assailant's head and chest area and in the case of Mrs Borden in the lower part of the body. Dolan agreed that when he examined the hatchet he said only that there were appearances that looked like blood. He also found hairs which he does not now think are human hairs.

Dolan said under cross-examination that the assailant was not necessarily covered with blood, because the blood would spurt in the opposite direction, but he or she would be likely to be spattered with blood. He said the wounds varied from ½ an inch to four inches in length, He would not think that the wounds gave any indication of the size of the weapon which inflicted them. This would undermine the prosecution case that the handleless hatchet was the murder weapon).

Edward Wood then gave evidence. Professor of chemistry in the Harvard Medical School. He dealt with the times of death of the victims: roughly one-and-a-half-hours between the two. Margin of error half-an-hour either way.

> "On August 10 at Fall River, I received from Dr Dolan the large hatchet known as the claw hammer hatchet, the two axes and other items relevant to the investigation.
>
> The claw hammer hatchet had several stains on it which appeared to be bloodstains, on handle, side and edge. All the stains on the head of the hatchet were subjected by me to chemical and microscopic tests for blood, and with absolutely negative results. The two axes, which I designated A and B, had stains which appeared like blood, but tests showed them absolutely free from blood."

Moody: Did you make an examination to be able to determine whether it was reasonably possible that the hatchet could have been used in inflicting the wounds which you have described, and then have been washed soon afterwards so that traces of blood might or might not be found upon it?

Professor Wood: It could not have been washed quickly on account of these cavities in between the head and the handle [This was the handleless hatchet which the prosecution put forward as the one which was the murder weapon].

Moody: Could blood have been washed off it so it couldn't be detected?

Prof. Wood: Absolutely, if the weapon was very thoroughly washed with cold water. But it couldn't be done by a careless washing. The broken hatchet would have to be washed before the handle was broken, because it would be almost impossible to quickly wash blood off that broken end.

Moody: Please describe the handleless hatchet.

Prof. Wood: The head was broken off from the handle, there was a white film, like ashes, over both sides of the blade. There were more ashes in the middle of the blade.

Questioned about the small hatchet Professor Wood gave similar replies.

Moody: I will ask you the same question I did with reference to the other hatchet, whether in your opinion that hatchet could have been used and then cleaned in a manner so as to remove any trace of blood beyond the power of your discovery, as you examined it?

Prof. Wood: It couldn't have been done by a quick washing.

Moody: Why not?

Prof. Wood: It would cling in those angles there and couldn't be thoroughly removed, the coagula would cling. It would have to be very thoroughly washed in order to remove it. It could be done by cold water, no question about that. But it couldn't be done by a careless washing.

Moody: And is that the same reason why you gave the same answer as to that hatchet?

Prof. Wood: Yes sir.

Moody: On account of the fibres of wood?

Prof. Wood: And the hole between the head and the handle.

Both sides of the hatchet were rusty. There were several suspicious spots on the side of it but they were not blood. When Wood received it, there was a white film, like ashes, on it.

Moody: How much of it when you first saw it had the appearance of being marked by this adherent film of white matter which looked like ashes?

> **Prof. Wood:** Both sides. One side you can hardly see now, and the other side you can see, more in the middle side of the hatchet, not near the edge.
>
> **Moody:** Did it appear to you to be the sort of covering that would result from being exposed to ordinary dust in the air (implying that it must have been deliberately put there by a person)?

Objection by the defence—objection upheld.

What then are we to make of the evidence regarding the weapon? Clearly, from the prosecution point of view it lost much of its force from the very start when Moody opened the case. In saying that the Commonwealth could only say that there was a probability that the hatchet head was the murder weapon he weakened the government's case on that point. No all-male jury in 1882 was likely to condemn a young woman of spotless character to death on a probability.

Clearly it was important for the prosecution to prove, if it could, that the weapon of death originated from inside and not outside of the house. Lizzie, on her own admission, knew where the axes and the hatchets were to be found, and what kind of killer would enter a house in the mere hope of finding the right implement for his diabolical purposes. But the testimony necessary for this simply wasn't enough.

The serious discrepancy in the police evidence on the question of the missing handle was very damaging for the prosecution, and the scientific evidence as to the possibility of every spot of blood being removed by washing did not inspire confidence in the prosecution claim that this was what Lizzie had succeeded in doing.

The prosecution badly needed to score on this point, and they failed to do so. That, taken with the questionable and potentially unjust exclusion of evidence by the court, gave Lizzie Borden her escape route.

CHAPTER TWELVE

The Burning of a Dress

The prosecution case was as follows: The light blue cotton dress was the dress Lizzie wore on the morning of the murders. She burnt it to destroy bloodstains. The heavy silk dress she claimed to have worn and handed to the police is not the dress she wore. It would have been too heavy for such an extremely hot day and not suitable for wearing about the house. Lizzie lied about this.

The defence case was that the heavy silk dress was the one she wore on the fatal day. There were no bloodstains on it. In any case, no bloodstains were seen by witnesses on the light blue dress and marks were because that dress had paint stains. Burning took place when police were about the premises. Emma was concerned that the burning would look suspicious as was Alice Russell. Adelaide B Churchill said:

> "I am a widow and have been a resident of Fall River more than forty three years, and have lived in my present house nearly all my life. It is the house next north of the Borden house. My household consists of my mother, sister, son niece and a man who works for us. I have known the Borden family for twenty years; I have been on calling terms with them".

Mrs Churchill, who was a strong and reliable witness, proceeded to describe the day of the murders when she spoke to Bridget and Lizzie. Lizzie asked her to come over because "someone has killed father". Her evidence completely contradicted that of Lizzie:

William H Moody: Will you describe the dress that she had on while you were there?

> **Mrs Adelaide Churchill:** It looked like a bright blue and white ground work; it seemed like calico or cambric, and it had a white groundwork with a dark navy blue diamond printed on it.
> **Moody:** Was the whole dress alike, the skirt and waist?
> **Mrs Churchill:** It looked so to me (the heavy silk dress was shown to Mrs Churchill).
> **Moody:** Was that the dress she had on that morning?
> **Mrs Churchill:** It does not look like it.
> **Moody:** Was it?
> **Mrs Churchill:** That is not the dress I have described.
> **Moody:** Was it the dress she had on?
> **Mrs Churchill:** I did not see her with it on that morning.
> **Moody:** Didn't see her with this dress on that morning?
> **Mrs Churchill:** No sir.

In cross-examination, Robinson, realising how damaging her evidence was, tried to establish that her memory was faulty.

> **George Dexter Robinson:** What dress did Bridget have on that morning?
> **Mrs Churchill:** I don't know, a light calico I think.
> **Robinson:** Do you know anything about it?
> **Mrs Churchill:** No sir.
> **Robinson:** You could not tell could you?
> **Mrs Churchill:** No sir.
> **Robinson:** Have not thought of that at all?
> **Mrs Churchill:** No sir.
> **Robinson:** Have you since that August 4th 1892, ever thought what clothes Bridget had on?
> **Mrs Churchill:** No sir.
> **Robinson:** And if we were now making the same enquiry about Bridget you could not tell, could you, her dress?
> **Mrs Churchill:** I never took particular notice of it.
> **Robinson:** Took no notice?
> **Mrs Churchill:** No. Not of the dress.
> **Robinson:** Did Mrs Bowen come there sometime in the morning?

Mrs Churchill: Yes sir.
Robinson: What did she have on?
Mrs Churchill: I don't remember, I think it was a white groundwork — light calico with a black vine or something on it, but I don't know.
Robinson: I don't doubt you know what you had on yourself?
Mrs Churchill: Yes sir I do.
Robinson: Could you tell us all about that?
Mrs Churchill: Yes sir.
Robinson: But when you get beyond that and what you say of Miss Lizzie's dress, you would not say much more about it, would you? Tell what Mrs Russell had on?
Mrs Churchill: No, I don't know what she had on.
Robinson: You had been there with Miss Lizzie all the time?
Mrs Churchill: Yes sir.

Alice Russell like Mrs Churchill was a patently honest woman.

Moody: Are you able to give us any description of the dress which she (Lizzie) had on that morning?
Alice Russell: None whatsoever. When Lizzie went upstairs, I went upstairs with her — at least I have always thought so, she had not yet changed her dress. She said "when it is necessary for an undertaker I want Winwood". I went downstairs and waited for Dr Bowen. I sent for him. Spoke to him and went upstairs to Lizzie's room again. She was coming out of Miss Emma's room, tying the ribbon of a wrapper — a pink and white striped wrapper. I stayed at the house all that night, having gone home once that day and returned, I did not suggest to Miss Lizzie that she change her dress; did not hear anyone suggest it.

Alice stayed for several days and nights. On the morning of Sunday 7th August she left the house for a while, returning before noon (by this time Lizzie knew she was a suspect).

Moody: Will you state what you saw after you returned?

Alice Russell: I went into the kitchen and I saw Lizzie at the other end of the stove. I saw Miss Emma at the sink. Miss Lizzie was at the stove, and she had a skirt in her hand, and her sister turned and said "what are you going to do?" and Lizzie said "I am going to burn this old thing up; it is covered with paint".

Moody: Do you recall anything else she said then?

Alice Russell: No sir.

Moody: What did you do then?

Alice Russell: I am quite sure I left the room.

Moody: Did you speak to either of them at that time?

Alice Russell: No sir. I don't remember that I did. I don't think I did.

Moody: Did you come into the room again?

Alice Russell: Yes sir.

Moody: What did you see then.

Alice Russell: Miss Lizzie stood up towards the cupboard door. The cupboard door was open, and she appeared to be either ripping something down or tearing part of this garment.

Moody: What part?

Alice Russell: I don't know for sure it was a small part.

Moody: A smaller part? Go on and state.

Alice Russell: I said to her "I wouldn't let anybody see me do that Lizzie". She didn't make any answer. I left the room.

Moody: Did she do anything when you said that?

Alice Russell: She stepped just one step further back up towards the cupboard door.

Moody: Did you notice where the waist of the dress was when she held her skirt in her hands as you first came in?

Alice Russell: I didn't know that it was the waist, but I saw a portion of this dress up on the cupboard shelf.

Moody: Inside the cupboard?

Alice Russell: Yes. The door was wide open.

Moody: When you came back the second time and she was tearing the smaller part, did you see the skirt?

Alice Russell: Well I am not positive; I think I did.

Moody: Did you have any talk with her that day or did she say anything to you about it?
Alice Russell: No sir.
Moody: At that time were there any police officers in the house?
Alice Russell: No sir.
Moody: Were there any officers about the house?
Alice Russell: Yes, sir.
Moody: Do you know whether there was anyone else in the house except yourself, Miss Emma and Miss Lizzie Borden?
Alice Russell: I don't think there was.

Alice Russell then referred to seeing Lizzie and Emma again in the dining room — "I said to them — 'I am afraid Lizzie, the worst thing you could have done was to burn that dress. I have been asked about your dress.'"

Moody: What was the reply?
Alice Russell: She said "oh what made you let me do it? Why didn't you tell me?"

Examination-in-chief resumed.

Moody: Miss Russell, will you tell us what kind of a dress — give us a description of the dress that she burned, that you have testified about on that Sunday morning?
Alice Russell: It was a cheap cotton Bedford cord.
Moody: What was its colour?
Alice Russell: Light-blue ground with a dark figure — small figure.
Moody: Do you know where she got it?
Alice Russell: I am not positive.
Moody: Well about when she got it?
Alice Russell: In the early spring (the witness was familiar with the dress).
Moody: Of that same year do you mean, or some other year?
Alice Russell: Yes sir, I think that same year.

Moody: To make it clear, between the time when you saw it on Miss Borden and had the talk about it in the spring. You did not see it again until the Sunday morning after the homicide?

Alice Russell: I never remember of ever seeing it, and I am quite sure I did not—that I never had.

Moody: Can you give me any further description of the dark-blue figure?

Alice Russell: No sir.

Moody: Can you give any further description?

Alice Russell: Nothing, only that it was small.

Moody: A small dark blue figure?

Alice Russell: Yes sir.

Cross-examined.

Robinson: You say you cannot tell us about a dress that she had on that morning?

Alice Russell: No sir [but she could describe the dress being burnt].

Alice Russell said under cross-examination that she saw no blood on Lizzie's clothing. That she saw nothing out of the way about the clothing or her person.

"The dress which I saw Sunday was neither calico or cambric; it was a Bedford cord. I did not take hold of it or examine it".

Under re-examination she said the dress was all cotton, not silk. Emma Borden was called for the defence by Jennings:

Andrew J Jennings: Have you an inventory, Miss Emma, of the clothes that were in the clothes closet on Saturday afternoon, the time of the search?

Emma Borden: I have.

Jennings: Will you produce it?

Emma Borden: I have, of the dresses.

Moody: Taken at the time?

The Burning of a Dress

Jennings: No.
Jennings: When was that made up?
Emma Borden: About a week ago.
Jennings: Was it made up from your recollection?
Emma Borden: Yes sir.
Jennings: You were there on the afternoon of the search?
Emma Borden: I was.
Jennings: Do you know what dresses were in there that afternoon?
Emma Borden: I do.
Jennings: Will you state either from your own recollection or by the assistance of that memorandum what the dresses were?
Hosea M Knowlton: Wait a minute, I do not object to the question except as to the memorandum.
Jennings: Well. How many dresses were in there?
Emma Borden: I can't tell you without looking at this paper.
Jennings: Well. Can you tell us about how many?
Emma Borden: Somewhere about eighteen or nineteen.
Jennings: And whose were those dresses?
Emma Borden: All of them belonged to my sister and I except one that belonged to Mrs Borden.
Jennings: How many of those dresses were blue dresses or dresses in which blue was a marked colour?
Emma Borden: Ten.
Jennings: To whom did these belong?
Emma Borden: Two of them to me and eight to my sister.
Jennings: Were you there on the afternoon of Saturday while the search was going on?
Emma Borden: Yes sir.
Jennings: Do you know how minute or extended that search was?
Emma Borden: I heard you say that every…
Jennings: You cannot say what you heard me say. Did you hear Dr Dolan or Marshall Hilliard?
Emma Borden: I asked Dr Dolan if they had made a thorough search…
Knowlton: Wait a minute, madam if you please, I pray your honours judgement as to that answer.

Judge: Question disallowed.

There then followed questions about the search of the house:

Jennings: Now then Miss Emma, I will ask you if you know of a Bedford cord dress which your sister had at that time?
Emma Borden: I do.
Jennings: Wont you describe the dress, tell what sort of dress it was?
Emma Borden: It was a blue cotton Bedford cord, very light blue ground with a darker figure about an inch long and I think about three quarters of an inch wide.
Jennings: And do you know when she had that dress made?
Emma Borden: She had it made in the first week in May.
Jennings: Who made it?
Emma Borden: Mrs Raymond the dress maker.
Jennings: Where was it made?
Emma Borden: At our home.
Jennings: What kind of material was it as to cost? Do you know what the price of it was?
Emma Borden: Very cheap.
Jennings: Do you know? Have you any idea what it cost?
Emma Borden: It was either 12 cents a yard or 15 cents.
Jennings: About how many yards do you think there were in it?
Emma Borden: Not over eight or ten.
Jennings: In what was it trimmed?
Emma Borden: Trimmed with just a ruffle of the same around the bottom. A narrow ruffle.
Jennings: How long were you in making the dress — do you know?
Emma Borden: Not more than ten days.
Jennings: Did you and Miss Lizzie assist the dressmaker in making the dress?
Emma Borden: Yes sir.
Jennings: That was your habit was it?
Emma Borden: Yes sir, I always do.
Jennings: And where was the dressmaking carried on?

Emma Borden: In the guest chamber.

Jennings: Was that where the dressmaking was always done?

Emma Borden: Always.

Jennings: Do you know whether or not they were painting the house at the time the dress was made?

Emma Borden: I think they did not begin to paint it until after the dress was done.

Jennings: Do you know anything about her getting the paint on it at that time?

Emma Borden: Yes. She did.

Jennings: Where was the paint upon it?

Emma Borden: I should say down the front and on one side towards the bottom and some on the wrong side of the skirt.

Jennings: Was that after it was made?

Emma Borden: Well, I think within two weeks; perhaps less in time than that.

Jennings: Now where was that dress, if you know, on Saturday, the day of the search?

Emma Borden: I saw it hanging in the clothes press over the front entry.

Jennings: How came you to see it at that time?

Emma Borden: I went in to hang up the dress that I had been wearing during the day, and there was no vacant rails, and I searched round to find a nail, and I noticed this dress.

Jennings: Did you say anything to your sister about that dress in consequence of you not finding a nail to hang your dress on?

Emma Borden: I did.

Jennings: What did you say?

Emma Borden: I said "you have not destroyed that old dress yet; why don't you?"

Jennings: What was the condition of that dress at that time?

Emma Borden: It was very dirty, very much soiled and badly faded.

Jennings: Was this material of which this dress was made in a condition to be made over for anything else?

Emma Borden: It could not possibly be used for anything else.

Jennings: Why?

Emma Borden: Because it was not only soiled, but so badly faded.

Jennings: When did you next see that Bedford cord dress?

Emma Borden: Sunday morning I think, about nine o'clock.

Jennings: Now will you tell the court and the jury all that you saw or heard that morning in the kitchen?

Emma Borden: I was washing dishes, and I heard my sister's voice and I turned round and saw that she was standing at the front of the stove, between the foot of the stove and the dining room door. This dress was hanging up on her arm and she says "I think I shall burn this old dress up". I said "why don't you?" or "you had better" or "I would if I were you" or something like that, I can't tell the exact words, but it meant "do it" and I turned back and continued washing the dishes and did not see her burn it and did not pay any more attention to her at that time.

Jennings: What was the condition of the kitchen doors and windows at that time?

Emma Borden: They were all wide open, screens in and blinds open.

Jennings: Were the officers all about at that time?

Emma Borden: They were all about the yard.

Jennings: Was Miss Russell there?

Emma Borden: Yes sir.

Jennings: Was anything said by Miss Russell in the presence of Miss Lizzie, in regard to this dress?

Emma Borden: Miss Russell came to us in the dining room and said that Mr Hanson asked her if all the dresses were there that were there the day of the tragedy and she told him "yes", and of course she said "it is a falsehood". Now I am ahead of my story. She came and said she told Mr Hanson a falsehood and I asked her what there was to tell a falsehood about, and then she said that Mr Hanson had asked her if all the dresses were there that were there the day of the tragedy and she told him "yes". There was other conversation, but I don't know what it was. That frightened me thoroughly. I cannot recall it, I know the carriage was waiting for her to go on some errand, and when she came back we had some conversation, and it was decided to have her go and tell Mr Hanson that she had told a falsehood, and to tell him that we told her to do so. She went into the parlour and told him, and in a few minutes she returned from the parlour and said she had told him.

Jennings: Now at the time when Miss Russell said: "it was the worst thing that could be done...".

Emma Borden: Oh yes sir, she said that Monday morning when she came into the dining room and said she had told Mr Hanson that she had told him a falsehood, we asked what she told it for. And she said "the burning of the dress was the worst thing Lizzie could have done" and my sister (Lizzie) said to her "why didn't you tell me? Why did you let me do it?"

Cross-examined by Knowlton for the Commonwealth:

Hosea M Knowlton: Do you recall what the first thing you said was when Miss Lizzie was standing by the stove with the dress?

Emma Borden: Yes sir.

Knowlton: What was it?

Emma Borden: I said "you might as well" or "why don't you?" something like that. That is what it meant. I can't tell you the exact words.

Knowlton: Wasn't the first thing said by anybody: "Lizzie what are you doing with that dress?"

Emma Borden: No sir. I don't remember it so.

Knowlton: Do you understand Miss Russell so to testify.

Emma Borden: I think she did.

Knowlton: Do you remember whether that was so or not?

Emma Borden: It doesn't seem so to me — I don't remember it so.

Knowlton: Why doesn't it seem so to you, if I may ask you?

Emma Borden: Why. Because the first I knew about it, my sister spoke to me.

Knowlton: That is what I thought you would say. Now, you don't recall that the first thing you said to her, the first thing that was said by anybody was "what are you going to do with that dress Lizzie?"

Emma Borden: No sir. I don't remember saying it.

Knowlton: Do you remember that you did not say it?

Emma Borden: I am sure I did not.

Knowlton: Miss Russell was in the room was she not?

Emma Borden: I don't know. When I turned to hear what my sister had to say I saw Miss Russell, but she wasn't in the room with her then, She was in the dining room with the door open.

Knowlton: The reason that you don't think you said so was because you had previously spoken with your sister about destroying the dress?

Emma Borden: Yes sir, I had previously spoken about it. I don't think I had thought of the dress all the time. I had spoken to her about it.

Knowlton questioned Emma regarding the figure on the dress, the condition of the dress, and the paint stains including the fact that Lizzie wore it in that condition.

Mrs Mary A Raymond gave evidence. A dress maker, she gave evidence that she had made the Bedford cord dress and had seen it after it had received the paint stains.

Dr Seabury Bowen

Dr Bowen's evidence, taken in conjunction with that of Mrs Churchill must have made it obvious to the jury that the dress exhibited at the trial as being the dress Lizzie wore on the morning of the murders was no such dress. He was an honest witness and would not be drawn beyond his statement at the final trial. At the inquest he had been more specific. This illustrates the benefit to Lizzie of the judge's exclusion of the inquest testimony.

We can contrast the English rule of evidence which is that even where it would otherwise be inadmissible such evidence can be admitted when to do so would be in the interest of justice, provided the interests of justice outweigh the element of prejudice to the defendant.

The evidence, if accepted, did not prove that Lizzie was the murderer, but it raised a question mark as to her honesty of—and if the jury concluded that she had lied deliberately it would have been within their province to ask why she had done so.

Dr Bowen again:

The Burning of a Dress

Moody: Doctor, did you at any time in the course of the morning notice anything with reference to the dress that Miss Borden had on?

Dr Bowen: Yes sir.

Moody: Will you describe it as well as you can?

Dr Bowen: The only time I noticed anything was when she changed it after she went up to her room. I noticed she had on a different dress when she went to her room.

Moody: What did you notice in reference to that dress?

Dr Bowen: I noticed the colour of the dress.

Moody: What was it?

Dr Bowen: A pink wrapper, morning dress. [The dress handed to the police was blue].

Moody: Did you notice anything with reference to the dress she had on prior to that time?

Dr Bowen: No sir.

Moody: Did you testify to this subject at the inquest?

Dr Bowen: I presume I was asked questions about it.

Moody: At that time was your memory as good as it is now or better?

Dr Bowen: Well about the same I should judge.

Moody: Do you recall making this reply to the questions that I am about to read? "Question: Do you recall how Lizzie was dressed that morning? Answer: It is pretty hard work for me. Probably if I could see a dress something like it I could guess, but I could not describe it; it was sort of drab, not much colour to it to attract my attention — a sort of calico morning dress I should judge."

Moody: What did you say as to the colour?

Dr Bowen: That is very indefinite there.

Moody: What did you say as to the drab?

Dr Bowen: I should say the colour is very indefinite.

Moody: I did not ask you to criticise your answer sir?

Dr Bowen: I made the best answer at the time that I could.

Moody: Do you assent at the present time to that statement of the colour of the dress (pink).

Dr Bowen: With the modification I make now.

Moody: What modification do you desire to make?

Dr Bowen: I don't remember anything distinctly about the colour [A clear contradiction of his earlier evidence].

Moody: Do you desire to say that the dress appeared to you to be a drab dress or not?

Dr Bowen: I merely meant to say that the dress is a common...

Moody: Answer my question.

Dr Bowen: Wait...

Moody: No answer my question, and this is the question; Did it appear to you to be a drab—coloured dress or not?

Dr Bowen: It was an ordinary unattractive, common dress that I did not notice specifically.

Moody: Will you answer my question?

Chief Justice Mason: Answer the question of you can, if you cannot, say so.

Dr Bowen: I don't think I can answer it better than I did, I don't know.

Moody: I would like to try it once more doctor. Did it appear to you to be a drab dress?

Dr Bowen: I did not pretend to describe a woman's dress, and I do not intend to now.

Dr Bowen is being clearly evasive—why? This is commented on in the book *Lizzie Borden*, by Arnold Brown, as follows: "Regardless of the effort required, Dr Bowen finally agreed to his initial inquest statements and conceded that the dress Lizzie had turned over to the police was drab. Couple his testimony with Mrs Churchill's no-nonsense testimony on the same subject and you can be sure that the dress being exhibited was not the first or only dress Miss Lizzie wore the morning of that bloody Thursday."

If the jury concluded that once again Lizzie is lying, and had agreed to an exhibit which created an entirely false impression as to the truth, they were entitled to ask the question—"Why has she done this if she is innocent?" When Emma's evidence conflicts with that of Alice Russell there is no doubt that Alice's is to be preferred. Emma was slanting her testimony in favour of her sister. This is plain from the answers she gave relating to the feeling which Lizzie had for her step-mother when cross-examined by Knowlton.

Emma proved to be a stubborn witness:

"I have an Aunt Mrs Morse, who is living now. She lives in Fall River. Her maiden name was also Morse. I do not visit her very often. My father had a great many cousins, one sister and no brothers. The sister is Mrs Harrington. She sometimes came to our house. Mr Harrington did not, except to call at the house to enquire for my sister or for me. My step-mother had a half-sister in Fall River Mrs Whitehead. She owned half her house and my step-mother the other half. My father bought the interest in the house and gave it to my step-mother. This was five or six years ago. I think he paid $1,500 for it."

Knowlton: Did that make some trouble in the family?
Mr Robinson: Five or six years ago. I object.
The Chief Justice: She may answer.
Knowlton: Did that make some trouble in the family?
Emma Borden: Yes.
Knowlton: Between whom?
Emma Borden: Between my father and Mrs Borden and my sister and I.
Knowlton: And also between you and your sister and your step-mother?
Emma Borden: I never said anything to her about it.
Knowlton: If you will observe the question, I did not ask you that; it is a very natural answer, I find no fault with it. Did it make any trouble between your step-mother and Lizzie and you?
Emma Borden: Yes sir.

Here Knowlton, as the cross-examiner of a basically hostile witness, had to tread carefully. Emma clearly sees the direction in which the questions are going. They are aimed at showing a strong course of resentment felt by Lizzie towards Abby Borden over this arrangement, and hence a motive for eventual murder. That is why Emma is beginning to hedge her replies.

Knowlton: Did you find fault with it?
Emma Borden: Yes sir.

Emma Borden: And did Lizzie find fault with it?
Emma Borden: Yes sir.
Knowlton: And in consequence of your finding fault did your father also make a purchase for you or give you some money?
Emma Borden: Yes sir.
Knowlton: How much?
Emma Borden: Grandfather's house on Ferry Street.
Knowlton: And was there some complaint that that was not an equivalent?
Emma Borden: No sir, it was more than an equivalent.
Knowlton: That it wasn't so productive of rent as the other?
Emma Borden: I don't know what the other house rented for, but I should think ours rented for more than hers.
Knowlton: Were the relations between you and Lizzie and your stepmother as cordial after that occurrence of the house that you have spoken of as they were before?
Emma Borden: Between my sister and Mrs Borden they were.
Knowlton: They were entirely the same?
Emma Borden: I think so.
Knowlton: Were they so on your part?
Emma Borden: I think not.
Knowlton: Did your sister change the form of address to her mother at that time?
Emma Borden: I can't tell you whether it was at that time or not.
Knowlton: She formerly called her "mother" didn't she?
Emma Borden: Yes sir.
Knowlton: She ceased to call her "mother" didn't she practically?
Emma Borden: Yes sir.
Knowlton: And wasn't it about that time that she ceased to call her "mother"?
Emma Borden: I don't remember.
Knowlton: Wasn't it five or six years ago?
Emma Borden: It was some time ago.
Knowlton: What address did she give her after that time?
Emma Borden: Mrs Borden.

Knowlton: And up to the time when she changed she had called her mother?

Emma Borden: Mostly.

Knowlton: From her childhood?

Emma Borden: Yes sir.

Knowlton: And don't you recall that was sometime in connection with the transaction in relation to the house?

Emma Borden: No sir, I don't know when it was.

Knowlton: Do you say that you have not said that the relations were not cordial between your sister and your mother?

Emma Borden: I don't remember that I have.

At this point once again Knowlton has to change his tactics; it is plain that Emma understands the object of his cross-examination — to establish, as far as possible that the events relating to the property created such ill-feeling between Lizzie and Mrs Borden that they provided ample motivation for the former to murder the latter. Consequently her answers tend to play down that possibility. However Knowlton has the information as to what Emma said at the inquest and he knows that this is not entirely consistent with her evidence now. She has not proved an entirely hostile witness to the prosecution, and so in reminding her of the discrepancy he must pursue a careful line.

Knowlton: You testified at the inquest did you not?

Emma Borden: I did.

Knowlton: Where you were asked questions in relation to that matter.

Emma Borden: I don't remember what you asked me.

Knowlton: Do you remember the answers that you gave?

Emma Borden: Only two.

Knowlton: Do you remember whether you answered the questions truly or not?

Emma Borden: I tried to.

Knowlton: Do you remember I asked you if your relations were cordial between you and your mother?

Emma Borden: I think you did either then or before the grand jury. I don't remember which.

Knowlton: Do you remember you said that they were not?

Emma Borden: I don't know whether I did or not.

Knowlton: And do you remember that I then asked you if the relations between your sister and your mother were also cordial?

Emma Borden: I do not.

Knowlton: Do you still say that the relations between your step-mother and your sister Lizzie were cordial?

Emma Borden: The last two or three years they were very.

Knowlton: Notwithstanding that she never used the term "mother"?

Emma Borden: Yes sir.

Knowlton: They remained cordial?

Emma Borden: For the last three years they were.

Knowlton: For how many years before that were they not cordial?

Emma Borden: I can't tell you, I don't know.

Knowlton: Now I want to ask you if you didn't say this: "Were the relations between you and your step-mother cordial?" Answer "I don't know how to answer that, we always spoke".

Emma Borden: That was myself and my step-mother.

Knowlton: Do you remember that answer?

Emma Borden: I do now.

Knowlton: That might be, and not be at all cordial?

Emma Borden: Well, perhaps I should say no then.

Knowlton: Do you remember that, talking about yourself?

Emma Borden: No sir, I don't remember it.

Knowlton: Were the relations between you and your sister and your mother what you would call cordial.

Emma Borden: I think more than they were with me.

Knowlton: Do you remember that answer?

Emma Borden: Yes sir.

Knowlton: The next question is pretty long. "Somewhat more than they were with you, but not entirely so, you mean perhaps? I do not want to lead you at all. I judged from your answer you meant that, or don't you mean that? You say somewhat more than your relations were. Do you mean that they were entirely cordial between your step-mother and your sister Lizzie? Answer "no?"

Emma Borden: Well I shall have to recall it, for I think they were.

Knowlton: That is, do you remember giving that answer?

Emma Borden: No sir.

Knowlton: How does it happen that you remember the answer in which you did not explicitly state whether they were cordial or not, but can't remember an answer, if one were given. In which you said they were not cordial, which was the following question?

Emma Borden: I don't understand.

Knowlton: This is a little involved perhaps. You do recall a question next precluding that in which you said "somewhat more than they were with me"?

Emma Borden: Not until you read it I did not.

Knowlton: You did recall it then?

Emma Borden: Yes, I think I did.

Knowlton: But when the next question, if I may assume to say so, was put to you, if it was put and such an answer was given by you, you don't now recall that answer?

Emma Borden: I don't seem to remember it.

Knowlton: Will you say you didn't say that?

Emma Borden: No sir, not if you say I did.

Knowlton: And would you say that was not true—I haven't said you did at all, Miss Borden, if you will pardon me. Don't understand me as saying that you said anything, so that I think that answer is not particular to my question. Do you recall now that it is read to you as saying that?

Emma Borden: No sir, I don't. I don't say I didn't say it, if you say I did. I don't remember saying it.

Knowlton: Do you remember saying I do? Now, I do not say you did, and I have no right to say you did. I haven't said anything about it. I am asking whether you gave that answer to such a question as that: do you mean they were entirely cordial between your step-mother and Lizzie? Answer "no?"

Emma Borden: I can only say I don't remember giving it.

Knowlton: Whether you said it or not, do you say that is true, that the relations were not entirely cordial between your step-mother and your sister Lizzie?

Emma Borden: I think they were for the last three years.

Knowlton: So whatever you said then you say so now; you say that is not now?

At this point Robinson objected. Knowlton did not press the questions.

Knowlton: Now I will read you this question and answer: "Can you tell me the cause of the lack of cordiality between you and your mother, or was it not any specific thing?" Answer "Well we felt that she was not interested in us, and at one time father gave her some property, and we felt that we ought to have some too; and he afterwards gave us some". Do you remember that?

Emma Borden: No sir.

Knowlton: Is that true?

Emma Borden: It was true at the time, he gave us a house.

Knowlton: I will read another question: "That however did not heal the breach, whatever breach there was? The giving of the property to you did not entirely heal the feeling?" Answer "No sir".

Emma Borden: It didn't. Not with me, but it did with my sister after.

It is plain to anyone acquainted with advocacy that Knowlton is facing an uphill task in cross-examining Emma Borden. Firstly he is clearly confronted by a hostile witness who is clever enough not to allow her hostility to become too apparent. Whenever he appears to be making any progress she digs in her heels and pleads a lack of memory. Knowlton is at a disadvantage because although he has the record of the inquest he can only use it in the form of questions. He cannot confront her with the actual record. This is because a judge who is clearly favourable to the defence has ruled the record inadmissible. Therefore counsel is "bound" by the answers to his questions. The rightness of the judge has been debated by lawyers ever since the trial, but his ruling applied at the time.

The Burning of a Dress

But perhaps the biggest handicap under which Knowlton was working was the unconvincing nature of the hypothesis which he was advancing. This was that the evidence of the past ill-feeling between Lizzie and her step-mother was sufficient to raise the belief that her hatred for the latter was great enough to prompt the hideous murders of both Abby and Andrew. The jury would have known from personal experience the prevalence from time to time of ill-feeling within families. In the Borden case this amounted to little more than Lizzie's derogatory remarks to some others about Abby Borden and resentment over a dispensation of property by her father in her step-mother's favour. That line by the prosecution was largely neutralised by the testimony of Emma to the contrary and that of Bridget who stated that Abby and Lizzie were conversing normally that morning and without acrimony shortly before the murders.

Perhaps the greatest unspoken problem for the prosecution was that the real truth was not such as could be placed before the jury as evidence at all. Let us consider what that is. For it involves the mystery and unfathomable compulsions of the human mind. Thus irritation can grow into resentment, resentment into anger and anger into a blind rage that finally expresses itself in an explosion of violence; this is a phenomenon that both psychiatrists and criminal lawyers are familiar with. It is true sometimes in cases of murder, and particularly so where close emotional and family relationships are concerned. A case in point is the *Wallace Case* which was heard at the Liverpool Assizes in 1931. Like Lizzie Borden the defendant Wallace was a man of hitherto unimpeachable character. In 1931, William Herbert Wallace was indicted for the murder of his wife Julia. Although the victims were in different categories there are similar factors in each case. In both instances the evidence was purely circumstantial; in spite of the substantial amount of blood from the wounds on the bodies none was found on the person or the clothing worn by the accused. In both cases the defendants stuck to their story and in each case the likelihood of an intruder committing the crime seemed remote. Unlike Lizzie, Wallace was convicted by the jury but escaped on appeal.

The judge at the trial court, Mr Justice Wright, a greatly respected jurist, commented many years later when he said:

"Never forget that Wallace was a chess player...I should say that, broadly speaking, any man with common sense would have said that Wallace's alibi was too good to be true, but that is not an argument you can hang a man on. So many strange things happen in life. I should not, and never did, demand a motive for any crime. Very often, the motive is merely impulse and you must remember that Wallace was a highly strung man".

Julia Wallace fell before a rain of blows to the head with a metal object. Professor MacFall the Home Office pathologist described the attack as "frenzied". The same surely could be said of the onslaughts on Andrew and Abby Borden.

Let us therefore sum up the position as to the burning of the dress, an incident which was not disputed by the defence. First of all it is one of the many coincidences we find in the whole case. It was a coincidence that the side door may not have been locked when Bridget was cleaning the windows; it was a coincidence that Abby returned from her alleged absence just before the murder; it was a coincidence that Lizzie was upstairs at the time Abby was killed; it was a coincidence that just before Andrew was murdered Lizzie had suddenly decided to abandon her ironing and go to the barn to search for a lead sinker; and it was coincidence that she stayed in a ferociously hot barn for the precise time required by the murderer to commit the crime. Strangest of all it was a coincidence that Lizzie changed her dress after the murders and some days later decided to destroy a dress which answered the description of the one identified by Mrs Churchill as worn by Lizzie on the day of the murders.

There were three places in the Borden home where water was to be obtained. The kitchen, the cellar and the barn. The minimum time in which Lizzie could have washed blood from her clothes and from the weapon after the murder of Abby was one hour. This was agreed by both sides in the trial. Andrew Borden was away in the town and Bridget was outside the house washing the windows. One hour was ample time for Lizzie to go to the kitchen or the cellar to extinguish the bloodstains.

With regard to the killing of Andrew, Judge Robert Sullivan in his book *Goodbye Lizzie Borden* makes reference to his own visit to the Borden house on Second Street:

"As to the murder of Andrew Borden, the explanation for the absence of blood on Lizzie's person is equally clear. Anyone who visited the Borden premises on Second Street, as this writer, and as the jury had done on the view—indeed as anyone who studies the ground-floor plan of the Borden residence, an illustration here, and an exhibit at the trial—can readily discern that the head of the couch upon which Andrew Borden lay was exactly flush with the door leading into the dining room. Andrew Borden, when he slept that morning of the 4 August slept with his head only inches from the open interior door leading to the dining room, he was within easy range of a well-directed blow or blows delivered by Lizzie standing shielded by the door opening, very probably with her feet in the dining room. Thus, shielded from blood stains, Lizzie had ample time to go to the cellar, wash the axe and plunge it into the ashes. Add to this the medical evidence that blood may spurt away from the person administering the blows and the defence claim that the absence of blood on Lizzie was a sure indication of innocence loses much of its strength".

CHAPTER THIRTEEN

The Alibi

One of the crucial aspects of the criminal trial was Lizzie's alleged alibi. This was that at the time of the murder of her father she was in the barn at the rear of the premises. The word "alibi" is defined in the *Oxford English Dictionary* as "a claim or piece of evidence that one was elsewhere when an alleged act took place". In modern-day English law where the defence is an alibi provision has been made by statute that the defence must give the prosecution advance notice of this, the form which the alibi will take and the evidence in its favour which it is proposed to present at the trial.

This gives the prosecutor an opportunity to check out the alibi, if necessary, by interviewing witnesses, and thus avoid being "ambushed" by the defence springing on them unexpectedly a story which cannot be verified or exposed as false. In his work *Trial of Lizzie Borden*, Edmund Pearson has this to say of Lizzie's alibi:

> "That anyone ironing handkerchiefs on a hot morning, should desert this torrid occupation and deliberately seek out the stuffiest, dustiest place on the premises, and do this for precisely the time needed to give the murderer a chance to commit his crime and make his escape, seems doubly hard to believe. It was not only a queer thing to do, but it was an extraordinary coincidence that it should be done at a time so favourable to the murderer's plans".

Pearson lists the accounts given by Lizzie on the day of the murders to various people who questioned her:

To Mrs Adelaide Churchill: "I went to the barn to get a piece of iron. I heard a distressing noise and came back and found the screen door open".

To Miss Alice Russell: "I was out in the barn getting a piece of tin or iron to fix the screens".

To Officer Fleet: "I was up in the barn for half an hour".

To Dr Bowen: "I was in the barn to get some iron".

To Officer Doherty: "I was in the barn, I heard no screams, I did hear some noise like scraping".

To Officer Harrington: "I went out in the barn, and remained there twenty minutes... I was up in the loft".

What are we to make of the various accounts?

To suggest, as some have, that Lizzie's replies to questions regarding her whereabouts at the time of the murder differ only in peripheral details is plain nonsense. These questions were put to her on the very day of these atrocious crimes when her memory should have been clear. Let the reader place herself or himself in the shoes of Lizzie Borden. Would not your own situation at the very time your father was being slaughtered be indelibly printed upon your memory in every detail? Yet Lizzie's description of her whereabouts at the crucial time consists of three stories. Firstly she was going to the barn when she heard a distressing sound. She does not enlarge upon the nature of that sound. Secondly she was actually in the barn when she heard some noise like scraping — whatever that may have been. Thirdly she remained twenty minutes in the loft of the barn. At the inquest on the 9th to the 11th of August Lizzie said, not that she wanted the iron to fix the screen, but also in order to use as sinkers for fishing. She adds the further embellishment that she lingered under the pear tree to get some pears, which she ate in the barn.

So here we have two basically different accounts. Firstly, that Lizzie was outside the house going to the barn when a distressing sound made her return to the house where she found her murdered father. Secondly that she was up in the loft of the barn and decided to return to the house, she entered and put her hat down intending to remove the shoes in her room when, on entering the sitting-room, she finds her father killed.

Lizzie was no fool; she was a highly intelligent woman. Did she realise that the weak point of her account of her movements to various witnesses on the 4th August was that Andrew Borden was killed with the first blow while he was asleep.

In such circumstances the victim could not possibly emit a groan or other sign of distress. He died instantly. Where the alleged scraping sound comes in baffles the investigation. Hence a variation became necessary and this was done at the inquest after Lizzie had time to think things over. It is not surprising that Edward D Radin in his attempt to exonerate Lizzie in his book *Lizzie Borden*, skirts over this aspect of the case.

What then are we to make of Lizzie's "alibi". First she says that going to the barn she heard a distressing sound which caused her to return to the house where to her horror she found her dead father. Then she states that while in the barn she hears a scraping sound which led her to go back. Later the story is that she returned to the house, laid down her hat preparatory to mounting the stairs to her room when she discovered the body of her father. She gives at first the reason for going to the barn in sweltering heat to acquire some lead to repair the screen. Later that becomes to obtain sinkers for the fishing lines which she had not used for five years. How could any court give credence to such a tale? And all without a word of corroboration. A well supported alibi, such as that of Morse or Emma can and should result in a suspect being cleared. A poor one may rebound on the teller and rightly bring about a conviction. We shall see when we come to the trial how the prosecution strove to counter this difficulty, assisted by the decision of the court to exclude the evidence of the inquest.

At the inquest Lizzie was questioned about the barn by Knowlton:

> **Hosea M Knowlton:** How long was your father in the house before you found him killed?
>
> **Lizzie Borden:** I don't know exactly because I went out to the barn. I don't know what time he came home. I don't think he had been home more than 15 or 20 minutes; I am not sure.

Lizzie is saying that she was 15 or 30 minutes in the barn; during that time the "interloper", having hidden in the house and already killed Mrs Borden was concealed for at least 45 minutes (in line with the medical evidence). He risked murdering Mr Borden without knowing Lizzie had gone to the barn or that Bridget might enter the sitting room where Mr Borden lay, at any time.

> **Knowlton:** When you went out to the barn where did you leave your father?
> **Lizzie Borden:** He had lain down in the sitting-room lounger, taken off his shoes and put on his slippers, and taken off his coat and put on the reefer. I asked him if he wanted the window left that way.
> **Knowlton:** Was he asleep?
> **Lizzie Borden:** No sir.
> **Knowlton:** Was he reading?
> **Lizzie Borden:** No sir.
> **Knowlton:** What was the last thing you said to him?
> **Lizzie Borden:** I asked him if he wanted the window left that way, then I went into the kitchen and from there to the barn.

Lizzie's claim to be attentive to her father's comfort is undermined by the photo of his body showing his boots still on!

> **Knowlton:** Whereabouts in the barn did you go?
> **Lizzie Borden:** Upstairs [An exceedingly hot and dusty place to stay 20 minutes. There was no sign of dust having been disturbed when later viewed by a detective].
> **Knowlton:** To the second story of the barn?
> **Lizzie Borden:** Yes sir.
> **Knowlton:** How long did you remain there?
> **Lizzie Borden:** I don't know; fifteen or twenty minutes [In that heat!].
> **Knowlton:** What doing?
> **Lizzie Borden:** Trying to find lead for a sinker.
> **Knowlton:** What made you think there would be lead for a sinker up there.
> **Lizzie Borden:** Because there was some.
> **Knowlton:** Was there not some by the door?

Lizzie Borden: Some pieces of lead by the open door, but there was a box full of old things upstairs. [Why not look at that by the door first?].

Knowlton: Did you bring any sinkers back from the barn?

Lizzie Borden: I found no sinkers.

Knowlton: Did you bring a sinker back from the barn?

Lizzie Borden: Nothing but a piece of chip I picked up on the floor [That took all of twenty minutes?].

Knowlton: Where was that box you say was upstairs, containing lead?

Lizzie Borden: There was a kind of workbench.

Knowlton: Is it there now?

Lizzie Borden: I don't know sir.

Knowlton: How long since you have seen it there?

Lizzie Borden: I have not been out there since that day.

Knowlton: Had you been in the barn before?

Lizzie Borden: That day? No sir.

Knowlton: How long since you had been to the barn before?

Lizzie Borden: I don't think I had been into it, I don't know as I had, in three months.

Knowlton: When you went out did you unfasten the screen door?

Lizzie Borden: I unhooked it to get out.

Knowlton: It was hooked until you went out?

Lizzie Borden: Yes sir.

Knowlton: It had been left hooked by Bridget, if she was the last one in?

Lizzie Borden: I suppose so; I don't know.

Knowlton then questioned Lizzie over the question of sinkers for the fishing lines—putting it to her that there were sinkers at the farm together with fishing lines. Therefore she had no reason to go looking for them at the barn (remember, Miss Russell was told by Lizzie that she wanted some metal to mend her screen). Lizzie was questioned by Knowlton about the sinkers:

Knowlton: Can you give me any information how it happened at that particular time you should go into the chambers of the barn to find a sinker to go to Marion with, to fish the next Monday?

Lizzie Borden: I was going to finish my ironing; my flats were not hot; I said to myself "I will go and try and find that sinker, perhaps by the time I get back the flats will be hot". That is the only reason.

Knowlton: How long had you been reading an old magazine before you went to the barn at all?

Lizzie Borden: Perhaps half an hour.

Knowlton: Had you got a fish line?

Lizzie Borden: Not here we had some at the farm.

Knowlton: Had you got a fish hook?

Lizzie Borden: No sir.

Knowlton: Had you any apparatus for fishing at all?

Lizzie Borden: Yes over there.

Knowlton: Had you any sinkers over there?

Lizzie Borden: I think there were some, it is so long since I have been there. I think there were some.

Knowlton: You had no reason to suppose you were lacking sinkers?

Lizzie Borden: I don't think there were any on my lines.

Knowlton: Where were your lines?

Lizzie Borden: My fish lines were at the farm.

Knowlton: What made you feel there were no sinkers at the farm on your lines?

Lizzie Borden: Because some time ago when I was there I had none.

Knowlton: How long since you used the fish lines?

Lizzie Borden: Five years, perhaps.

Knowlton: You left them at the farm then?

Lizzie Borden: Yes sir.

Knowlton: And you have not seen them since?

Lizzie Borden: Yes, sir.

Knowlton: It occurred to you after your father came in it would be a good time to go to the barn after sinkers, and you had no reason to suppose there was not abundance of sinkers at the farm and abundance of line?

Lizzie Borden: The last time I was there there was some lines.

Knowlton: Did you not say before, you presumed there were sinkers at the farm?

Lizzie Borden: I don't think I said so.

Knowlton: Had you any sinkers over there?

Lizzie Borden: I think there were some. It is so long since I have been there. I think there were some.

Knowlton: You did say so exactly. Do you now say you presume there were no sinkers at the farm?

Lizzie Borden: I do not think there were any fish lines suitable to use at the farm; I don't think there were any sinkers on any line that had been mine.

Knowlton: Do you remember telling me you presumed there were lines, and sinkers and hooks at the farm?

Lizzie Borden: I said there were lines, I thought, and perhaps hooks. I did not say I thought there were sinkers on my lines. There was another box of lines over there besides mine.

Knowlton: You thought there were not sinkers?

Lizzie Borden: Not on my lines.

Knowlton: Not sinkers at the farm?

Lizzie Borden: I don't think there were any sinkers at the farm. I don't know whether there were or not.

Knowlton: Did you then think there were no sinkers at the farm?

Lizzie Borden: I thought there were no sinkers anywhere, or I should not have been trying to find some.

Knowlton: That is the reason you went into the second story of the barn to look for a sinker?

Lizzie Borden: Yes sir.

Knowlton: What made you think you would find sinkers there?

Lizzie Borden: I heard father say, and I know there was lead there.

Knowlton: You thought there might be lead made into sinkers?

Lizzie Borden: I thought there might be lead with a hole in it.

Knowlton: Did you examine the lead that was downstairs near the door?

Lizzie Borden: No sir.

Knowlton: Why not?

Lizzie Borden: I don't know.

Knowlton: You went straight to the upper storey of the barn?

Lizzie Borden: No I went under the pear tree and got some pears first.

Knowlton: Then went to the second storey of the barn to look for sinkers for lines you had at the farm as you suggested, as you had seen them there five years before that time?

Lizzie Borden: I went to get some sinkers if I could find them. I did not intend to go to the farm for lines; I was going to buy some lines down here.

Knowlton: You then had no intention of using your own lines and hooks at Marion?

Lizzie Borden: I could not get them.

Knowlton: What was the use of telling me a little while ago you had no sinkers on your line at the farm?

Lizzie Borden: I thought I made you understand that those lines at the farm were no good to use.

Knowlton: Did you not mean for me to understand one of the reasons you were searching for sinkers was that the lines you had at the farm, as you remembered them, had no sinkers on them?

Lizzie Borden: I said the lines I had at the farm had no sinkers on them.

Knowlton: I did not ask you what you said. Did you mean for me to understand that?

Lizzie Borden: I meant you to understand I wanted the sinkers, and was going to have new lines.

Knowlton: You had not then bought your lines?

Lizzie Borden: No sir, I was going out Thursday noon.

Knowlton: You had not bought any apparatus for fishing?

Lizzie Borden: No hooks.

Knowlton: You have not bought anything connected with your fishing trip?

Lizzie Borden: No sir.

Knowlton: Going to go fishing next Monday were you?

Lizzie Borden: I don't know that we should go fishing Monday.

Knowlton: You had no fishing apparatus you were preparing to use next Monday until then?

Lizzie Borden: No sir not until I bought it [Lizzie could have purchased sinkers at the same time].

Knowlton: You had not bought anything?

Lizzie Borden: No sir.

The Alibi

Knowlton: You had not started to buy anything?
Lizzie Borden: No sir.

Knowlton then proceeded to question Lizzie regarding the box of oddments in which she looked for sinkers and about the fact that after spending several minutes searching she was eating pears in a very hot barn. The total time according to Lizzie being 15 to 20 minutes!!!

At the trial Officer William Medley described an experiment he conducted in the upper floor of the barn to indicate nobody including Lizzie had been there prior to his arrival:

William Medley

Called for the prosecution on the 6th day of the trial by Mr Moody:

William H Moody: You are at present doing special work on the Fall River Police Force?
Officer Medley: Yes sir.
Moody: Under the title of Inspector?
Officer Medley: Inspector.
Moody: And last year you were a patrolman?
Officer Medley: Patrolman.

Mr Medley testified that he arrived at the house about 19 or 20 minutes past 12; and that after a brief talk with Lizzie, who said that she was "upstairs in the barn" during the murders, he went to the barn himself.

Moody: After you went into the barn what did you do? Describe in detail.
Officer Medley: I went upstairs until I reached about three or four steps from the top, and while there part of my body was above the floor, above the level of the floor, and I looked around the barn to see if there was any evidence of anything having been disturbed, and I didn't notice anything had or seemed to have been disturbed, and I stooped down low to see if I could discern any marks in the floor of the barn having been made there. I did that by stooping down and looking across the

bottom of the barn floor. I didn't see any and I reached out my hand to see if I could make an impression on the floor of the barn, and I did so by putting my hand down (demonstrates) and found that I made an impression on the barn floor.

Moody: Describe what there was on or about the floor by which you made an impression?

Officer Medley: Seemed to be accumulated hay dust and other dust.

Moody: How distinctly could you see the marks which you made with your hand?

Officer Medley: I could see them quite distinctly when I looked for them.

Moody: Go on and describe anything else which you did.

Officer Medley: Then I stepped up on the top and took four or five steps on the outer edge of the barn floor, the edge nearest the stairs, then came up to see if I could discern those, and I did.

Moody: How did you look to see if you could discern those footsteps which you had made?

Officer Medley: I did it in the first place by stooping down and casting my eye on a level with the barn floor. And could see them plainly.

Moody: Did you see any other footsteps on that dust other than those which you made yourself?

Officer Medley: No sir.

Moody: After you had made that examination what did you do?

Officer Medley: I came downstairs and searched around the pile of lumber and other stuff there was in the yard, looking for anything that we could find, and after a while I met Mr Fleet.

Moody: Wait a moment now. Did you notice what the temperature was in the loft of the barn as you went up there?

Officer Medley: Well I know it was hot, very hot. You know it was a hot day.

Moody: Did you notice whether the windows or the hay door were open or closed?

Officer Medley: They were closed at that time.

Medley Cross-Examined by Robinson:

Robinson: Did you go up, Mr Medley, to the Borden house with anybody?

Officer Medley: No sir.

Robinson: When you arrived there I think you called the gentleman you first saw, a Mr Sawyer?

Officer Medley: Yes sir.

Robinson: Was there anyone else you saw on the outside of the house?

Officer Medley: Yes.

Robinson: Who were they?

Officer Medley: I cannot recall now—some officers, one or two, Mr Doherty...

Robinson: Mr Doherty is an officer?

Officer Medley: Yes sir. He was in citizen's clothes, I mean, in speaking of officers in that connection, officers in uniform, and Mr Doherty was in citizen's clothes.

Robinson: Now, tell me just what your movements were.

Officer Medley: I went into the room where Mr Borden lay dead, and from there I went upstairs in the room where Mrs Borden lay dead, and then I came out from there and spoke to an officer in the front hallway upstairs and rapped on the door occupied by Miss Borden.

Robinson: When you went to Miss Lizzie's room did Mr Fleet go with you?

Officer Medley: No sir.

Robinson: You went in alone?

Officer Medley: I did.

Robinson: Who else was there?

Officer Medley: Miss Borden, Mr Buck and I think Miss Russell, but I won't be sure.

Robinson: Was that the time that you had conversation with Miss Borden?

Officer Medley: Yes sir.

Robinson: And the only time I think you said.

Officer Medley: The only time.

Robinson: That is the time when you asked her where she was, and she told you up in the barn?

Officer Medley: Yes sir.

Robinson: And there was nothing more said; you have given it all?

Officer Medley: As near as I can recall.

Robinson: Where did you go then?
Officer Medley: I came downstairs and went out and upstairs in the barn, as I described to the head of the stairs. Then I came out from there and spoke to an officer in the front hallway upstairs and rapped on the door occupied by Miss Borden.

Officer Medley then described a conversation with Lizzie in which she said that at the time of the murders she was in the upper part of the barn. He then said he went to the upstairs in the barn, to the head of the stairs.

Robinson: When you went in the barn do you know what time it was?
Officer Medley: I only know by the length of time that I think I was in the house.
Robinson: Perhaps you cannot tell any more than the rest of us can infer from where you say you went. Did you stop anywhere there in the house, in any of the rooms other than in Miss Lizzie's?
Officer Medley: That is the only place I stopped.
Robinson: Then you went into the barn and looked about you, as you said.
Officer Medley: Yes sir.
Robinson: And you did not see any evidence of any tracks in the dust?
Officer Medley: No sir.
Robinson: Did not see any at all?
Officer Medley: No sir.
Robinson: Anywhere?
Officer Medley: No sir.
Robinson: It was all perfect?
Officer Medley: Seemed to me.
Robinson: You went in alone?
Officer Medley: Yes sir.
Robinson: Do you know whether the window on the west end had a curtain or not?
Officer Medley: I cannot say about that. I don't know.
Robinson: You don't remember about that?
Officer Medley: I don't.
Robinson: How about the windows on the east?

Officer Medley: Well. I don't remember that, but I think there was a curtain on one of the windows, but I can't say which.

Robinson: Did you look at the boxes or baskets up there?

Officer Medley: I did not go on the floor other than the time I have described, and I stood round there with my body halfway above the floor and looked around; and on the south side of the barn there was a bench, I think it had some things on it. What they were I don't know, but I think there was quite a large basket, a basket of some kind or other.

Robinson: Do you think this is the one here?

Officer Medley: I could not say whether it was or not, because I am not sure of it.

Robinson: How long were you up there in the barn?

Officer Medley: Two or three minutes.

Robinson: What were you doing?

Officer Medley: I was looking around.

Robinson: Do I understand you that you did not go round on the barn floor?

Officer Medley: No sir, I did not.

Robinson: Your looking round consisted of the time you occupied standing on the stairs and looking about?

Officer Medley: Yes sir.

Robinson: You did not go up on the floor except when you went up two steps and came back. As you said?

Officer Medley: No sir.

Robinson: You did not go over to the window?

Officer Medley: No sir.

Robinson: And you did not examine over there at all?

Officer Medley: No sir. I did not.

Robinson: Then two or three minutes would be consumed in standing there and looking about generally, taking a general look?

Officer Medley: Yes.

Robinson: That was all you did?

Officer Medley: That was all.

Robinson: Then you came right down?

Officer Medley: Yes sir.

Medleys evidence was undermined by Everett Brown and Thomas Barlow who were upstairs in the barn two hours before Medley and would have disturbed the dust which Medley said was undisturbed.

The defence called witnesses to support Lizzie's alibi. One of these was Hyman Lubinsky. Examination by the defence:

"I am an ice-man peddler working for Mr Wilkinson of 42 N Main Street. I peddle ice cream by the team driving wagon. On the day of the murder, I left the stable a few minutes after eleven and drove by the Borden House. I saw a lady come out of the way from the barn right to the stairs at the back of the house, the north side stairs. She had on a dark coloured dress, nothing on her head. She was walking very slowly. I did not see her go into the house. I know it was a few minutes after eleven because I was worried that I was late that morning and I looked at my watch when I left the stable. I have seen the servant Bridget Sullivan at that house. I delivered ice-cream there two or three weeks earlier. The woman was not the servant, I am sure of it."

Cross-Examined by Mr Knowlton:

Knowlton: How long after 11 am was it that you looked at your watch?
Hyman Lubinsky: I cannot say.

Knowlton very strongly cross-examined Lubinsky about his peddling movements through various streets, but he could not shift the witness on what he had seen at the Borden house, nor regarding the time he claimed to have seen it.

Knowlton: Did you actually see the woman leave the barn?
Hyman Lubinsky: No.
Knowlton: Did you actually see her go into the house?
Hyman Lubinsky: No. I saw her about two or three feet from the kitchen door.
Knowlton: Did you look at any other yards besides the Borden yard?
Hyman Lubinsky: I looked all over the yard.

Knowlton: What were you looking around for?

Hyman Lubinsky: Because I am acquainted with looking round.

Knowlton: Were you looking in any other yard beside the Bordens?

Hyman Lubinsky: I don't think there is any other yards—no other yards more, I looked all over yards.

Knowlton: Had you got by the house when you saw the woman?

Hyman Lubinsky: I don't know what you mean.

Knowlton: Why?

Hyman Lubinsky: Because not educated in the English Language.

Knowlton: Had you passed the house when you saw the woman?

Hyman Lubinsky: Certainly, I had.

Knowlton: Do you remember seeing anyone in the Borden yard any other day before that day?

Hyman Lubinsky: I don't remember.

Knowlton: You go down the street every day don't you?

Hyman Lubinsky: Every day.

Knowlton: You didn't take any notice any other day.

Hyman Lubinsky: Something made me look at it that day. What has a person got eyes for, but to look with?

Knowlton: You don't remember whether you ever saw anybody before that day or not?

Hyman Lubinsky: What do you mean?

Knowlton: If you don't understand I will not ask it.

Hyman Lubinsky: You ask too fast, I can't understand what you mean.

Knowlton: That is all sir.

Here was an obviously honest witness doing his best to tell the truth. Hyman Lubinsky was a foreign Jew with a poor command of English. Knowlton's rough handling may have;

(1) Given rise to sympathy for the witness on the part of the jury; and
(2) Made the jury aware that his evidence put Knowlton in a difficulty.

Lubinsky said the woman had no hat—Lizzie referred in her evidence at the inquest to removing her hat when she got into the house. This was part of the evidence excluded by judge. If Lubinsky was wrong about the time, the woman could not have been Lizzie. Lubinsky was partially corroborated by Charles Gardiner. Lubinsky never saw the woman in the barn or in the house.

The police did not place any importance on Lubinsky's evidence — he was not a prime witness. Lubinsky did not recognise the woman — he knew it was not Bridget. Surely he had seen Lizzie if he had previously called at the house. He never stated that the woman was Lizzie. The evidence of Charles E Gardiner followed. Gardiner was owner of the stables where Lubinsky kept his horse. Knowlton, in cross-examination, cast considerable doubt on the times reported by Gardiner. Asked by his counsel the time when Lubinsky left the stables Gardiner said, "Between 11.05 and 11.10 am".

He said he was sure of the time because Lubinsky arrived while the horses were still feeding. He looked at his watch and the time was 11.08 am.

Cross-examined he said he left the stables about 15 minutes after Lubinsky had left. About 11.30, when he arrived at the Borden house he said he saw no activity. In fact there was a great deal of activity. This greatly undermines Gardiner on times and is in fact no real corroboration of Lubinsky.

Charles Newhall, called on behalf of the defence to corroborate Lubinsky was of no assistance on the question of times. Further evidence was called by the defence regarding the barn alibi. Everett Brown said:

> "My name is Everett Brown, living at 117 Third Street, Fall River. On the day of the murder, with another party, I left my house somewhere around 11 am and went down to the Borden house. I saw Officer Doherty come out of the Borden yard. We went in the yard, and tried to get in the house; Mr Sawyer would not let us in. I did not see Officer Medley there. We then went to the barn. The party who was with me tried the door, and we went in. We stood a minute to see who would go upstairs; he said he wouldn't go up, somebody might drop an axe on him. We went upstairs, looked out of the window on the west side, and went over to the hay and were up in the barn about five minutes and then came down and out into the yard. We went to

the south east corner of the house, tried to look in and couldn't. There were other people trying to look in the window. I saw Officer Fleet coming up the walk. This other fellow was with me then. He was Thomas Barlow. Then we got out of the yard. Everybody that was in there got put out".

As a witness, Brown was of no help to anyone. He was completely unable to say at what time he got to the scene. He did not see anyone go up into the barn upstairs before himself and Barlow. They both went out of the barn and hung about outside until about 5 pm. He might have seen Medley and he might not. They went into the barn because he hoped to see the murderer inside.

Thomas E Barlow gave evidence maintaining, contrary to all the other evidence, that the barn was a cool place. He said he stayed at Brown's place for about eight minutes before going to the barn. He was unable to give that time at that moment or when he came to testify, and said that he had not looked at the time that day. He and Brown went into the barn to see if anybody was in there.

The fact is that Lubinsky, Brown and Barlow were such unreliable witnesses that Medley's evidence was not seriously undermined. Lubinsky had a fleeting glance of a woman very near to the side entry to the house and not even near the barn. Lizzie claimed at the inquest she was wearing a hat. Lubinsky said the woman was hatless. Lubinsky never identified the woman. He could only say who it was not. His evidence conflicted with Gardiner on the amount of activity going on at the house.

Brown and Barlow were hopelessly unreliable. They were only upstairs in the barn for a few minutes and both were completely vague about the time factor.

Quite apart from the varying accounts which Lizzie gave for her presence in the barn and the reasons for her returning to the house it is difficult to see how Lizzie's "alibi" can be called an alibi at all. She alone gives the account of her movements, and her story has not a word of corroboration. The nearest thing to corroboration is the word of Lubinsky, but his view was fleeting and did not identify Lizzie as the person he claims to have seen.

In her book *A Private Disgrace,* Victoria Lincoln points out the coincidence that Lizzie was absent from the house in the barn, as she alleges, for the precise time necessary to cover the murder of Mr Borden. It might be added that Emma was away from home, as was Uncle John Morse, while Bridget was upstairs in her attic room. Victoria Lincoln adds "even in my day hook, line and sinker could be had complete for a dime and if you lost your sinker a nickel would buy you a small fist of them". She further writes:

> "In our part of the world, Lizzie's and mine, professional fisherman trawled the deep waters with nets. The rest of us fished the shallows of the tidal inlets using a small wooden hand-reel, like four clothes pins fastened together in a square, with the fish line wound round it".

Neither Lizzie Borden at the inquest nor Bridget Sullivan at the trial gave the exact time when Mr Borden came home prior to his murder.

The only evidence regarding the precise time when Lizzie said she left the house and went to the barn is her own wholly uncorroborated statement at the inquest. Nobody saw her leave the house. Nobody saw her enter the barn. Nobody saw her leave the barn and re-enter the house. The fact the she declined to go into the witness box and tell her story undermines Lizzie's alibi.

Now let us see what Bridget and Alice Russell said at the trial and what Lizzie said at the inquest. Bridget Sullivan was examined by Knowlton:

Knowlton: Have you ever gone to let Mr Borden in on any other day at the front door?
Bridget Sullivan: No sir. I don't remember.
Knowlton: What?
Bridget Sullivan: No sir. I did not.
Knowlton: Let us see if we understand it right. All the time that you lived there did you ever go when he came to the door and couldn't unlock the door?
Bridget Sullivan: I don't remember.
Knowlton: Don't remember that you did.

Bridget Sullivan: No sir, I don't.

Knowlton: After you let Mr Borden in you say you heard Miss Lizzie laugh?

Bridget Sullivan: Yes sir.

Knowlton: And you say she was upstairs somewhere?

Bridget Sullivan: Yes sir.

Knowlton: And you didn't see her on the stairs?

Bridget Sullivan: No sir.

Knowlton: Didn't see her at all.

Bridget Sullivan: No sir. I didn't look.

Knowlton: You heard the sound of the laugh?

Bridget Sullivan: Yes sir.

Knowlton: Was that all?

Bridget Sullivan: Yes sir.

Knowlton: And there was talk with her father about the mail?

Bridget Sullivan: Yes sir.

Knowlton: And what did he say?

Bridget Sullivan: I don't know.

Knowlton: You don't know what was said?

Bridget Sullivan: I only heard her tell her father her mother had a note and gone out.

Knowlton: Did you hear what he said about that?

Bridget Sullivan: No sir.

Lizzie Borden was questioned by Knowlton at the inquest regarding her movements on the day of the murders: Questioned as to when her father left the house to go to town, she replied as follows:

Knowlton: What was the next thing that happened after you got down [downstairs in the morning]?

Lizzie Borden: Maggie went out of doors to wash the windows, and father came out into the kitchen and said he did not know whether he would go down to the post office or not. And then I sprinkled some handkerchiefs to iron.

Knowlton: Did your father go downtown?

Lizzie Borden: He went down later.
Knowlton: What time did he start away?
Lizzie Borden: I don't know.
Knowlton: What were you doing when he started away?
Lizzie Borden: I was in the dining room I think. Yes I had just commenced to iron, I think.
Knowlton: It may seem a foolish question. How much of ironing did you have?
Lizzie Borden: I only had eight or ten of my best handkerchiefs.
Knowlton: Did you let your father out?
Lizzie Borden: No sir, he went out himself.
Knowlton: Did you fasten the door after him?
Lizzie Borden: No sir.
Knowlton: What time do you think your father went down town?
Lizzie Borden: I don't know. It must have been after nine o'clock.

Somewhat surprisingly Knowlton did not press Lizzie on the time factor. This would have given an indication of the time of Mr Borden's return and hence of Lizzie's alleged departure to the barn.

Knowlton: How long was your father gone?
Lizzie Borden: I don't know sir. Not very long.
Knowlton: An hour?.
Lizzie Borden: I should not think so.

It was clear from her evidence that Lizzie left for the barn shortly after her father had come in and lain down on the sitting room sofa. If Mr Borden left home after nine o'clock and was gone for under an hour — say 30 to 40 minutes, he would have returned about 10 am. A few minutes, after he arrived, Lizzie left for the barn where she estimates staying for 15 to 20 minutes. She would have emerged about 10.20 am. Lubinsky claims to have seen her walking away from the barn a few minutes after 11 am.

With regard to her movements at the time when Mr Borden returned home Lizzie contradicted herself several times. We shall consider the significance of this in connection with the desperate battle conducted by her counsel at the trial to get the evidence of the inquest excluded, For it to be admitted might have been disastrous to her chance of an acquittal.

Alice M Russell gave evidence:

> "Lizzie was there after the murders. I think she was standing in the door, leaning against the door frame. I asked her to sit down in the rocking chair, which she did. I cannot tell it in order, for it was disconnected. People came around; I don't know who they were. Later when she told us about going into the barn I asked her what did you go to the barn for Lizzie?' And she said 'I went to get a piece of iron or tin to fix my screen'. She said my screen. I heard about the note to Mrs Borden; I didn't know who told it. I started to loosen her dress, thinking she was faint, and she said 'I am not faint'".

Here is the clearest possible discrepancy from the account of the sinker.

Lizzie Borden and the Massachusetts Axe Murders

CHAPTER FOURTEEN

The Exclusion of the Inquest Evidence

When the trial of Lizzie Borden began the prosecution had two valuable points in their favour and one against. The defence likewise enjoyed two favourable circumstances and one against.

The significant facts for the Commonwealth which were not in dispute were, firstly, that Mrs Borden as well as her husband had been murdered and secondly that only Lizzie was in the house at the time of the first of the two homicides and in the precincts at the time of the second. The main difficulty for the prosecution team was the absence of blood on Lizzie's clothing following the murders which gave rise to a great deal of blood.

The strong points for the defence were the absence of blood on Lizzie and the absence of any direct evidence of her involvement. The weakness of the defence was the double killing.

Many other issues were raised, but they were all subsidiary to these. There was, however one over-riding factor which made an acquittal inevitable, notwithstanding the brilliant performance of Moody—the court was biased in favour of the defendant. There is no conceivable way of interpreting the rulings which the court made, which were grossly slanted in Lizzie's favour and impossible to understand for anyone conversant with the law of evidence in either the English or American courts of law. This is not for a moment to suggest that any of the three judges hearing the case was deliberately biased, but that they favoured the defence is undeniable.

The importance from the prosecution's point of view was the poor performance which Lizzie put up in the witness box at the inquest—frequently changing her story. This was something she could have been cross-examined about at the trial; she did not give evidence. Therefore any witness who was cross-examined was bound by the answer and could not press the question further. For the same reason it was vital for the defence to persuade the judge to reject the evidence because the effect on the jury, if it were admitted, might be extremely damaging to Lizzie's case.

The English rule with regard to out-of-court statements is as follows: If a statement is to be used in a way which falls within the scope of the hearsay rule then the next question must be whether the situation falls within the exception to the rule against hearsay covering certain contemporaneous assertions by a person as to his or her own state of mind or body.

This exception provides that wherever the physical condition, emotions or state of mind of a person are in issue, or are directly relevant to an issue, his or her statements indicative thereof made at or about the time in question may be given in evidence (*Phipson on Evidence*). The exception is preserved in criminal cases by the Criminal Justice Act 2003. A similar exception is found in the Evidence Act 1995 of the Commonwealth of Australia 572 and the Federal Rules of Evidence (United States of America) rule 803.

In English law the specimen directions by the influential Judicial Studies Board to a judge in cases of trial by juries declare: "You decide intent by considering what the defendant did or did not do (and the effect of his actions or inaction) and by what he said or didn't say. You should look at his actions before, at the time of and after [the alleged offence]. All these may shed light on his intention at the critical time".

Arguments for and against excluding inquest evidence

Moody opened the case for the admission of the evidence. He referred to the statute law under which the inquest was held.

In 1892 August 9th to 11th, the dates of the inquest, the coroner had been superseded by a medical examiner—a qualified physician.

The inquest was held under Chapter 26 of the public statutes which provided that a medical examiner, upon view or personal inquiry in respect of a body that is found by evidence, shall notify the justice of a district, police, or municipal court of the district attorney.

Section 13 of the public statutes provides:

> "The court or trial justice shall thereupon hold an inquest, which may be private, in which case any or all persons, other than those required to be present by the provision of the chapter, may be excluded from the place where such inquest is held, and said court or trial justice may also direct the witness[es] to be kept separate, so that they cannot converse with each other until they have been examined. The district attorney, or some person designated by him, may attend the inquest and examine all witnesses".

Moody:

> "Of course the implication from that language is that the privacy or the degree of privacy of the inquest is entirely within the control of those representing the Commonwealth. Because the language is that 'any or all persons may be excluded from attending upon the inquest'".

Moody then pointed out that the general rule was that the evidence of the defendant, who appeared as a witness under subpoena at the inquest, was that such declaration that she made, if material to the charge upon which she was now being tried, was competent and admissible at the trial.

The question was, Moody submitted, was there anything in the agreed circumstances which would take the evidence of Lizzie Borden at the inquest out of the general rule. Moody, anticipating objection by the defence, quoted authority showing that a statement of a deceased person made after an indictment was not admissible in a subsequent trial. But that comment and declarations as showing a concession of guilt were admissible. It was not a confession which he was offering to the court but a statement of the accused which tended to show her guilt.

Moody:

> "The proposition which I desire to submit to your honour is this; that the true rule is declarations voluntarily given, no matter where or under what

circumstance, are competent; declarations gained by compulsion are never competent".

Moody then turned to the authorities on this subject and began his address by saying that no help could be obtained from the English precedents. Moody cited a New York case—*People v Hendrickson*, 10 New York 721 (1854). The defendant, who was indicted for murder, had made statements at the coroners court which were denials not a confession. He was not under arrest or under suspicion. The court admitted the defendant's statements made at the inquest and the appeals court upheld that decision. He contrasted this with another decision—*People v Monsdon*, 103 New York 211 Appeal Court in which the defendant who had been arrested without a warrant, had while in custody been examined as a witness before the coroner's jury. He was ignorant of the English language and had not been cautioned as to his rights. His declarations were excluded at the trial. Moody quoted Mr Justice Rapallo, who, having quoted the cases, cited said:

"[T]hey [the cases cited] draw the line sharply and define clearly in what cases the testimony of a witness examined before a coroner's inquest can be used on his subsequent trial, and in what case it cannot. When a coroner's inquest is held before it has been ascertained that a crime has been committed or before any person has been arrested or charged with the crime, and a witness is called and sworn before the coroner's jury, the testimony of that witness, should he afterward be charged with the crime, may be used against him on his trial, and the mere fact that at the time of his examination he was aware that a crime was suspected and that he was suspected of being the criminal, will not prevent his being regarded as a mere witness whose testimony may be afterwards given in evidence against himself.

But if, at the time of his examination, it appears that a crime had been committed and that he is in custody as the supposed criminal, he is not regarded merely as a witness but as a party accused, called before a tribunal vested with the power to investigate primarily the question of his guilt, and he is to be treated in the same manner as if bought before a committing magistrate and an examination not taken in conformity with the statute cannot be used against him on his trial for the offence".

Moody concluded:

"That decision was in the year 1886 and it is to be observed that the line may be stated in a single word; it is whether the person is then under arrest or not".

"It is very clear by all", said Moody, "so far as I am aware of them, at least by all the authorities of weight, that upon enquiring into the death of a person, if one then under suspicion and informed that he is under suspicion, responds to the subpoena of the state, and in the eye of the law voluntarily gives testimony at that enquiry, if he is subsequently arrested upon the accusation of being guilty of that death, what he has said at the inquiry is admissible against him".

Robinson's reply maintained that the inquest was directed to extracting from the defendant something that could be used against her at her trial—not to discover if a crime had been committed, as an inquest should. Robinson made his argument clear in the following words:

"In the present case Miss Borden had been under suspicion. She had been put under a personal charge or accusation, to use another word, of the Chief Officer of the City. She had been proceeded against; in other words, proceedings formally, had been instituted against her, and the warrant issued and it was in the hands of the City Marshall directing him, not permitting him, but directing him to take her into custody. He had not any right when he received the mandate of that court to choose whether he would execute it or not, and it was not in the power of the district attorney to instruct him to disobey the order of that court, It was a pocket warrant, but that pocket did not belong to Marshall Hilliard, but was the pocket of the Commonwealth, and Hilliard was but the instrument or agent directed to execute it."

Robinson made the following points:

(1) The murders were committed August 14th 1982 — the medical examiner took immediate possession of the bodies.
(2) The defendant's testimony was given on August 9th to 11th, 1892.
(3) The defendant was accused of the crimes by the Mayor on August 6th.
(4) The defendant was kept under police observation from August 6th until her arrest.
(5) On or before August 9th the defendant was subpoenaed to appear and testify at the inquest.
(6) Before testifying the defendant requested counsel which was denied. She was surrounded by police, confronted by the City Marshall and unrepresented.
(7) She was not properly cautioned.
(8) A warrant for her arrest was placed in the hands of the City Marshall on August 8th — which was before she testified.
(9) At the conclusion of her testimony she was not allowed to depart. She was arrested two hours later on another but similar warrant.

Robinson concluded:

"I have stated my position as a matter of law — nay rather the defendant's position. If I have given the court emphasis on it, it is her's rather than mine. I stand by those rights which are her's by the constitution, and to depart from their preservation, will be peril, not alone to her, but to everybody hereafter who may be placed in a similar position, and may desire to find the constitution his protection".

Moody in reply commented on his opponent's argument —

"It is magnificent, but it is not law".

He claimed that Lizzie's liberty was not restrained at all. The warrant had not been seen by her ad therefore did not act upon her mind. The Chief Justice concluded:

"The Common Law regards substance more than form. The principle cannot be evaded by avoiding the form if arrest of the witness at the time of such testimony is practically in custody. From the agreed facts and the facts otherwise in evidence, it is plain that the prisoner at the time of her testimony was, so far [as] relates to this question, as effectively in custody as if the formal precept had been served; and without dwelling on other circumstances which distinguish the facts of this case from those of cases on which the government relies, we are all of opinion that this consideration is decisive, and the evidence is excluded".

This ruling was the subject of widespread criticism. Writing in 1975 Judge Robert Sullivan noted:

"But with all the law which the Warren Court has given us, today admissions—confessions of criminal defendants are as they always have been; admissible when it is established that they were voluntarily made, before or after arrest. And certainly the mere fact of arrest does not in and of itself destroy voluntariness."

CHAPTER FIFTEEN

The Exclusion of the Prussic Acid Evidence

The exclusion of the Prussic acid evidence is nothing short of outrageous. It is outrageous for two reasons. Firstly it was plainly wrong in law. Secondly, if true, it enabled a woman who was guilty of one of the most terrible crimes known to human society, the murder of both one's parents, to escape the consequences of her abominable crimes. Over the days before the murders a woman entered a chemists shop, the nearest in town to the Borden house, namely D R Smith at the corner of South Main and Columbia Street, and asked for ten cents worth or Prussic acid. This was between 10 am and 10.30 am. The reason given for the purchase was to clean a sealskin cape. Three witnesses identified the woman as Lizzie Borden. This was good identification and the reason for admitting it was in order to establish intent to kill. Evidence was also available that to use Prussic acid for cleaning sealskin was not only unheard of but also very dangerous to the user.

In the High Court of Justiciary in Edinburgh in June 1857 at the trial for murder of Madeleine Smith evidence of purchase of arsenic was admitted. There is no reason for any distinction in the context between purchase and attempt to purchase. The state of mind is the same in both instances.

The Prussic Acid Evidence and Its Exclusion

There is little in the earlier history of the Borden family that provides any real clue to the events of the 3rd and 4th of August 1892. It was the absence of a motive for murder of any real substance on the part of Lizzie which presented the Commonwealth lawyers with a difficulty. There was of course the resentment on the part of the sisters over their father's property arrangements, but Andrew Borden had sought to rectify the position by making recompense. There were the hostile words used by Lizzie when referring to her step-mother. There were the tales about Lizzie's acts of cruelty to cats which would never be admissible for one moment in a court of law as evidence of a predisposition to commit an act of murder.

As against those things, there was the testimony of Bridget, a patently honest witness, that she had never witnessed friction in the Borden household. Motive does not have to be proved to establish a charge of murder, but a jury will normally be hesitant to convict without it especially in the absence of other overwhelming evidence. It is for that very reason that the lawyers of the Commonwealth wished to call evidence that on the very day before the murders Lizzie Borden visited not one, but two chemists shops in the vicinity of Second Street and attempted to purchase Prussic acid.

This aspect of the Borden trial has been skirted over by some writers on the subject . This author begs to differ from those writers. The reason for this is three-fold. Firstly the evidence was clearly admissible on the ground that, if true, it would show an intention on Lizzie's part to commit an act of murder. It could not have been more proximate to the killing. Secondly, the jury had every right, in the exercise of its function, to decide whether the allegation was true or not; and thirdly the identification by three witnesses was sound by any test of the law of evidence. This author will explain why, in his view, the ruling of the court excluding the proposed testimony of Eli Bence, Frank Kilroy and Frederick Marks was nothing short of outrageous.

Professor Edward S Wood was called as an expert witness in Medico-legal cases. He gave evidence regarding the contents of the stomachs of the two victims. He also spoke about the time differences between their deaths. He gave further evidence about the hatchet which had been produced as probably the murder weapon. Which will be dealt with later. Knowlton then asked Wood these questions:

> **Hosea M Knowlton:** What is the nature of Prussic acid?
> **Professor Edward S Wood:** It is a poison acid, gaseous. It consists of gas, and that gas is soluble in water.

Knowlton: In reference, I mean now, to its poisonous effects?
Prof. Wood: It is one of the most deadly poisons we know.
Knowlton: And how instantaneous or otherwise is it?
Prof. Wood: Death is caused anywhere from a few seconds to a couple of minutes.
Knowlton: And what quantity of Prussic acid is sufficient to cause the death of a human being?
Prof. Wood: Any solution of Prussic acid which contains a grain of acid is a fatal dose. That is, it is less than a teaspoonful of the solution which is ordinarily used in drug stores, which is two per cent solution.
Knowlton: And what is the solution used for, if you know?
Prof. Wood: For medicine.
Knowlton: Alone, or in prescriptions?
Prof. Wood: Prescription.

In this passage we can see that Knowlton is laying the foundation for what will follow towards the end of the prosecution case where the witnesses are called who describe, or are called to describe, Lizzie's visit to the chemists.

When Moody called Eli Bence, the drug clerk at D R Smith's pharmacy at the corner of South Main and Columbia Street's in Fall River, Mr Robinson, counsel for the defence rose to object. After a short discussion between counsel, the Chief Justice ordered: "The jury may retire with the officers and remain until sent for. The witness may return downstairs". The jury and the witness withdrew from the court.

The testimony of Eli Bence had been heard at the preliminary hearing and at the inquest. This witness had first been spoken to by two police officers who visited the D R Smith's drug store and learned from him that Lizzie Borden had entered the drug store within 36 hours ago and had enquired about purchasing Prussic acid. He was closely questioned about the details of the attempted purchase and then taken to an address on Second Street where Lizzie was present at that time. Bence did identify her. In his address to the court Moody quoted the words of Bence to Lizzie when she tried to obtain a purchase:

"This party came in there and enquired if I kept Prussic acid. I was standing out there, I walked in ahead. She asked me if we kept Prussic acid. I informed her that we did. She asked me if she could buy ten cents worth off me. I informed her that we did not sell Prussic acid except by a physician's prescription. She then said that she had bought this several times, I think she said several times before. I said 'well my good lady, it is something we don't sell unless by a prescription from the doctor, as it is a very dangerous thing to handle'. I understood her to say she wanted it to put on the edge of a seal skin cape, if I remember rightly".

William H Moody: She did not buy anything, no drug at all, no medicine?
Eli Bence: No sir.

Eli Bence was a respected young man in Fall River and his testimony had the ring of truth. He knew Lizzie by sight since she frequently passed by his shop which was near her home. He was adamant both about his correct identification and about the details of the sale. What possible motive could he have had for inventing such a story? And who else might have put forward the absurd suggestion that such a dangerous poison could properly be used to kill moths in a cape?

Asked at the preliminary hearing by Knowlton, "Is this the woman?" the reply was "Yes sir". Asked "Are you sure?" he answered "positive". Beyond extracting an admission that Bence could not remember the exact colour of the dress, hat, purse or gloves of the woman who had entered his store or other sales he had made that morning to other women, Bence was not shaken in cross-examination.

Bence further said that he had talked to the authorities about the incident, and that when he identified Lizzie he was fully in her view. The significant factor about Bence's evidence is that it was corroborated, and the corroboration was good. Frank H Kilroy was a medical student who was in the drug store talking to Bence when Lizzie entered and requested Prussic acid. He knew Lizzie by sight and made a positive identification:

"I was sitting in the front shop under the fan and conversing with Mr Bence, and this lady came in and Mr Bence left me and went behind the counter, and I heard her say 'Prussic ccid'. Mr Bence said 'I cannot sell it without a prescription'. She said something that I could not understand, except 'seal skin cape'; and she left the store".

Another clerk at Smith's drug store also testified. He was Frederick B Harte; he said at the inquest that Lizzie Borden came in, asked Bence for Prussic acid, was refused by Bence and then left. He never doubted that the lady in question was Lizzie Borden. He could only fix the time as between ten and half past eleven. He could not say what she had been wearing.

An important question is: Where was Lizzie on the morning and early afternoon of Wednesday August 3rd? Under questioning concerning her movements in the early part of that day when Uncle John Morse arrived, Lizzie gave answers that give the impression that she was out of the house.

> **Melvin O Adams:** When did he (Morse) come to the house the last time before your father and mother were killed?
> **Lizzie Borden:** He stayed there all night Wednesday night.
> **Adams:** My question is when he came there.
> **Lizzie Borden:** I don't know; I was not at home when he came, I was out.

On 27th August, Bridget the maid gave evidence at the preliminary hearing before Judge Blaisdell. The defence advocate, Adams, endeavoured to coax Bridget into saying that Lizzie was at home the whole of the Wednesday morning and early afternoon. He failed:

> **Adams:** And Lizzie complained of being sick?
> **Bridget Sullivan:** Yes sir.
> **Adams:** Lizzie stayed in her room all that afternoon did she not?
> **Bridget Sullivan:** I suppose so, I did not see her until she came to dinner.
> **Adams:** You knew she was upstairs? They were all sick and ailing that day?
> **Bridget Sullivan:** Yes sir.
> **Adams:** She did not go out at all that day, did she as far as you know?
> **Bridget Sullivan:** Miss Lizzie? I did not see her.
> **Adams:** So far as you know she did not go out?

Bridget Sullivan: I could not say whether she went out or not.

Adams: They ate a little breakfast, and Lizzie went back upstairs to her room?

Bridget Sullivan: I suppose so. She went out of my sight. I do not know where she went.

It is also significant that Smith's drug store was in the South Main Street area of Fall River. This was the unfashionable district where Lizzie or persons of her class most certainly would not go shopping. It would however be a part of town where she was not likely to be noticed or recognised.

It is little wonder that the defence fought desperately to persuade the court to exclude the testimony of Bence, Kilroy and Hart. It was dynamite and the identification was strong. In the leading English Court of Appeal authority on this subject, *R v. Turnbull* (1977) QB 224 the court laid down the correct rules to be applied in testing the value of identification evidence:

> "The judge should direct the jury to examine closely the circumstances in which the identification by each witness came to be made. How long did the witness have the accused under observation? At what distance? In what light? Was the observation impeded in any way? As for example by passing traffic or a press of people? Had the witness ever seen the accused before? How often? If only occasionally had he any special reason for remembering the accused? How long elapsed between the original observation and the subsequent identification by the police? Was there any material discrepancy between the description of the accused given to the police by the witness when first seen by them and his actual appearance?"

On every one of these points the evidence identifying Lizzie Borden as the woman attempting to purchase Prussic acid is very strong indeed. Once that fact is established the remaining question is—why give as her reason the absurd explanation that the poison was required to clean a fur cape? This, in the words of Judge Robert Sullivan in his work *Goodbye Lizzie Borden* is the equivalent of using dynamite to destroy a wasps' nest.

But would the evidence so potentially damaging to Lizzie's plea of innocence, be admitted by the court?

At this point I pause. These are matters which are more familiar to the lawyer than the layman. However they are of vital importance, not only because the decision of the court made a vast difference to the trial, but also because it gave rise to the continuing question of whether the Commonwealth of Massachusetts itself was fairly treated by the presiding judges.

As to the application by Moody to call the three witnesses, I cannot do better than quote Robert Sullivan in his book *Goodbye Lizzie Borden*:

> "I recognise that the exclusion of this evidence is, or may to a certain extent be, considered discretionary with the court. Nonetheless I am completely at a loss to understand the exclusion of the evidence offered to show that on the afternoon before the murders, Lizzie Borden attempted to purchase the deadliest of poisons, Prussic acid, in order, she said to mothproof a fur cape—a pretence so thin that even the most naïve would equate it for absurdity with using dynamite to destroy a wasps' nest.
>
> Since the attempted purchase took place only hours before the murders, it could not conceivably have been considered too remote in time to be material to a determination of the state of mind before the crimes. Certainly these actions of Lizzie manifested a clear intent to kill, or a pre-disposition to kill. Why else would she attempt to purchase the deadly poison? If it was to be purchased for some innocent use, and in the unlikely event that she had an innocent purpose (for there is quite obviously no commercial use for Prussic acid) should not the jury determine this, or have the opportunity to determine this?
>
> Finally it is specious to argue that merely because Lizzie ultimately used another deadly weapon, a hatchet, the jury should not be told that hours before the murder she was attempting to buy deadly poison. We are here only concerned with a determination of her state of mind prior to the murders, whether or not she was predisposed to kill. That and that alone was the sole purpose of offering the Prussic acid testimony.

> The admissibility of this evidence in the circumstances and in this time frame seems so basic to the law of evidence that it is sound common sense and hardly requires the support of legal authority, although there is considerable support.
>
> Both of these evidentiary problems when they arose had been argued by District Attorney William H Moody for the prosecution. He presented a formidable array of case authority to support the propositions of law he advanced. His statements of the law demonstrate careful preparation and profound grasp of the problems. The court rejected his arguments.
>
> Robinson in turn had argued both issues in the manner which characterised his trial technique. As he himself declared he 'relied on good common sense' as a substitute for legal authority—probably as a substitute for adequate preparation. His arguments were short, yet somewhat rambling. The court was compliant. Lizzie Borden prevailed".

Robinson was invited to place his objection to the evidence before the court. He put forward one or two extraordinary propositions. Let us consider some of his statements:

> "She is charged in this indictment with slaying or killing these two people with a sharp instrument; committing the murder with an axe, for instance. Nothing else. Now here, if it has any force at all, suppose it were carried away up to its legitimate result, it is an attempt to charge her with an act causing death by a wholly different means, for which she is not now on trial."

In fact there was no such attempt by the prosecution and to suggest as much, coming from an experienced and able trial lawyer as was Robinson, is a mischievous representation of the purpose for which the evidence was offered. Robinson continued:

"It must be shown, I maintain, that any act which is to be put in evidence on the part of this defendant must have some natural tendency to show that she has committed the act for which she stands on trial".

This was to expound a doctrine unknown to the law of Massachusetts or the Common Law of England. Sullivan again:

"The prosecution was of course offering this evidence—foreshadowed at the end of Dr Woods testimony—as being supportive of the fact that Lizzie Borden had had a pre-disposition to kill on the afternoon before the murders; in short pre-determination. This issue was not was she planning to kill with an axe but did she have murder on her mind? Moody made this point very clearly: 'The whole discussion, as I understand it, evades the precise bearing of this testimony. This indictment not only charges that the person killed Mr and Mrs Borden, but that she did it with a certain intent and with premeditation, and the purpose for which this testimony is offered is upon the intent and the premeditation, or in other words, upon the state of mind of the defendant just prior to this homicide".

Moody accurately stated the principle of law:

"It seems to be that there, in general terms [summing up the authorities] we have laid down the rule which should govern us in this inquiry, and it seems to me that any act or any declaration of this prisoner which is sufficiently near in point of time or significant in point of character of the state of mind which she had at or about the time of this homicide, is competent against her, and its bearing and proper weight is for the consideration of the jury".

The ultimate decision of the court to exclude the evidence of the attempted purchase of Prussic acid was extraordinary and unjustified by all the known principles of the law of evidence. Moody was minded to discontinue the case there and then. Knowlton however did not agree. Certainly the issue was swung strongly in favour of the defence and undermined what should have been a powerful case for the Commonwealth.

Judge Sullivan surely has the last word:

"How can one evaluate the impact of the court, its actions, its rulings, its instructions upon the jury and upon the jury verdict? It cannot be done with reasonable accuracy; there are too many...This fact, however, is certain: there is an impact, there is an influence, and when the court's actions, rulings and instructions to the jury are done with propriety, with dignity and in accordance with the law, there should be an impact, an effect which combined with an..., honest, objective search for the truth by the jury produces justice".

How did the handling of the Borden case fit this pattern for achieving justice? Can it be fairly said that it was a shining hour in the long and glorious history of Massachusetts jurisprudence? I think not.

CHAPTER SIXTEEN

Lizzie's Failure to Give Evidence

There must be strong reasons why Lizzie Borden was not called by Jennings and Robinson in her own defence. In the English appeal case of *Cowan and Others* certain principles were laid down which we shall look at shortly.

Until 1995, the prosecution in England were not permitted to comment on the failure of the defendant to give evidence. The judge was allowed to do so. The law was changed by section 35 Criminal Justice and Public Order Act 1994. The defendant is not compellable to give evidence but inferences may now be drawn from his or her silence.

The section does not apply if:

"(a) the guilt of the defendant is not in issue; or (b) it appears to the court that the physical or mental condition of the accused makes it undesirable for him to give evidence."

Further, a direction under section 35 is appropriate where there is no dispute on the central facts, the issue being whether these facts amount to the offence charged.

If it is indicated at the conclusion of the evidence for the prosecution that the defendant will give evidence, the section does not apply. Unless such an indication is given, the court must satisfy itself that the defendant is aware that he or she can give evidence and that if he or she chooses not to do so inferences can be drawn. A warning is given to the defendant in trials on indictment in the presence of the jury. In cases to which section 35 applies, the court or the jury, in determining whether there is guilt "may draw such inferences as appear proper" from the failure to give evidence.

In *Cowan and Others* ([1996] 1 Cr App R 1) the Court of Criminal Appeal laid down the principles which the judge should follow:

(1) The judge should have told the jury that the burden of proof remained on the prosecution throughout and what the required standard of proof was (i.e. beyond reasonable doubt).

(2) It was necessary for the judges to make clear to the jury that the defendant was entitled to remain silent. That was his or her right and choice. The right of silence remains.

(3) An inference from failure to give evidence cannot on its own prove guilt.

(4) Therefore the jury must be satisfied that the prosecution have established a case to answer before drawing any inferences from silence. Of course the judge must have thought so or the question whether the defendant was to give evidence would not have arisen.

But the jury may not have believed the witnesses whose evidence the judge considered sufficient to raise a prima facie case. It must therefore be made clear to them that they must find a case to answer on the prosecution evidence before drawing an adverse inference from the defendant's silence.

(5) If despite any evidence relied upon to explain his or her silence, or in the absence of any such evidence, the jury conclude the silence can only be attributed to the defendant having no answer, or none that would stand up to cross-examination they may draw an adverse inference.

So much for the law. But what of the tactics which counsel may decide to employ in court.

Whether or not to call his or her client is a crucial decision for the defending advocate. If the defendant is called and makes a poor impression it reduces his or her chances of an acquittal. On the other hand if counsel does not put the client in the witness box the jury will wonder why not. Has the accused got something to hide? Is this a sign that the defence lawyer does not have much faith in the client's story? This is strictly speaking not a relevant issue—but juries are free to come to conclusions of their own.

The failure of the accused person to give evidence completely changes the nature of a criminal trial, however much the defendant may try to minimise the effect of this by emphasising to the jury his or her right of silence. The defendant, who at that point has a case to answer, has chosen not to put forward his or her own defence. The jury has been deprived of the opportunity to hear what the defendant has to say about the allegations.

It is a fair assumption that the jury would like to see and hear from the defendant in the witness box and to make a judgement regarding his or her veracity. In fact only one side of the case has been heard—the prosecution's. That is why it would be grossly improper for the defence lawyer, either by way of comment or during his address to the jury, to indicate, or even hint what his client would say, or would have said had he or she given evidence. The advocate cannot say to the jury, "You have heard the defendant's account of the matter". The most he or she can say is, "You have heard the prosecution evidence. I submit to you that this is not sufficient evidence on which a reasonable jury, properly directed, can or should convict in this case". It will be interesting to see, in due course, to what extent Robinson's closing address in the case of Lizzie Borden conformed to this ethical standard.

The sole purpose of the defence when they are not calling the defendant is to attack and discredit the prosecution case by cross-examination and persuade the jury that there is no convincing case against the defendant and that therefore there must be a doubt and they should acquit.

It is open to the defence, at the conclusion of the prosecution case, to submit to the court that there is no case to answer—or put another way, that taken as a whole the state of the evidence is such that no reasonable jury, properly directed, could convict the accused. The danger for the defence in taking this course is clear. Firstly it throws upon the judge the responsibility of deciding whether the evidence is sufficient to constitute a case at this stage of the trial. Secondly, although the jury will be absent from court while this issue is argued by the counsel, they will sense, if the trial continues, that the judge is of the opinion that the evidence against the accused is not without weight, and this may influence their findings.

The judge's ruling on a submission of no case to answer contravenes the usual rule that facts are the province of the jury and the law is for the judge. There is a divergence between the English and American jurisprudence in this regard. English judges, when summing-up, in addition to instructing the jury on the law and the rules of evidence will elucidate the facts shown by the evidence. They have a considerably wider authorisation in the extent to which they are entitled to comment on those facts than is usual for the judge in an American court.

This function is, however, a delicate one. Some judges acquire a name for being "prosecution minded" while others have a reputation for leaning towards the defence. If the judge is unfairly biased or prejudicial in his approach to a case it may be a cause for an appeal. We shall consider this further when we come to study Justice Dewey's charge to the jury.

A famous English trial in which the crucial decision by an advocate whether or not to put his client in the witness box is illustrated in that of the King against Frederick Bywaters and Edith Thompson heard at the Central Criminal Court, Old Bailey, London on the 6th December 1922.[1] They were charged with the murder of Edith's husband, Percy Thompson, a London shipping clerk. Bywaters was a good looking young man of 20 who was a ship's writer. He was eight years younger than Edith, who in her turn was a good deal more youthful than her husband with whom she had a difficult and unsatisfactory marriage. Mr and Mrs Thompson befriended Bywaters and a fatal attraction developed between Edith and the young man. Percy was naïvely unaware of this, or if he was aware does not seem to have worried about it. For Edith and Frederick however love developed into an all-powerful passion and for both of them Percy Thompson was seen as an obstacle to the fulfilment of their dreams.

In that era divorce was rare and infrequently resorted to, and there is no indication that Percy Thompson would even consider such a course.

---

1. For a fuller account of this case, see my book, *Three Cases That Changed the Law*, Waterside Press 2016.

Bywaters was away at sea a great deal and consequently he and Edith conducted a prolific and passionate correspondence. It led to a discussion about murder. In the case of Bywaters there is no doubt at all that it was murder that he seriously contemplated, and indeed in due course carried out. In a few of her letters Edith appeared to encourage him to kill her husband, but it must be remembered that she was a lovesick youngish woman who was desperate not to lose her young lover. Whether Edith was fantasising or seriously intended to kill Percy has to be a matter of some doubt. Foolishly, Bywaters kept her letters and after they were both arrested they formed the basis of the case against her as an accessory to the murder of her husband. At the trial Edith, against the advice of her counsel, Sir Henry Curtis Bennet KC, insisted on giving evidence.

She appeared over-confident and unaware of the gravity of her situation. This made a bad impression on the jury, and this, together with a summing up by the judge Mr Justice Shearman, which at times has more to do with Victorian morality than law, sufficed to bring about her conviction. There was evidence that, when Thompson was stabbed to death by Bywaters, Edith Thompson was heard to call out, "Oh don't, oh don't". When sentence of death was passed on her Edith cried out, "I am not guilty, oh God, I am not guilty".

In his introduction to the account of this trial in the *Notable British Trials Series*, the barrister and legal expert Filson Young considered the problem arising from calling or not calling the accused to give evidence:

> "The dilemma is an acute one. On the one hand there is the adverse comment which the judge in his summing-up is entitled to make on the silence of the accused person; the jury are asked to draw the inference that if there was any true story to tell, the accused would be the first to wish to tell it. There is the advantage, in the case of an attractive woman, of the effect of her personality and the appeal to humanity through the pathos of their position; although in my opinion of modern juries, the value of that effect should not be put too high.
>
> On the other hand there is the terrible danger of the cross-examination to which the accused giving evidence is subjected; the risk of the one word

too much, or the failure of mental endurance at a critical moment, that may turn the scale of opinion against the accused. And, of course, there is always the possibility, if a person who is not giving evidence is convicted, of the awful misgiving that if he or she had gone into the witness box the jury might have found a different verdict. The reason against Mrs Thompson going into the witness-box were, however, so strong that when she insisted on doing so she threw away her case.

There is nothing about which our law is so scrupulous as in seeing that the facts of a case, against which no defence is made except that of denial, are proved against the prisoner beyond all shadow of doubt. The case for the prosecution on the indictment was that Bywaters and Mrs Thompson on the 4th day of October 1922 in the county of Essex and within the jurisdiction of the Central Criminal Court, murdered Percy Thompson? That is what the jury were asked to find. If the defence had said, on behalf of Mrs Thompson 'I did not murder Percy Thompson; I had nothing to do with it; I had no knowledge of it, and I was stunned and horrified when it took place, and I defy the prosecution to introduce any evidence with which that denial is not absolutely compatible' and had rested in that, I do not think you would have found a British jury to convict her".

From the accused's point of view, Robinson was right not to put Lizzie Borden in the witness box. It was the saving of her life.

CHAPTER SEVENTEEN

Closing Speeches and Charge to the Jury

Any lawyer who is familiar with the criminal courts, in this country or in America, would have to admit that the closing speech for the defence of Lizzie Borden by George D Robinson was a brilliant exhibition of obscurantism, guile evasions, and disingenuous forensic fog that was ever heard in a court of law from an advocate. Once or twice it spilled over into plain deception. Only a speaker of Robinson's gifts would have got away with it, and only a presiding judge so indulgent towards the defendant would have allowed him to.

Robinson commenced his address to the jury with a description of the crime which could not be faulted by anyone conversant with the facts. The point to note however, is that in doing so he was laying the foundation for his whole attack on the Commonwealth case — namely that for a young woman of impeccable character, known for her allegiance to her church and for her charitable activity, to have perpetrated such horrors is unthinkable. Let us take a look at that opening:

> "May it please your honours, Mr Foreman and gentlemen: One of the most dastardly and diabolical of crimes that was ever committed in Massachusetts was perpetrated in August 1892, in the city of Fall River. The enormity and outrage startled everybody, and set all into the most diligent enquiry as to the perpetrator of such terrible acts. Our society is so constituted gentlemen that every man feels that the right must be done and the wrong punished, and the wicked doer brought to his account as promptly as due procedure of law will permit.

> Here there was a crime with all its horrors, and well may those who stood first to look at the victims have felt sickened and distressed at heart, so that the experiences of a lifetime will never bring other such pictures.
>
> The terrors of those scenes no language can portray. The horrors of that moment we can all fail to describe. And so we are challenged at once, at the outset, to find somebody that is equal to that enormity, whose heart is blackened with depravity, whose whole life is a tissue of crime, whose past is a prophecy of that present. A maniac or a fiend, we say. Not a man in his senses and with his heart right, but one of those abnormal productions the deity creates or suffers, a lunatic or a devil".

It is not surprising that such a slaughter should be described in somewhat colourful and extreme terms, but nevertheless the analogy is a false one.

The history of crime in both England and America is replete with cases of murder of the utmost savagery committed by people whose heart is not "blackened by depravity" nor who's "whole life is a tissue of crime". Examples abound. As mentioned earlier in this book, in 1931 William Herbert Wallace was convicted by a jury of a brutal murder upon his wife Julia by beating her brains out with a weapon which was never found. Wallace was a mild mannered insurance agent who had a previous history of impeccable behaviour all of his life. In 1933 in the French town of Le Lemans two servant girls, Christine Popin and her sister Lea, for no identifiable causes attacked their employer and her daughter with a knife and hammer and slaughtered them with diabolical ferocity. In 1966 in England when Ian Brady and Myra Hindley where convicted of the torture and murder of three young people in a case in which the very depths of evil were plumbed, neither defendant had any criminal records nor was it suggested that either was not perfectly sane.

Robinson goes on to discuss the position with the police:

> "Now, suspicion began to fall here and there. Everybody about there, even, called to account so far as could be.

> That is proper. That is right and necessary investigation proceeds. The police intervene. They form their theories. They proceed to act. They concern this one and that one. They follow out this and that clue with care. They are human only and when once a theory possesses our minds you know how tenaciously it holds its place, and how slow the mind is to find lodgement in something else.
>
> Now no decent man complains of investigation. No one says there ought not to have been anything done. Everything ought to have been done. Nay, more, we say, everything was not done and that the proper pursuit was not taken".

In an example of how rapidly Robinson can change direction, a few passages later he criticises the police for making what in the circumstances were perfectly reasonable enquiries: "They make themselves, as a body of men, ridiculous, insisting that a defendant shall know everything that was done on a particular time, shall account for every moment of that time, shall tell it four times alike, shall never waver or quiver, shall have tears or not have tears, shall make no mistakes".

In fact there has been no evidence in the case, either from Lizzie herself or anyone else that the Fall River police employed bullying, still less violent tactics in the course of their investigation. Clearly Robinson is concerned that the jury will have heard of Lizzie's contradictions and variations in her story — even though the inquest testimony had been excluded.

Then comes a statement from Robinson who is at straight variance with the evidence:

> "I say then, at the outset, as you begin to contemplate this crime and it's possible perpetration by this defendant, you must conclude at the outset that such acts are morally and physically impossible for this young woman defendant. To foully murder and then go straight away and slay her own father is a wreck of human morals; it is a contradiction of her physical capacity and certainty".

This statement is contradicted by Dr Frank W Draper. "A hatchet is consistent with these wounds, in my opinion the wounds could have been made by the use of an ordinary hatchet in the hands of a woman of ordinary strength". Robinson had heard this evidence but nevertheless made his statement regarding Lizzie's alleged physical incapacity for the murder.

Worse still, however, it is Robinson's appeal to the Almighty on behalf of his client. The Almighty surely, only wants justice to be done. There is nothing in the scriptures to suggest otherwise. Other than that there is no reason to suppose that he has any other interest. To suggest that he has Lizzie under his special protection — and therefore she must be innocent — is a disgraceful position to take:

> "I noticed one day, as we were proceeding with this trial, a little scene that struck me forcibly. It was one morning as the court was about to open, when you were coming into your seats and standing there, and the judges were passing to the bench to take their positions; and the defendant was asked to pass around from the place where she now sits in order that she might come in so as to be near her counsel, and right at that moment of transition she stood there waiting between the court and the jury, and waited in her quietness and calmness, until it was time for [her to] properly to come forward, it flashed through my mind in a minute; there she stands, protected, watched over, kept in charge by the judges of this court, and by the jury who have her in their charge.
>
> If the little sparrow does not fall unnoticed to the ground, indeed, in God's great providence, this woman has not been alone in this courtroom, but ever shielded by his providence from above, and by the sympathy and watchful care of those who have her to look after".

Another tactic of Robinson was equally wrong in his exploitation of the fact that, if convicted, Lizzie would face execution.

The province of the jury in a criminal trial is whether the defendant is guilty or not. It is not the consequences of a conviction. It was wrong for a defending advocate to arouse feelings of guilt in the members of a jury by reminding them of the horrors of the capital penalty. In any event it was probably unnecessary to emphasise this. Today in Britain and some American states the death penalty has been abolished, therefore this problem does not arise there. But for Robinson to say: "You are trying a capital case, a case that involves her human life, a verdict which against her, calls for the imposition of but one penalty, and that is that she should walk to her death" is a deliberate manoeuvre to play on sympathy rather than to concentrate on evidence—and that alone.

Robinson was less than fair in his reference to the two elements in the trial which had been ruled out by the court—the attempted purchase of Prussic acid and Lizzie's evidence at the inquest:

> "You have not heard any such evidence; it is not proved; the court did not allow it to be proved and it is not in the case. Now you will not go to the jury room with the thought, if it had been allowed, you would have considered that it was proved. But it was not allowed, no such evidence came before you, and I shall expect the district attorney, Man fashion to get up and say so, and I think you will, and I shall be disappointed in him if he does not".

The whole purpose of a matter of admissibility of evidence being argued in the absence of the jury is because, until it is accepted, the jury do not and should not hear it or take it into consideration at all in their deliberations. Robinson knew that the prosecution could not answer his comments, notwithstanding the fact that many legal experts considered that the testimony was wrongly excluded. He twisted the position to sound as though the Commonwealth lawyer's had tried to give substance to something which in fact had none.

Another strategy of Robinson is to put forward a theory which had never been advanced by the Commonwealth, and then to demolish it. It has never been suggested that the murderer, whoever he or she was, had an accomplice. Yet Robinson saw fit to say:

> "I am at a loss to know where there is any evidence about an accomplice or anybody else connected with it at all, and so it is only my enquiry to find out if there is any proof as to this defendant".

The most misleading part of Robinson's address was his misinterpretation of the law about motive. It has never been the law either of England or the United States that to succeed the prosecution must prove motive. This clearly has to be the case because in many trials, particularly for violence, including murder, there is no apparent motive, or one that is either so comparatively trivial or completely irrational, that it would give little clue as to why a defendant acted as he or she did. Yet Robinson would have the jury believe that this aspect must be proved. After a broad and seemingly correct statement of the law, Robinson continued:

> "Now why is the Commonwealth bound in this case to attempt to show a motive for doing it? Merely for this gentlemen: Because they say: Here are the crimes. There sits the defendant, now in order to hold her responsible for the crimes, we have yet to bind her up to the crimes. We have no direct evidence that puts her there; we have some circumstances that look as if she might get there; and so in order to bring her to it we must show a reason why she would do it, what moved her to do it; and that is the motive. That is to say the motive in this case is only to explain the evidence".

Needless to say Robinson made the most of the absence of blood on Lizzie and the missing hatchet handle — as was his right. He dwelt on the view of Abby's body which Lizzie might or might not have seen from her position on the stairs. This, however, was a red herring because the issue was not Lizzie's view of the body but whether or not she was the murderer. If she was not, she could have innocently failed to see the body. If she was the question is irrelevant.

At the end of the day there are two items of evidence which Robinson either misunderstood or, one hesitates to say of a respected figure in both law and politics, misrepresented.

The first concerns the alleged note which caused, or was said to cause Abby to leave the house. The one thing that is certain is that if Abby Borden had really answered a note by going to town to visit a sick person she would not have remained in the house to meet her death. She was in the house and she did meet with her death. Let us see how Robinson dealt with this:

> "Now she (Lizzie) told about the note, they say, and that is evidence of guilt. She told about Mrs Borden having a note. Now there is considerable interest in that question, and I ask your attention to it. You know that after the tragedies, when Miss Lizzie was asked about where Mrs Borden was, she told Bridget, so Bridget tells us, that Mrs Borden had a note and had gone out. 'I said who is sick? I don't know; she had a note this morning, it must be in town'.
>
> Now that is what Bridget says. Then Mrs Churchill comes, and she says 'I said, meaning herself, 'I said, where is your mother. She said 'I don't know she has got a note to see someone who is sick'. Next question, listen to it 'what did Bridget tell you about having a note? Answer 'she said Mrs Borden had a note to go and see someone that was sick, and she was dusting the sitting room, and she hurried off, and said she didn't tell me where she was going, she generally does'. Now that is what Bridget told Mrs Churchill. You get the idea. Both Bridget and Lizzie had learned from Mrs Borden that she had had a note. Mrs Borden had told Lizzie. Mrs Borden had told Bridget."

This conclusion of Robinson's is totally unjustified by the evidence. To see this one only has to look at the evidence of Bridget Sullivan:

> "Miss Lizzie came downstairs and came through the front entry into the dining room. I heard her ask her father if she had any mail and they had some talk between them which I didn't understand. But I heard her tell her father that Mrs Borden had a note and had gone out.
>
> She [Lizzie] said 'Maggie, are you going out this afternoon?' I said 'I don't know; I might and I might not. I don't feel very well. She says 'if you go out be sure and lock the door, for Mrs Borden has gone out on a sick call and I might go out too'. Says I 'Miss Lizzie, who is sick?' 'I don't know; she had a note this morning; it must be in town'."

This testimony makes it crystal clear that Bridget heard the note story from Lizzie and not from Abby. It completely refutes the statement of Robinson.

It only remains to say that Robinsons reasons given to Lizzie's visit to Alice Russell on the eve of the murders border on the absurd.

Closing for the Commonwealth: Hosea Knowlton

Knowlton, like Robinson, addressed the jury eloquently and at length. Yet informed opinion had always been that he spoke with less conviction than his rival. It will be recalled that from the start Knowlton was less than enthusiastic about this prosecution. Why? Moody, his associate counsel never showed the slightest hesitation. The crime was appalling; there was at the very least a prima facie case against Lizzie. At the preliminary proceedings she had been found "probably guilty". She had proved an unconvincing witness at the inquest. The basic situation was that there was no reasonable likelihood of anybody but Lizzie having killed Abby.

This was made abundantly clear when Knowlton mocked the "intruder theory":

> "He came into the house where there was no chance to get in, he hid in closets where no blood was found, he went from room to room where no traces of blood were found in passageways or stairs, he came out when there was no opportunity to come out without being see by all the world, that unknown assassin who knew all the ins and outs of the family, who knew Bridget Sullivan was going upstairs to sleep when she didn't know it herself, who knew when Lizzie was going to the barn when she didn't know it herself, who knew that Mrs Borden would be up dusting the guest room when no person could have foreseen it, who knew that he could get through and escape the eye of Lizzie and would find the screen door open at the exact time when it was possible to run in; that unknown assassin never would have carried the weapon away, carried the bloody weapon with him in the streets. It would have been left beside his victims. The fact that no hatchet was found there is itself evidence."

In his peroration Knowlton said:

> "What is the defence Mr Foreman? What is the answer to this array of impregnable facts? Nothing; Nothing. I stop and I think and I say again,

Nothing. Some dust thrown upon the story of Mrs Reagan which is not of the essence of the case; some question about time put upon the acts of Mr Medley which is not of the essence of the case, some absurd and trifling stories about drunken men the night before, and dogs in the yard the night before, of men standing quietly on the street the same day as the tragedy exposing their bloody persons for the inspection of passers-by, of a pale and irresolute man walking up the street in broad daylight. Nothing, nothing. The distinguished counsel with all his eloquence, which I vainly hope to match or approach, has attempted nothing but to say 'not proven'. But it is proven; it is proven."

With one powerful declaration Knowlton had demolished the theory of an interloper committing the crimes. He had made the absurdity of that idea as plain as two plus two equal four or in this case two minus one equals one.

That one person was Lizzie Borden. Yet the jury acquitted her. Why? The true mystery of the Borden case is not the question of who was the killer? The real puzzle is why the jury acquitted her, and after such a short retirement. In saying that I am sure I shall have my critics, although many people who once favoured Lizzie have subsequently had second thoughts.

I do not propose to weary my readers with a long recapitulation of the salient points in Knowlton's speech. Suffice it to say that although it has been suggested that he did not have his heart in his work his approach was efficient and thorough. He forcibly made the important points which the Commonwealth advocate maintained throughout the trial. But the 12 good men and true were not persuaded. To find the reason for this we must now turn to the charge to the jury, or to use the English expression the summing-up of Justice Dewey.

The Charge to the Jury

Whatever may be said regarding Dewey's charge to the jury one thing is certain; it was a direction to acquit. Dewey began with an accurate statement of his function of judge as against the function of the jury. If he had followed his own guidance his instructions would have been impeccable, but he did not.

In both English and American law the basic rule for both jurisdictions is the same; the law is for the judge and the facts are for the jury. That is to say, the jury must take the judge's advice on the law, and the judge is bound by the jury's finding on the evidence. However, there is a difference. In English courts judges are allowed greater latitude when discussing the evidence than is the situation in the United States. Hence the distinction between summarising the facts and summing them up. In the latter instance, for example, a point or points made forcefully by one side or the other may appear to the judge to have little real weight. He may regard the arguments advanced in that particular matter to be of no significance or even to be a stratagem of counsel in order to impress or even mislead the members of the jury. In that case the judge may direct the jury to take little notice. It is, after all, within his or her prerogative to indicate to the jury which are and which are not issues of importance for their consideration. Equally, if he or she thinks that there is an important matter which has been overlooked or only mentioned in passing it is his right and duty to bring that to the notice of the jury. Of course if the judge is seen to be biased in favour of the prosecution or the defence, and this is blatantly obvious he is in excess of his proper role and if a conviction results it may found the basis of an appeal.

Now let us take a look at the commencement of Justice Dewey's charge to the Borden jury:

> "Mr Foreman and gentlemen of the jury, you have listened with attention to the evidence in this case, and to the arguments of the defendant's counsel and the district attorney. It now remains for me, acting on behalf of the court to give you such aid towards a proper performance of your duty as I may be able to give within the limits for judicial action, prescribed by law; and to prevent any erroneous impression, it may be well for me to bring to your attention at the outset, that it is provided by a statute of this state that court shall not charge juries with respect to matters of fact, but may state the testimony of the law."

Next comes this vital passage:

"Without attempting to define the exact scope of this statute, it is not to be doubted in view of the expectations made of it by our court of last resort, that it was intended to prevent the judges presiding at the trial from expressing any opinion as to the credibility of the witnesses or the strength of evidence, while it does not preclude them from defining this degree of weight which the law attaches to a whole class of testimony, leaving it to the jury to apply the general rule to the circumstances of the case."

Notwithstanding this direction, Dewey proceeded to make clear his personal opinion on a whole range of subjects. He rightly pointed out that the preliminary proceedings, including the inquest (which he had ruled out) were not before the jury to adjudicate upon and he reminded the jury of Lizzie's previous excellent character in the eyes of the law. On the question of ill-feeling between Lizzie and her step-mother he again rightly stressed that the mere fact that Lizzie had called Abby "a mean old thing" could hardly found a basis for intent to murder. Justice Dewey rightly said that the case for the Commonwealth was purely circumstantial and he gave an accurate summary of the meaning of circumstantial. Then Dewey turned to the question of the note. He correctly stated the position of the Commonwealth to be that no such note existed, but that Lizzie had fabricated the story lest her father had wanted to see her step-mother who at that time was lying dead upstairs. Since Andrew was tired and wanted to rest, Lizzie was playing for time until she was able to murder him. Dewey said, "What motive had she to take upon herself the responsibility of giving utterance to this distinct and independent fact of a letter or note received with which she might be confronted and which she might afterwards find it difficult to explain, if she knew that no such thing was true".

Here the obvious comment is that if Lizzie was lying about the note she knew full well that there was no prospect of her being confronted with it. Dewey then posited an extraordinary scenario of there being a second assassin who planned to draw Mrs Borden out of the house. He continued: "If he afterwards came in there, came upon her. Killed her. Might he not have found the letter or note with her, if there was one already in the room?"

It must be said that neither side envisaged or suggested the possibility of two murderers. This emanated entirely from Dewey's imagination. Dewey emphasised the importance of the absence of bloodstains and questioned whether a person of the defendants sex and size could be the assailant. He dismissed as of no importance Lizzie's contradictory accounts regarding the reason for being in the barn and was less than polite about the scientific witnesses:

> "Now the government has called as witnesses some gentlemen of scientific and medical knowledge and experience, who are termed experts, and there has been put into the case considerable testimony from them. Now, following a distinction which I have pointed out, I think I may say to you that expert testimony constitutes a class of evidence which the law requires you to subject with careful scrutiny. It is a matter of frequent observation to see experts of good standing expressing conflicting and irreconcilable views upon questions arising at trial. They sometimes manifest a strong bias or partisan spirit in favour of the party employing them. They often exhibit a disposition to put forward theories rather than to verify or establish or illustrate the facts."

Then this remarkable passage. "So whether certain wounds in the skull were caused by a particular hatchet head or could have been caused by that hatchet head only, if you have the hatchet head and the skull, you may think you can apply them to each other and judge as well as the expert".

Dewey then put his own slant on the evidence of Alice Russell as to Lizzie's visit to her the night before the murder with her premonitions of tragedy, which the prosecution understandably held was a sign that Lizzie herself was contemplating bringing about those terrible events:

> "Suppose some person in New Bedford contemplated the perpetration of a great crime up the person or property of another citizen in New Bedford, contemplated doing it soon. Would he naturally, probably, predict a day or two beforehand, that anything of the nature of that crime would occur? Is

there reasonable construction to be put on that conversation that of evil premeditation dwelt upon, or only of evil fears and apprehensions."

However one views Justice Dewey's charge to the jury it seems certain that its intention was to secure the acquittal of Lizzie Borden — which it did.

Lizzie Borden and the Massachusetts Axe Murders

CHAPTER EIGHTEEN

The Conclusion

How much does the expression of public sentiment influence the decision of a court? Hopefully never, because the due course of law should not be at the whim of passing emotions. Yet public feeling can run high where there is a powerful human element involved. An extreme example, in a very different trial from that of Lizzie Borden which took place in England at the end of the second world war.

William Joyce was charged with treason.[1] During the war he had made a number of broadcasts from Germany to England predicting Britain's defeat and emphasising the virtues of the Third Reich. Before war broke out he was a member of the British Union of Fascists and had been active in the rough and tumble of street fighting in the 1930s. He was in fact an American citizen, that being the country where he was born, but he had lived most of his life in Northern Ireland. At the outbreak of Second World War he had travelled to Germany under a British passport to which he was not entitled. Once in Germany he had divested himself of the passport, which in his case was not valid anyway. He then proceeded to make broadcasts on behalf of his adopted country. The court held that while he was in possession of the passport he owed allegiance to the King because he could claim the protection of the British Crown should he wish to do so. There was little evidence as to when he obtained the passport.

After his conviction he appealed, first to the Court of Appeal and lastly to the House of Lords, now the Supreme Court of Justice in England and Wales at that time. It was argued that as he was an alien the jurisdiction

---

1. For a fuller account of this case, see my book, *Three Cases That Changed the Law*, Waterside Press 2016.

of the appeal court did not apply to a crime committed abroad by an alien. It was also argued that the time when he divested himself of the passport was not a matter of law, but a matter of fact for the consideration of a jury. Both arguments, which would seem to be of considerable strength, were dismissed by the Lords and Joyce was executed.

There is no doubt that had the case been dismissed there would have been an outcry since Joyce's broadcasts, while treated by most with jocularity, had been listened to by a great many people. But one cannot avoid wondering whether on that particular occasion public feeling exerted a degree of pressure on the judicial system.

Juries are invariably warned by the judge that they must not be influenced in their decision by anything which they have heard or read about the case before they are sworn in for jury service. Justice Dewey did not omit this duty. But juries are themselves members of the public, and in a case which attracted the enormous publicity such as that of the Lizzie Borden it would be fanciful to think that this jury had not been fully apprised of the basic facts before the trial began. From the moment that news of the tragedy broke the furore began. Huge crowds gathered on Second Street. Excitement was intense. Workers briefly abandoned their occupations and traffic jams blocked the streets. Some people were not far from hysteria. This was murder with a difference. It was parricide of the most terrible kind and the suspect, after several obvious misidentifications, became a young woman known for her impeccable character and good works. At first it was thought by many that only a demented maniac of the nature of "Jack the Ripper" could be responsible. In this respect the sheer authority of the crime was helpful to Lizzie's cause.

In an age before radio and television the newspaper was the only source of information for members of an information hungry populace. The *Fall River Globe* was particularly active and took a position violently opposed to Lizzie. All the papers increased their circulation and some of the other eastern cities sent reporters. The case was rapidly becoming known throughout the United States.

Friends of Lizzie and organizations with which she had been associated took her side. When she was detained after the inquest there were petitions for her release. Sermons were preached by Congressionalist

Ministers protesting her innocence. The Women's Christian Temperance Union maintained that Lizzie, a teetotaller, could not have done such a dreadful thing.

Judge Sullivan amply sums up the atmosphere:

> "The Bloomer Girls and other articulate feminist organizations had rallied militantly around her. Shortly before the trial Mrs Susan S Fessenden, president of the powerful Women's Christian Temperance Union, had thrilled the annual meeting of that national organization with her maudlin oratorical praise of Lizzie 'the poor helpless child'. 'Is Lizzie Borden guilty?' Mrs Fessenden screamed, rhetorically at the WCTU. Then in a line which was to become the lead lyric of a popular son, she answered herself, 'No, No, a thousand times No'."

Lizzie's past though somewhat spasmodic, endeavours for the Christian Endeavour Society and for the Fruit and Flower Mission of the Central Congregational Church were rewarded by a thousand fold. These coupled with the cloak of sanctimony lent to her by two now well-publicised clerical escorts, the Reverend Jubb and the Reverend Buck, won for her the support of various well-meaning religious groups of all denominations and persuasions.

Bear in mind that the jurymen, although no doubt honourable and honest men, would have learnt all of this before attending the trial. An interesting question is to what, if any, extent was the Borden jury influenced by the existence of the death penalty. Robinson took more than one opportunity to remind the 12 members of the consequences following a verdict of guilty. To the good men and true in who's hand the fate of Lizzie lay the vision of the virtuous young lady, innocent under the law until proved guilty, hanging by her neck from a rope like a piece of meat suspended from a hook in a butchers shop must have seemed terrible. Remember also this was an all-male jury. It is common knowledge among trial lawyers in the United States and criminal advocates in England that women jurors are less chivalrous towards their own sex than are men.

The death penalty in England was reduced in 1861 to four crimes: murder, treason, arson in the Royal Dock Yards and piracy with violence. But the public mood was sceptical about capital punishment for some time before abolition came about. It was the execution of two women which intensified this feeling of abhorrence. Edith Thompson in 1922 and Ruth Ellis in 1955. In the former case the evidence was somewhat ambivalent and in the latter, where the defendant shot her lover after a quarrel, many thought the recommendation to mercy which the jury made should have been acted upon by the Home Secretary.

But it was the hanging of Timothy Evans in 1966 and Derek Bentley in 1968 which finally swung the pendulum decisively. In both cases there were grave doubts concerning the unsatisfactory nature of the evidence, and the convictions resulted in posthumous pardons. But in the public mind the pardons came too late for the deceased pair and the argument that capital punishment cannot be reversed, if found to be mistaken, gained considerable force.

Following a Private Members Bill in 1965, Parliament voted to suspend the death penalty for five years. Since the beginning of the century capital punishment had been the only sentence a judge could pass for the crime of murder. A jury could add to its verdict a recommendation to mercy, but the Home Secretary could accept or reject this. There lay an appeal to the Court of Criminal Appeal but this was limited to a few categories such as the judge misdirecting the jury on matters of fact or law or the finding of the jury being against the weight of the evidence.

If the Home Secretary accepted the recommendation to mercy the sentence of death would be commuted to life imprisonment. This would almost certainly not be available to an appellant convicted of murder on the scale of the Borden crimes.

On the 20th May 1998, during a debate on the Human Right's Bill, members of Parliament decided by 294 to 136 to adopt the provisions of the European Convention On Human Rights outlawing capital punishment for murder except in times of war or imminent threat of war. The Human Rights Act 1998 incorporated the European Convention into UK law. The Criminal Justice Act of that year removed high treason or piracy with violence as capital crimes, thus effectively ending capital punishment. It was finally outlawed for any theoretical residual situations, such as in time of war, when Home Secretary Jack Straw signed the 6th Protocol to the Europe Convention in 2003 (though arguably if the UK leaves the European Union as is presently the position this might one day be reversed by English law, again at least in theory).

Perhaps a greater question is: Was the court biased in favour of Lizzie Borden? Bias in a judge is a very serious charge. If made during his or her lifetime it would certainly be defamatory unless fully substantiated. We have already seen the contrast between English and American jurisprudence on this subject.

Since Justice Dewey was appointed to his position on the Superior Court by the defending advocate Robinson when the latter was governor of Massachusetts, it would seem to have been wise of him not to sit on this particular case. How much difference did it make to the result of the trial that the evidence of the attempted purchase of Prussic acid was excluded? Would it have ensured Lizzie's conviction had it been admitted? Not necessarily. Two trials in the same area in England and Scotland indicate this possibility.

Madeleine Smith was a young Scottish girl of good family who fell in love with a French packing clerk named L'Angelier. Madeleine, during their courtship, had written a number of love letters to the young Frenchman. When she, in due course, became engaged to a more "appropriate suitor", she was very anxious to recover the passionate letters.

L'Angier began to suffer from severe stomach pains, and in due course died in great agony. An autopsy disclosed the presence of a very large quantity of arsenic in his stomach. Madeleine protested that she had not seen L'Angier recently and knew nothing of his ailment, However it was discovered that she had made purchases of arsenic, which she maintained was used externally to improve he complexion (compare: to clean a seal skin coat). Madeleine Smith was charged in 1857 with the murder of her erstwhile lover but the jury returned a verdict of 'not proven' (a verdict only available in Scotland).

In 1885 Adelaide Bartlett was charged with the murder of her husband by administering to him a quantity of chloroform which was subsequently found to be in his stomach. A young Methodist Minister named the

Reverend George Dyson was charged with being an accessory. A young girl of 19, Adelaide had become trapped in a loveless marriage with a husband a great deal older than herself—Mr Bartlett even sent his young wife to boarding school and on her return paid her scant attention. He rejected her wish to have children and her life became lonely and friendless.

The entry of a cultured young man onto the scene was a classic ingredient for trouble. Dyson, the newly found friend of Adelaide purchased a quantity of chloroform allegedly to assist her to "calm" her husband, but at his death both were charged with murder. In the event both were acquitted.

The evidence of Lizzie's testimony at the inquest is a different matter. It is less convincing as to intent than the attempted purchase of Prussic acid. Allowing Lizzie to testify on that occasion was a near disastrous mistake. She proved a poor witness under Knowlton's searching cross-examination. It was a sufficient warning to her defence team as to what the consequences might be if she were to do the same thing at her trial. It was a great piece of good fortune for the defence that Justice Dewey ruled the testimony inadmissible. Nevertheless at the time of the hearing before Judge Blaisdell the full material does not appear to have been published. However, when it was offered in evidence at the trial on June 13th 1892, copies of it were released for press publication. Could word of its contents have reached the jury?

One thing is certain. The admission in evidence of Lizzie's contradictions, hesitations and prevarications would have been highly damaging to her defence. Robinson's decision not to call her as a witness at her trial was absolutely the right one. He was then able to say to the jury—you have heard the prosecution witnesses. Do you really think what you have heard is sufficient to send this young woman to her death? When a defendant has not given evidence the result of the trial depends entirely upon whether the witnesses for the prosecution, assuming that they have come up to proof, have satisfied the jury that the defendant has been proved to be guilty beyond reasonable doubt.

As to the burden of proof, which remains throughout the trial, upon the prosecution, Justice Dewey's direction would seem to be perfectly sound:

> "The law requires that before the defendant can be found guilty upon either count in the indictment, every material allegation in it shall be proved beyond a reasonable doubt.
>
> Now what do the words 'beyond reasonable doubt' mean? Some courts do not favour an attempt to define them, thinking that the jury can judge as well without any suggestion. But I am unwilling to omit any further explanation, and I can in no way give you so accurate a description of their meaning, as by reading to you an excerpt from an opinion of the court by whose views it is our duty to be governed.
>
> The court says — Proof beyond reasonable doubt is not beyond all possible or imaginary doubt, but such doubt as precludes every reasonable hypothesis or theory except that which it tends to support. It is proof to a moral certainty, as distinguished from absolute certainty! As applied to a judicial trial for crime, the two phrases 'beyond reasonable doubt' and 'to a moral certainty' are synonymous and equivalent. They mean the same thing. Each has been used by eminent judges to explain the other, and each signifies such proof as satisfies the judgement and conscience of the jury as reasonable men, and applying their reason to the evidence before them, that the crime charged has been committed by the defendant, and so satisfies them as to leave no other reasonable conclusion possible. In other words they must have as clear and strong a conviction in their own minds of the truth of that conclusion to be acted on by them as in matters of the highest importance to themselves."

Very pertinent to the situation in the Borden case of the summing up in the *Wallace Case* in Liverpool (mentioned earlier in this book) in 1931 by the great English judge Mr Justice Wright:

"The question is not: Who did this crime? The question is: Did the prisoner do it? — Or to put it more accurately: Is it proved to your reasonable satisfaction and beyond reasonable doubt that the prisoner did? It is a fallacy to say: If the prisoner did not do it, who did? It is a fallacy to look at it and say it is very difficult to think the prisoner did not do it. Who did? And it may be equally difficult to think the prisoner did do it. The prosecution must discharge the onus cast upon them if establishing the guilt of the prisoner, and must go far beyond suspicion or surmise or even probability, unless the probability is such as to amount to a practical certainty; and when a jury is considering circumstantial evidence they must always bear other considerations in mind, and must not be led by any extraneous considerations to act upon what cannot be regarded as — well, I cannot say mere suspicion — but cannot be regarded as establishing beyond all reasonable doubt the guilt of the accused man."

Justice Dewey's direction on circumstantial evidence seems impeccable:

"This is a legal and not unusual way of proving a criminal case, and it is clearly competent for a jury to find a person guilty of murder, upon circumstantial evidence alone. Indeed judges and juries have been somewhat divided in their views at to the comparative strength and volume of circumstantial and direct evidence."

Mr Justice Wright:

"There is some circumstantial evidence which is as good as the evidence of the actual eye-witness. In other cases the only circumstantial evidence which anyone can present still leaves loopholes and doubts, and still leaves possibilities of other explanations, of other persons and still leaves the charge against the accused man little more than a probability and nothing that could be describes as reasonably conclusive."

The criticism levied against Justice Dewey was not his basic direction, but that he allowed his opinion to influence his judgement.

The Conclusion

It has been suggested that Knowlton was lacking in enthusiasm to take on the prosecution. A much quoted letter he wrote to Pillsbury the Attorney General of Massachusetts makes this plain. Pillsbury was unable to take on the prosecution due to illness, which came as very unwelcome news to Knowlton. Knowlton's letter to Pillsbury makes this clear. David Kent quotes the letter in full in his book *Forty Whacks*:

"The Hon A E Pillsbury, Attorney General

My Dear Sir:

I have thought more about the Lizzie Borden case since I talked with you, and think perhaps that it may be well to write to you, as I shall not be able to meet you probably until Thursday, possibly Wednesday afternoon.

Personally I would very much like to get rid of the trial of the case, and feel that my feelings in that direction may have influenced my better judgement. I feel this all the more upon you're not unexpected announcement that the burden of the trial would come upon me!"

It is not clear exactly what he meant by "get rid of the trial of the case". Did Knowlton mean that the indictment should be quashed? If there was a prima facie case it would not have been open to the Commonwealth lawyers to offer no evidence. The letter continues:

"I confess however, I cannot see my way clear to any disposition of the case other than a trial. Should it result in disagreement of the jury, there should be no difficulty in disposing of the case by admitting the defendant to bail, but a verdict either way would render such a course unnecessary. The case has proceeded so far and an indictment has been found by the grand jury of the country that it does not seem to me that we ought to take the responsibility of discharging her without trial, even though there is every reasonable expectation of a verdict of not guilty".

This is an extraordinary statement. The equivalent test for the English Crown Prosecution Service in deciding whether to bring a prosecution is: Is there a reasonable prospect of a conviction—I suspect that the same principle applies in American jurisdiction. The letter goes on:

> "I am unable to concur fully in your views as to the probable result. I think that it may well be that the jury might disagree upon the case. But even in my most sanguine moments, I have scarcely expected a verdict of guilty. The situation is this: Nothing has developed which satisfies either of us that she is innocent; neither of us can escape the conclusion that she must have had some knowledge of the occurrence.
>
> She has been presented for a trial which, to say the least, was not influenced by anything said by the government in favour of the indictment.
>
> Without discussing the matter more fully in this letter, I will only say as above indicated that I cannot see how any other course than setting the case down for trial, and trying it, will satisfy that portion of the public sentiment, whether favourable to her or not, which is worthy of being respected.
>
> June seems to be the most satisfactory month, all things considered, I will write more fully as to the admission of her confession after I have looked the matter up."

Lizzie had made no confession.

On the 21st November the hearing before the grand jury took place. Robert Sullivan in his work *Goodbye Lizzie Borden* describes some very strange actions by Knowlton:

> "For most of the week County District Attorney Hosea M Knowlton presented his evidence and then, presumably having finished his presentation to the grand jury, he did an astonishing thing.
>
> He notified Andrew S Jennings, attorney for Lizzie Borden that Jennings would be allowed to present to the grand jury evidence for the defence.

This was a gesture, to my knowledge unheard of in Massachusetts if not in Anglo-American jurisprudence, before, or for that matter since the indictment of Lizzie Borden.

As has been pointed out, it is not and was not the function of the grand jury to weigh both sides of the case and determine guilt or innocence. That is the exclusive responsibility of the trial jury, the petit jury. The grand jury's duty and responsibility was and is only to weigh the evidence of the prosecution to satisfy themselves that there is enough evidence to warrant a trial by a petit jury to determine the issue of guilt or innocence.

The newspapers of the country carried these amazing and puzzling events on their front pages. Professionals in the law were completely dumbfounded. District Attorney Knowlton's disingenuous attempt to demonstrate complete fairness, if that were his motive in making his offer to Lizzie's attorney, seemed to have backfired. Or was it that Knowlton thought it a good tactic to induce his opponent to disclose his defence ahead of the trial so that the prosecution would be prepared for it."

In speaking of the good character of Lizzie and the distasteful task of prosecuting her for murder Knowlton would seem at times to be excessively apologetic, However one hesitates to criticise such an able and respected advocate who discharged his duty thoroughly and efficiently.

We come back again to the question of why what originally appeared to be a water-tight case for the Commonwealth of Massachusetts failed to achieve a conviction. One of the difficulties facing the prosecution becomes plain with the opening address by William H Moody. Moody made the most of what he had got, but to demonstrate an adequate motive for murder was close to "making bricks without straw". The jury were of course reminded several times by counsel for both sides and by Justice Dewey that motive does not have to be proved in a criminal trial — not even for murder. In this respect the unique horror of the Borden case assisted Lizzie. The gap between the enormity of the crime and any conceivable reason for its commission was so great that this was bound to impress the jury.

Moody, at the start of his opening address, plunged straight into the issue of motive and the result was something of a "damp squib". One only has to consider his words:

> "It will appear that some five years before the death of Mr and Mrs Borden some controversy had arisen about some property not important in itself. Mr Borden had seen fit to do some benefaction for a relative of Mrs Borden, and in consequence of that fact the daughter's thought that something should be done for them by way of pecuniary provision as an offset. The details of what happened at that time are, as I have said, by no means important."

Here is the prosecutor telling the jury that the cause of the dispute was not important. Surely the reaction of the jurors must be: "If the matter was not important how could it be an incentive to these ghastly killings?"

"It is significant however," said Moody,

> "that enough of feeling had been created by the discussion which arose to cause to charge the relations between the prisoner and Mrs Borden. Up to that time she had addressed her step-mother as 'mother'. From that time she substantially ceased to do so. We shall show to you that the spring before these homicides, upon some occasion when a talk arose between the prisoner and a person who did the cloak making for the family, the latter spoke of Mrs Borden as 'mother'. The prisoner at once repudiated that relation and said 'Don't call her mother, she is a mean thing and we hate her. We have as little to do with her as possible'. 'Well, don't you have your meals with her?' 'Yes we do sometimes, but we try not to, and a great many times we wait until they are over their meals and we stay in our own rooms as much as possible'.

To assistant City Marshall of Fall River John Fleet who asked her if she had any idea who could have killed her father and mother Lizzie replied, 'She is not my mother sir she is my step-mother. My mother died when I was a child'. Is this enough to promote murder?"

Moody built up what he submitted was a picture of discord in the Borden house, but this was undermined by the evidence of Bridget the maid. Who presented as a truthful witness. She was cross-examined at the trial by Robinson:

George Dexter Robinson: Did you have any trouble there in the family?
Bridget Sullivan: No sir.
Robinson: A pleasant place to live?
Bridget Sullivan: Yes sir. I liked the place.
Robinson: You never saw any conflict in the family?
Bridget Sullivan: No sir.
Robinson: Never saw the least of any quarrelling or anything of that kind?
Bridget Sullivan: No sir.

Bridget agreed that the sisters did not eat with the family all the time. They did from time-to-time. Emma Borden said that during the period of the last three years relations had been good between Lizzie and Abby.

Another example of a matter which may have caused the jury doubt and confusion is that of the handleless hatchet, Having said that the break in the handle might have been 24 or 48-hours-old, or indeed a week or a month old, Moody went on to say that the hatchet may have been the weapon. There was no weapon before the court which the prosecutor affirmed was the instrument of murder.

The contradictory statement made by Lizzie regarding her alleged visit to the barn are made less damaging to the defence due to the evidence of Lubinsky, Brown and Barlow.

Again and again what should have been a strong point for the prosecution is blunted by the ability of an extremely clever defendant to raise a possible doubt. Juries are not inclined to analyse precisely the measure of reasonableness when considering what is a "reasonable doubt". All the more so when a young woman of impeccable character stands at risk of being hanged.

The essence of the prosecution case in the Borden trial is simply: If Lizzie didn't do it who else could have done? But when that is the proposition before a jury trying a defendant who enjoys from start to finish the presumption of innocence that is not enough. Judges know too well the difference between feeling certain that the defendant is guilty—and the sufficiency of the evidence to prove it.

The method of criminal trial in Anglo-American jurisprudence is weighted in favour of the defendant. But as a system of justice it is, like democracy, though imperfect, better than all the others.

Select Bibliography

The Author wishes to acknowledge the following sources:

De Mille, Agnes. *Lizzie Borden—A Dance of Death* (1968, Little, Brown & Co., Boston, Toronto).
Engstrom, Elizabeth. *Lizzie Borden* (1991, Tom Doherty Associates, New York).
Flynn, Robert A. *The Borden Murders—An Annotated Bibliograph* (1992, King Philip Publishing Co., Portland, USA).
Kent, David. *Forty Whacks. New Evidence in the Life and Legend of Lizzie Borden* (1992, Yankee Books, Emaus, Pennsylvania).
Lincoln, Victoria. *A Private Disgrace* (1968, Victor Gollancz Ltd).
Lustgarten, Edgar. *Verdict in Dispute* (Reprint 2010, A. Wingate).
Pearson, Edmund. *Trial of Lizzie Borden*, Edited with a history of the case and contains the original transcript (1937). First Edition.
Radin, Edward D. *Lizzie Borden—The Untold Story* (1961, Victor Gollancz Ltd).
Rappaport, Doreen. *The Lizzie Borden Trial* (1992, Harper Collins).
Sullivan, Robert. *Goodbye Lizzie Borden* (1975, Chatto & Windus).

Index

A

accomplice *221*
acquittal *31, 83–84, 100, 191, 193, 212, 225, 229*
Adams, Melvyn *81, 84*
affection *20, 35, 118*
A G Borden Building *49*
Alford *82*
alibi *54, 62, 64, 104, 168, 171–191*
   alibi in reverse *73*
allegiance *231*
ambiguity *25*
anger *167*
animosity *24*
arrest *197*
arrogance *31*
arsenic *201, 235*
arson *46*
ashes *136–139, 145, 169*
assassination *15*
attack
   frenzied attack *90*
autopsy *39, 142, 235*
axe *32, 39, 41, 76, 90, 105–107, 136–140, 146, 169, 186, 208*

B

Barlow, Thomas *184, 187*
barn *21, 38, 49–80, 92, 171–191, 243*
   break in at *45*
   demolition *32*
Bartlett, Adelaide *235*
Beecher, Dr David *143*
Bence, Eli *202–203*
benevolence *24*
Bentley, Derek *234*
betrayal *90*
Betz, Eva *30*
beyond reasonable doubt *236*
bias *18, 123, 193, 214, 226, 235*
Birch, Mr *49*
Bladgett, Justice *81, 82*
Blaisdell, Judge *79, 205, 236*
blind rage *167*
blood *27, 39–40, 53–54, 113, 127–134, 135, 152, 167, 193, 222*
   blood splatter *143*
   bloodstains *105, 133, 144, 147, 168*
Bloomer Girls *233*
bodies *94, 113*
Borden, Abby *14, 25*
   murder of *89–109*
Borden, Andrew *14, 19, 22, 37, 59*
   murder of *111–118*
Borden, Anna *25*
Borden, Emma *19, 24, 152, 243*

alibi *54*
Borden family *19*
Borden, Lizzie
  buying poison *201*
  chopping off cat's head *31*
  credibility *79*
  cross-examination at inquest *78*
  mental state *30*
  peculiar look *30*
  skilful witness *52*
Boston University *84*
bottled up feelings *19*
Bowen, Dr Seabury *35, 38, 45, 54, 113, 128, 158, 172*
Brady, Ian *13, 218*
break in *45*. See also *barn; burglary*
Brigham, Mary *126*
Bristol (USA) *14, 81*
British Union of Fascists *231*
brother-in-law (of Andrew Borden) *52*
Brown, Arnold *160*
Brown, Everett *184, 186*
Brown University *84*
brutality *218*
Buck, Reverend E A *31, 123, 233*
bullying *219*
burden of proof *212, 237*
burglary *46–47*
burning
  burning of a dress *43, 53, 158–169*
  burning the house down *46*
butchery *52*
Bywaters, Frederick *214*

C

Caldwell, John *126*
callousness *31*
capital punishment *221, 233*
case to answer *212*
cellar *21, 27, 140*
character *19, 22, 227*
charity *24, 217*
  charity worker *31*
chemist *41–42, 43–44, 132, 201*
chloroform *235*
Christian Endeavour Society *31, 233*
church *23, 31, 217*
  Congregational Church *233*
Churchill, Adelaide *21, 38, 53, 59, 107, 128*
class *20*
closing speeches *217–229*
coincidence *75, 117, 168, 171*
coldness *20, 31*
Common Law *28, 199, 209*
common sense *17*
Commonwealth *81, 193, 217*
confession *240*
  voluntariness *199*
confidence *18*
contemporaneous statements *194*
contradictions *94, 236*
controversy *17*
cordiality *29–30, 162–164*
corroboration *72, 186, 187, 204*
counsel *52, 166, 186, 191*
Court of Appeal *231*
Criminal Justice Act 2003 *194*
Criminal Justice and Public Order Act 1994 *211*

cross-examination *123, 163, 213*
cruelty to cats *202*
Curtis Bennet, Henry *215*

D

Dartmouth College *84*
death
  death penalty. See *capital punishment*
  of friend in the night *32*
  times of deaths *144*
deception *217*
defence *15, 194, 211–216, 217*
  strongest argument *127*
democracy *244*
Denning, Lord *87*
depravity *218*
depression *46*
Devereux, Arthur *88*
Dewey, Justice *81, 82, 214, 225*
discord *243*
discourtesy *46*
discrepancy *78*
District Attorney *49, 53, 81*
Doherty, Officer *172*
Dolan, Dr William *113, 128, 130, 143*
double killing *193*
Draper, Dr Frank *133, 142, 220*
dress. See *burning: burning of a dress*
  silk dress *147*
D R Smith's pharmacy *203*
Dyson, Reverend George *236*

E

Edinburgh *201*
Ellis, Ruth *234*

emotion *16, 17, 231*
  emotional turmoil *19*
enemies *16, 24, 36, 45, 112*
envy *24*
ethics *213*
Europe *25*
Evans, Timothy *234*
evidence *25, 73, 82*
  circumstantial evidence *53, 83, 167, 238*
  direct evidence *85*
  Evidence Act 1995 (Australia) *194*
  excluded evidence *100, 112, 193–199, 221*
  Federal Rules of Evidence *194*
  interference with *123*
  Lizzie not giving *211–216*
  medical evidence *15, 73, 90, 111, 174, 202*
  police evidence *146*
  rules of evidence *21*
  scientific evidence *146*
evil *13, 218, 229*
execution *220, 232*
experts *228*
eyes
  emptiness in *30*

F

fact *28*
Fairhaven *54*
Fall River *13, 20*
falsehood *156*
Farm Mills Company *24*
farms *23*
fears *46*
feminists *233*
Ferry Street *49*

first blow *15*
First National Bank *24*
fishing *64*, *74*. See also *sinkers*
Fleet, John *26*, *112*, *137*, *142*, *172*, *242*
foreboding *36*
forensics *19*
fortress *26*
frenzy *15*, *168*
friends *43*
Fruit and Flower Mission *233*
funeral director *23*

G

gallows *14*
Gardiner, Charles *186*
generosity *32*
Germany *231*
Gifford, Hannah *25*
Grand Jury *81*
Gray, Oliver *32*
groan *76*
grudge *15*
guest bedroom *73*, *105*, *118*

H

Harrington, Captain Philip *113*
Harrington, Hiram *52*, *172*
Harrington, Mrs *161*
Hart, Frederick *205*
Harvard *49*
    Harvard Law School *83*, *84*
    Harvard Medical School *132*, *142*
hatchet *13*, *27*, *76*, *136*, *137–146*, *202*
    claw hammer hatchet *144*
    handleless hatchet *143*, *243*

hatred *16*, *167*
hearsay *194*
Hickey, Thomas *124*
High Court judge *82*
High Court of Justiciary *201*
Hilliard, City Marshall *38*, *123*
Hindley, Myra *13*, *218*
Holocaust *35*
Homes, Charles *125*
Home Secretary *234*
hooks *177*
hostility *25*, *166*
    hostile witness *161–163*
House of Lords *231*

I

ice-man peddler *184*
identification *201*, *206*
identity *16*
ill-feeling *32*, *50*, *163*, *167*, *227*
impulse *28*, *168*
incompatibility *95*
inconsistencies *40*
inferences *211*
inquest *30*, *40*, *49*, *76*, *78*, *163*, *173*, *189*, *194*, *227*
inquisitorial system *17*
insurance fraud *167*
intention *194*, *201*
interloper/intruder (theory of) *16*, *26*, *51*, *74*, *92*, *137*, *167*, *174*, *224*
investigation *16*, *26*
ironing *93*, *176*, *190*

J

Jack the Ripper *40, 232*
Jennings, Andrew *81, 84, 240*
Joyce, William *231*
Jubb, Reverend *233*
judges *17, 81–88, 212, 226*
Judicial Studies Board (UK) *194*
jurisdiction *231*
jury *13, 210, 212, 217, 232*
   grand jury *14*
   jury challenge *17*
   role of *226*

K

Kelly, Dr *37*
keys *27, 37, 56*
Kilroy, Frank *202, 204*
kindness *23*
Knowlton, Hosea *20, 49, 81, 82, 127, 224, 240*

L

lawyers *81–88*
layout of the house *x–xi, 15, 20*
left handed blow *130*
lettings *47*
lies *147*
life imprisonment *234*
Lincoln, Abraham *28*
Lincoln, Victoria *188*
Liverpool *13*
   Liverpool Assizes *167*
locks *16, 19, 26, 37, 92*
lovelessness *20*
Lubinsky, Hyman *184–186*

M

"Maggie" *33*
maid *32, 36, 54*
maniac *40*
Manning, John *124*
Marks, Frederick *202*
marriage settlement *50*
Mason, Chief Justice *81, 82*
Massachusetts *13, 20, 35*
   Massachusetts Legislature *49*
   Superior Court *81*
mass sentiment, etc. *17*
matricide *13*
McManus, Mr *49*
media/press *124, 232*
medical examiner *194*
Medley, William *179*
memory *79, 148, 166, 172*
Merchants Manufacturing Company *24*
mercy *234*
miscarriage of justice *17*
mistake *79*
mood swings *30*
Moody, William *20, 81, 83, 127, 241*
Moors Murders *13*
morality *215*
morphine *88*
Morse, John *14, 26, 35, 50, 55, 104, 205*
Morse, Sarah *24, 35*
motivation *52*
motive *19, 25, 26, 49, 85, 90, 109, 202, 222*
Mullaly, Police Officer *140*
murder *13*
mystery *136*

N

New Bedford *81*
New England families *20*
Newhall, Charles *186*
no case to answer *213*
Northern Ireland *231*

O

obscurantism, etc. *217*
orchard *21*

P

pardon *234*
parricide *232*
pathology *168*
patricide *13*
Pearson, Edmund *40, 141, 171*
perverting the course of justice *123*
petitions *232*
Pillsbury, H E *239*
plot to murder *73*
poison *36, 43–46, 88, 113, 133, 202, 207*
police *38, 113, 203, 219*
Popin, Christine and Lea *218*
Potter, Mrs *31, 32*
prejudice *17, 158, 214*
premonition *16, 36, 228*
press. See *media/press*
presumption of innocence *244*
prevarication *94, 236*
prison officer *123*
privilege *20*
Prussic acid *35, 41, 77, 87, 112, 201, 221*
psychopathy *30*
public sentiment *231*

Q

quarrelling *19, 54*

R

Radin, Edward *54, 173*
Rapallo, Mr Justice *196*
Raymond, Mary *158*
Reagan, Hannah *119–126*
real estate *23, 49*
reasonable doubt *21, 28*
recall *95*
red herring *222*
relationships *30*
resentment *161, 167, 201*
respect *24, 35*
Robinson, George *52, 72, 81, 84, 217*
Roman Catholicism *33*
Roosevelt, Theodore *84*
Russell, Alice *15, 16, 36, 39, 43, 78, 89, 112, 128, 149, 172, 188, 191, 228*

S

Safe Deposit and Trust Company *24*
sanctimony *233*
Scotland *235*
Second Street *21, 26, 202*
security *14*
sentiment *18*
  sentimentality *23*
sermons *232*
servants *20*
shareholding *23*
Shearman, Mr Justice *215*
sick note *105–109, 223*
silence *212*

sinkers 63–80, 172–179
skirt 76
skull 142
Smith, Madeleine 201, 235
speculation 17
stains 144
staring eyes 30
state of mind 207
sticking to a story 167
stranger 113, 137
Straw, Jack 235
subpoena 195, 197
Sullivan, Bridget 14, 19, 22–27, 32, 36, 59, 90–106, 188, 205–206
Sullivan, Judge Robert 21, 32, 83, 95, 141, 168, 199
summing-up 214, 225–229
Sunday School 31
Superior Court 80, 81
Supreme Court 84
Swansea (USA) 49
sympathy 112, 221

T

testimony 79
theft 46
Thompson, Edith 214, 234
Thompson, Percy 214
threats 89
time lapse 15, 73
tourists 14
tragedy 24
treason 231
trial 17, 40, 171
Troy Cotton and Woolen Manufacturing Company 24
truthfulness 43, 49, 87
Tufts College 49

U

Union Savings Bank 24

V

veracity 94, 213
verdict 210
violence 19, 90, 167
vomiting 45

W

Walker Jubb, Reverend 31
Wallace Case 13, 28, 167
Wallace, Julia 167
Wallace, William 85, 167, 218
warmth 20, 29
wealth 20, 49
weapons 27, 39, 74, 135–146, 243
Whitechapel Murders 40
Whitehead, Sarah 32, 161
will 50
witnesses 15, 40
  credibility of 227
  hostile witness 163, 166
  intelligence of 79
  unreliable witnesses 187
Women's Christian (Temperance) Union 31, 233
Wood, Professor Edward 53, 132, 137, 144, 202
wounds 114, 135, 143, 228

Wright, Mr Justice *167*, *237*

Y
Young, Filson *215*

The Tottenham Outrage and Walthamstow Tram Chase: The Most Spectacular Hot Pursuit in History
by Geoffrey Barton
With a Foreword by Mike Waldren QPM

Not since the days of highwaymen and footpads had armed robbery been seen in London. Geoffrey Barton explains the political backdrop to the arrival in the UK of armed revolutionaries driven by their own frenzied missions, causing citizens to go in fear. Laws were passed to deal with aliens and terrorism but as the author explains the civil police were ill-equipped to deal with the problem. Although well known to local people, the Tottenham Outrage of 1909 when two Latvian robbers, Jewish refugees, intercepted a payroll has been comparatively hidden to the wider world (unlike the notorious Siege of Sydney Street which took place two years later). Resulting in the most spectacular police pursuit in history it involved a hundred police officers and up to a thousand citizens in running to ground two desperate police killers. The book follows every inch of the six-and-a-half miles and minute of the two-and-a-half hours of the chase. It also pays minute attention to the people and places involved as well as the aftermath. As former Head of Firearms Training Operations for the Metropolitan Police Service, Mike Waldren writes in his *Foreword*, 'The officers… did their best relying on guts and determination to see them through an unprecedented incident.' The first in-depth account of an iconic event — fascinating police, social and local history based on extensive first-hand research.

Paperback | ISBN 978-1-909976-40-5 | January 2017 | 224 pages

Three Cases that Shook the Law
by Ronald Bartle

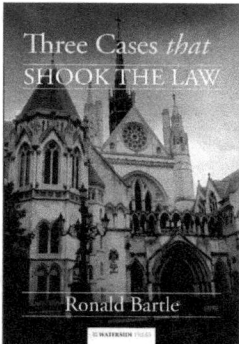

There are cases in the annals of English criminal law that forever resonate. In Three Cases that Shook the Law former district judge Ronald Bartle has selected three for close scrutiny: those of Edith Thompson who suffered due to her romantic mind-set, a young lover and the prevailing moral climate; William Joyce (Lord 'Haw Haw') where the law was stretched to its limits to accommodate treason; and—as portrayed in the BBC TV drama Rillington Place—Timothy Evans who died due to the lies of the principal prosecution witness Reginald John Halliday Christie who it later transpired was both a serial killer and likely perpetrator.

Paperback | ISBN 978-1-909976-36-8 2016 | Revised Edn. | 224 pages

Bow Street Beak
by Ronald Bartle
With a Foreword by Lord Hurd

From the cases of Michael Fagan and other Buckingham Palace intruders to those of West End pickpockets, over-zealous preachers, 'saucy' prostitutes and cockroaches in the kitchens of one of London's most prestigious clubs, Bow Street Beak is a roller-coaster ride through the judicial career of stipendiary magistrate Ronald Bartle at the iconic Bow Street Magistrates' Court.

'Her Majesty was interested to read your reminiscences, and has directed that the copy be held in the library at Windsor'— Chief Correspondence Officer, Buckingham Palace.

Paperback | ISBN 978-1-909976-36-8 | 2016 | Revised Edn. | 224 pages

www.WatersidePress.co.uk

www.ingramcontent.com/pod-product-compliance
Lightning Source LLC
Chambersburg PA
CBHW070340240426
43671CB00013BA/2380